D1129776

To:

From:

Date:

Your Every Day
READ AND PRAY
BIBLE
for Kids

Your Every Day Read and Pray Bible for Kids
©2016 (North America) International Publishing Services
Pty Ltd. Sydney Australia
www.ipsoz.com
External Markets © North Parade Publishing
Written by Janice Emmerson
Prayers by Annabelle Hicks
Illustrations by Netscibes and QBC Learning

Published by Harvest House Publishers
Eugene, Oregon 97402
www.harvesthousepublishers.com

ISBN 978-0-7369-6683-2

All rights are reserved. No part of this publication may be reproduced, stored in a retrieval system, or transmitted in any form or by any means—electronic, mechanical, photocopying, recording, or any other—except for brief quotations in printed reviews, without the prior permission of the publisher.

Printed in China

16 17 18 19 20 21 22 23 24 25 / IPS / 10 9 8 7 6 5 4 3 2 1

Your Every Day
READ AND PRAY
BIBLE
for Kids

HARVEST HOUSE PUBLISHERS
EUGENE, OREGON

CONTENTS

MOSES AND THE EXODUS

THE RISE OF ISRAEL

THE TIME OF THE PROPHETS

PSALMS AND PROVERBS

THE NEW TESTAMENT

THE GOSPELS

THE EARLY CHURCH

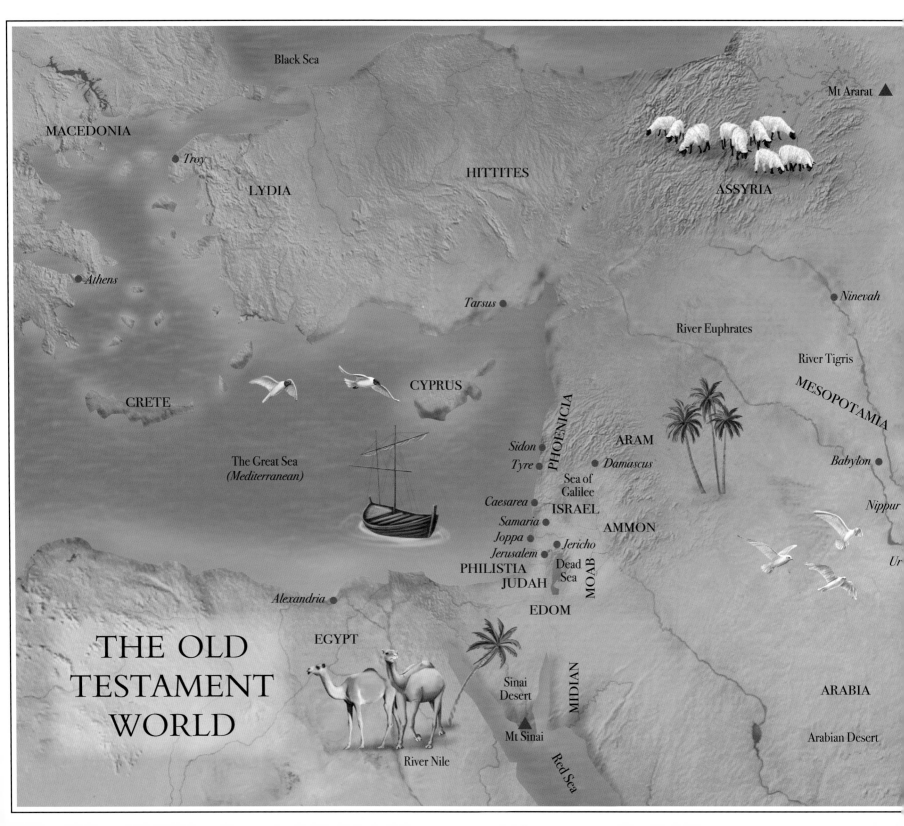

Black Sea

MACEDONIA

Troy

LYDIA

HITTITES

Mt Ararat ▲

ASSYRIA

Athens

Tarsus

Ninevah

River Euphrates

River Tigris

MESOPOTAMIA

CYPRUS

CRETE

PHOENICIA

ARAM

Babylon

The Great Sea
(Mediterranean)

Sidon

Tyre

Damascus

Sea of
Galilee

Nippur

Caesarea

ISRAEL

Samaria

AMMON

Ur

Joppa

Jericho

Jerusalem

Dead
Sea

MOAB

PHILISTIA

JUDAH

Alexandria

EDOM

THE OLD
TESTAMENT
WORLD

EGYPT

Sinai
Desert

MIDIAN

ARABIA

Mt Sinai ▲

Arabian Desert

River Nile

Red Sea

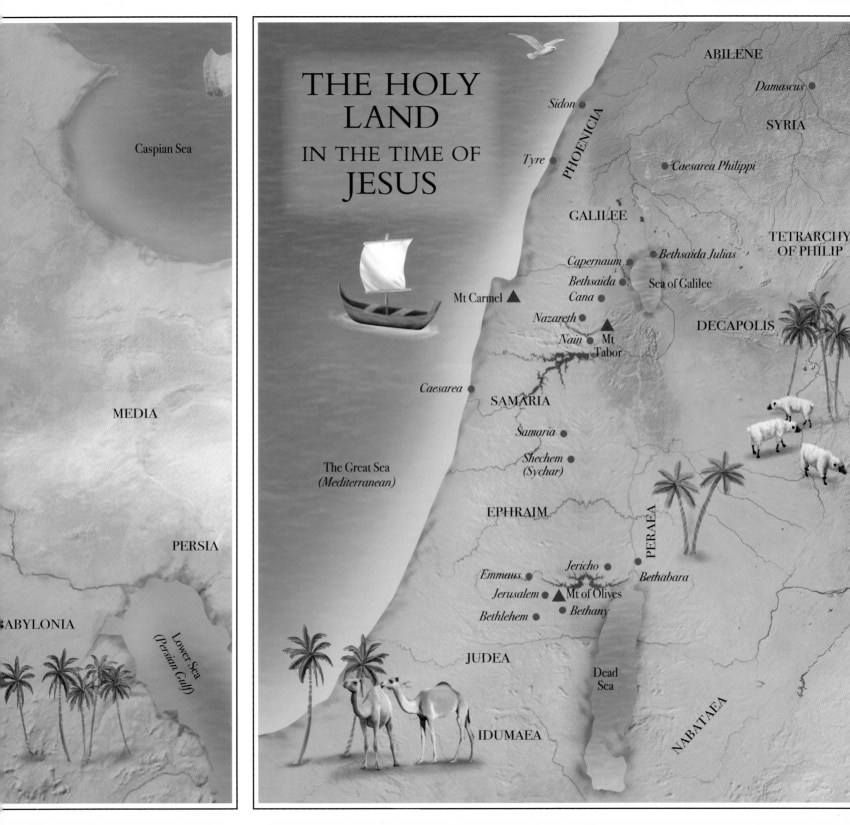

THE HOLY LAND
IN THE TIME OF JESUS

Caspian Sea

MEDIA

PERSIA

BABYLONIA

Lower Sea
(Persian Gulf)

Sidon

Tyre

PHOENICIA

ABILENE

Damascus

SYRIA

Caesarea Philippi

GALILEE

TETRARCHY
OF PHILIP

Capernaum

Bethsaida Julias

Bethsaida

Sea of Galilee

Mt Carmel ▲

Cana

Nazareth

DECAPOLIS

Nain

▲ Mt
Tabor

Caesarea

SAMARIA

Samaria

*Shechem
(Sychar)*

The Great Sea
(Mediterranean)

EPHRAIM

PERAEA

Jericho

Emmaus

Bethabara

Jerusalem ▲ Mt of Olives

Bethlehem

Bethany

JUDEA

Dead
Sea

NABATAEA

IDUMAEA

Every word of God proves true;
   he is a shield to those who take
   refuge in him.

Proverbs 30:5

GOD MAKES THE WORLD

In the beginning, there was nothing at all. Then God created the heavens and the earth, but everything was still covered in darkness, so God said, "Let there be light," and there was light! God called the light day and the darkness night, and that was the first day and the first night!

In the days that followed, God separated the water from dry land and covered the land with beautiful plants and trees. He made the sun to shine in the day and the moon and stars to light up the night sky.

Then God filled the seas with enormous whales and shiny fish, leaping dolphins and wobbly jellyfish, and he filled the skies with colorful birds. He made animals of all shapes and sizes—swift cheetahs, slow tortoises, huge elephants, and many more.

Last of all, God made man and told him to take care of this wonderful world and all the creatures.

God was pleased with all he had made and done, so on the seventh day, he rested and made that day a special day to rest and give thanks.

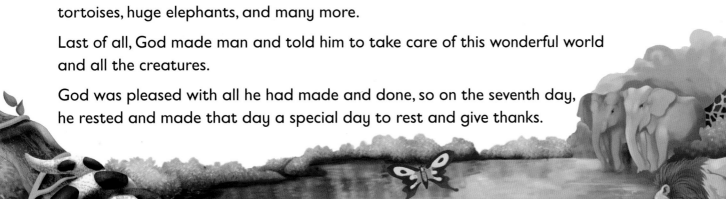

PRAYER
Dear Lord God,
help me to be amazed
with joy as I see more and
more of the wonderful
things you have made.
Help me to value and take
care of your creation.
Amen

THE BEAUTIFUL GARDEN

G od created the beautiful Garden of Eden for Adam—a marvelous paradise filled with green grass, colorful plants, and wonderful trees. God told Adam to help himself to fruit from any of these trees except for one: the Tree of Knowledge. But there were still plenty of other wonderful things for him to eat!

God brought all the animals and birds to Adam so that he could name them. But none of the animals were like him, and Adam was lonely, so God created a woman, Eve, to be his special friend.

PRAYER

Thank you, Lord God, that you have made all people and you made me just the way you want me to be. Help me to respect all people, because you made them.

Amen

DISOBEYING GOD

Now, of all the animals, the most cunning was the snake. One day, he said to Eve, "Did God really tell you that you couldn't eat fruit from any of the trees in this garden?" And she replied, "Oh, no, we can eat from any of them except from the one in the middle of the garden. We're not even allowed to touch it!"

"The Tree of Knowledge?" asked the wily snake. "But the fruit is delicious, and it won't harm you in the slightest! The only reason God doesn't want you to eat it is because it will make you wise like him. Go on, take a bite!"

The fruit looked so delicious that Eve picked some. She offered some to Adam, too, and they both ate it.

At once, it was as though their eyes had been opened. They realized they were naked and tried to cover themselves with some fig leaves that they sewed together to make clothes.

PRAYER

Dear Lord God, I am sorry that I hurt you and I hurt other people when I disobey your rules. Please make me strong to do what is right.

Amen

CAST OUT

Later that day, God was walking in the garden. When he found Adam and Eve hiding behind some bushes, he knew exactly what had happened. He was very angry. He cursed the wicked snake to crawl on its belly in the dirt for the rest of its life, and he banished Adam and Eve from the Garden of Eden. He told them that from now on they would need to work hard to get their food from the ground and would have to struggle with sharp thorns and choking weeds, for they had disobeyed him.

Then he used some animal skins to make clothes for them and sent them away from the beautiful garden. He placed an angel with a flaming sword to stand guard at the entrance.

PRAYER

Dear Lord God, help me to understand that you are holy, and help me to be glad that you are always fair and therefore you must punish wrong. Please help our police and judges to be fair too.
Amen

CAIN AND ABEL

Time passed, and Adam and Eve had two sons. Cain was a farmer who worked in the fields all day with his crops, while his younger brother Abel was a shepherd. One day both Cain and Abel brought offerings to God. Abel brought the very best meat he could, the finest and fattest of his lambs, and God was pleased. But God wasn't so pleased with the crops that Cain brought. When Abel brought his offering to God he had faith in his heart, and that is why God was pleased with him, but Cain was proud.

God saw that Cain was angry and said, "Why are you looking so cross? If you do what is right, then I'll be pleased with you. But watch out—if you don't do what is right, then you will find that sin is just around the corner! You must control it and not let it control you!"

Without faith we can't please God. We won't be accepted into the kingdom of heaven just because we have done good things. It isn't just what we do that matters—it is the way we do it and what is really in our hearts.

PRAYER

Thank you, Lord God, that Jesus has come as the Lamb of God, an offering for the sins of the whole world. Help me to trust in him and not try to bring any other offering.

Amen

MY BROTHER'S KEEPER

Cain was very jealous of his brother. He was angry with him—and he was angry with God! God hadn't accepted his offering, but he had accepted that of his younger brother!

With evil in his heart, Cain invited Abel to come with him into the fields, and there, filled with rage and bitterness, he killed his younger brother!

Later that day, God asked him where his brother was. Cain answered rudely, "How should I know? Do you expect me to watch over him? Am I my brother's keeper?"

But God saw Abel's blood on the ground and was angry. He knew what had happened. He punished Cain and sent him away from his home and family to wander from place to place without a home.

PRAYER
Dear Lord God, please help me to keep control of my temper. Help me not to be jealous of other people.
Amen

NOAH BUILDS AN ARK

Many years passed, and soon there were lots of people in the world. But they were becoming more and more wicked, and this made God very sad. He made up his mind to send a terrible flood to destroy everything that he had created.

But there was one good man on earth who loved and obeyed God. His name was Noah, and he had three sons. God told Noah to build an enormous boat, an ark, so that he and his family might be saved, along with two of every living creature.

When people saw Noah building a boat in the middle of the land, they laughed at him and made fun of him. But Noah ignored them, for he trusted God.

PRAYER

Dear Lord God, help me to trust and follow you at all times, even if it's hard and other people are against me.
Amen

TWO BY TWO

Noah built the amazing boat out of cypress wood. It had lots of rooms inside it and was three decks high! God told him exactly how it should be made and how big it should be. It took Noah and his three sons a long, long time to finish it.

When the ark was finished, Noah, his wife, and his sons and their wives loaded it with food for themselves and the animals. Then God sent the animals to the ark, two by two—one male and one female of every kind of animal and bird that lived upon the earth or flew in the skies.

Once they were all safely in, God closed the door behind them.

PRAYER

Thank you, Lord God, that you have a great plan for my life. Help me to follow your instructions.
Amen

THE FLOOD

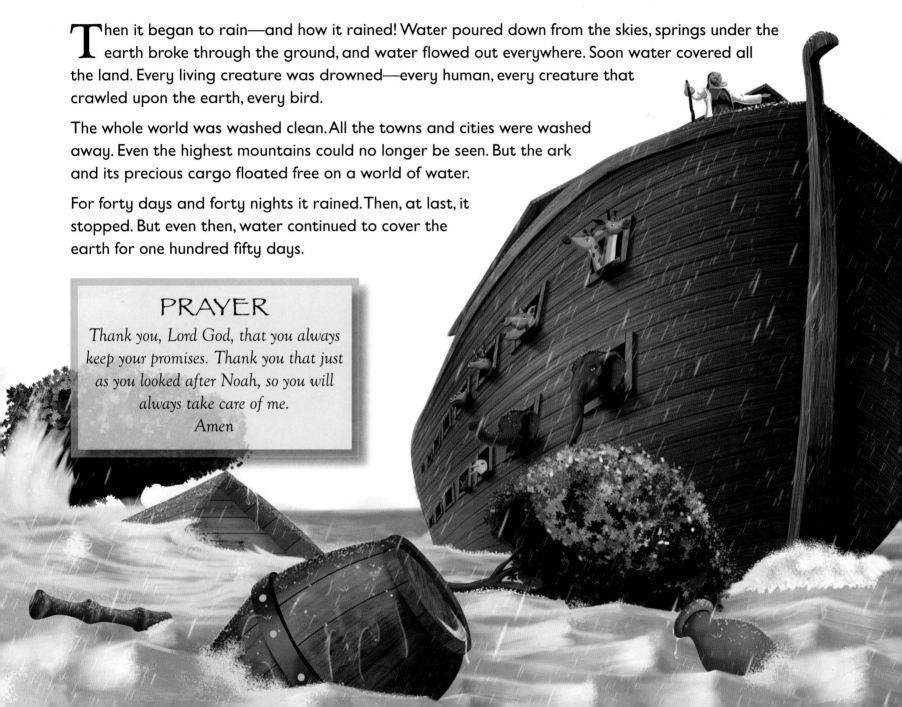

Then it began to rain—and how it rained! Water poured down from the skies, springs under the earth broke through the ground, and water flowed out everywhere. Soon water covered all the land. Every living creature was drowned—every human, every creature that crawled upon the earth, every bird.

The whole world was washed clean. All the towns and cities were washed away. Even the highest mountains could no longer be seen. But the ark and its precious cargo floated free on a world of water.

For forty days and forty nights it rained. Then, at last, it stopped. But even then, water continued to cover the earth for one hundred fifty days.

PRAYER

Thank you, Lord God, that you always keep your promises. Thank you that just as you looked after Noah, so you will always take care of me.

Amen

A BRAND-NEW START

The rain had stopped, yet the world was still covered with water. But God didn't forget about Noah or the animals. He made a wind blow over the earth, and slowly, slowly, the flood waters began to go down. At last the ark touched land—on the top of a mountain!

When the tips of the mountains began to emerge once more from the water, Noah sent out a dove to see if water still covered the world. But the dove could find nowhere to rest and came back to the boat.

One week later, Noah sent out the dove again—and this time it returned with an olive leaf in its beak! Now Noah knew that the flood was over, for the trees were growing again. It was time to leave the ark. Noah was filled with gratitude, and God promised to never again send such a dreadful flood. He put a beautiful rainbow in the sky as a reminder of this promise.

PRAYER

Thank you, Lord God, that when I see a rainbow, it will always remind me that you keep your promises. Thank you for beautiful rainbows.
Amen

THE TOWER OF BABEL

To begin with, the whole world had only one language, so everyone could understand everyone else. There came a time when a group of Noah's descendants decided to settle down and build a great city. It would be famous throughout the land and have a tower that would reach to the heavens.

But when God saw what they were doing, he was not happy. He feared they were becoming too proud and vain—they had forgotten about God!

So God made them unable to understand one other. Soon a great babble of voices was heard all over the city, with everyone speaking in a different language. No one could understand his neighbor!

PRAYER

Dear Lord God, please help me to appreciate and love all people, whatever their language or color.
Amen

In all the confusion, building stopped. The wonderful tower was left unfinished, the people scattered far and wide, and the tower became known as the Tower of Babel.

GOD CALLS ABRAHAM

Abraham was a good man who trusted in God. God asked Abraham to leave his home, his country, and his family and go to another land. He promised to bless him and to make him the father of a great nation.

Abraham had a good home with large flocks of sheep and cattle, but when God told him to leave, he did. He took his wife, Sarah, his nephew, Lot, and his servants and set out for Canaan.

Along the way, God appeared to Abraham and told him, "I will give this land to your children." Sarah and Abraham had been unable to have children, but Abraham was overjoyed at this news and built an altar to God and praised him.

Later, Abraham took his family to Egypt, for there was a terrible famine. By the time he left Egypt to return to Canaan, he had become very wealthy and owned many animals.

PRAYER

Dear Lord God, help me to trust you, like Abraham, so that I will obey your instructions and follow your plan for my life.
Amen

GOING SEPARATE WAYS

Abraham and his nephew Lot had large flocks of cattle, sheep, and donkeys—so large that there wasn't enough grazing land for them all, and their herdsmen began to fight. Abraham decided that they would have to split up. He gave Lot the first choice of where to go, and Lot chose to leave Canaan and go east to the green and fertile Jordan Valley. Abraham stayed in Canaan.

After Lot had left, God called Abraham to him. "Look as far as you can. All the land that you can see, I will give to you and to your children forever, and your children shall be like the dust of the earth—for there will be so many of them that no one will be able to count them!"

PRAYER

*Dear Lord God, when
I have choices to make,
please help me to choose the
pathway that pleases you.
Amen*

GOD'S PROMISE

Abraham and his wife were very old and hadn't had a child, but Abraham wasn't worried—he trusted God. God told him that he would be a father and that he would have too many descendants to count—as many as the stars in the sky!—and that all this land would belong to them. Then God told him to prepare a sacrifice.

That evening, God spoke to him again, telling him that his descendants would be slaves in a country not their own for four hundred years. But they would at last be free and would return to their own land, and those who had enslaved them would be punished.

When the sun had set and darkness had fallen, a smoking firepot with a blazing torch appeared and passed between the pieces of the sacrifice as a sign to Abraham from God.

PRAYER

Dear Lord God, teach me to trust you and learn to wait patiently even when it seems a long time, because your promises are always good and true.
Amen

ABRAHAM ENTERTAINS ANGELS

Not long after this, Abraham saw three strangers passing by. He hurried out to meet them and offered to bring water to wash their feet and food to eat while they rested in the shade of a nearby tree. Sarah baked some bread while Abraham brought his choicest meat for the men to eat and milk for them to drink.

Then one of the men, who was really God, asked Abraham where his wife was. When Abraham replied that she was inside the tent, God told him that he would come back within a year and that Sarah would have given birth to a son.

Sarah was listening in the tent and could not help laughing out loud. How ridiculous—she was far too old to have children!

But God asked, "Why is Sarah laughing? Nothing is too hard for the Lord." And sure enough, nine months later, Sarah gave birth to a baby boy. And she named him Isaac, which means "he laughs!"

PRAYER

Thank you, Lord God, that you are close to me and interested in the details of my life.
Amen

THE BAD CITIES

Sodom and Gomorrah were bad cities. The people had turned away from God and were wicked and cruel. God decided to destroy them. But Abraham was worried, for his nephew Lot lived in Sodom. He asked God if he would still destroy the city if there were any good men living in it, and God said to him, "If there are even ten good people, I will spare the city."

Lot was standing by the city gates when two strangers—angels in disguise —passed through. He begged them to spend the night in his house. He gave them water to wash their feet and prepared a meal for them, but an angry, violent crowd gathered, demanding that he send the strangers outside.

Lot begged them to leave the strangers alone, for they were his guests, but the mob became angry, and the angels had to pull Lot back inside. Then they struck the crowd with blindness so they could not find the door to break in!

PRAYER

Thank you, Lord God, for all the times your angels have watched over me and saved me from danger.
Amen

GOD DESTROYS SODOM

The angels warned Lot to leave the city with his wife and daughters that very night, as God was angry and the city would be punished. They took them by the hand and led them to safety, urging them to hurry. "Flee for your lives! Run to the mountains and don't look back!"

As Lot and his family hurried away, they could hear dreadful sounds as a storm of burning sulphur rained down on the city. Nothing and no one survived—not one building, not one person. But Lot's wife could not help looking back, and as she did so, she was instantly turned into a pillar of salt! Lot and his daughters were the only ones to survive the destruction.

PRAYER

Thank you, Lord God, that you are completely fair when you punish wickedness. Thank you, too, that you make a way of escape for those who trust you.

Amen

A GOOD MAN

Job lived in the days of Abraham. He was wealthy but was not boastful or selfish. He worshipped God and obeyed all his laws, and God was pleased with him. One day Satan said, "It's easy for Job to be good when things are going so well. I bet if life got hard, he would change his tune!" And God agreed that Satan could test Job's faith.

One day, shortly after this, when Job's children were all feasting at his eldest son's house, a messenger came running up. He was upset and told Job that all his cattle had been stolen. He had hardly finished speaking when another servant came to tell him that a ball of fire had fallen from the sky and burned all the sheep. But the worst was yet to come, for now another servant came to tell Job that all his children had been killed when a mighty wind from the desert had struck his son's house, and it had collapsed, killing all inside.

Job sank to the ground in sorrow, but he said, "Everything I have was given to me by God. What he has given, he can take away. I still praise his name."

Job had passed the first test.

PRAYER

Dear Lord God, help me to be glad for everything you give me, but not to depend on things I see around me for my happiness.
Amen

THE SECOND TEST

Satan went back to God. "That's all very well," he said, "but it would be a different story if Job himself had to suffer." God agreed that he could test him again, and the very next day Job woke up covered in boils from head to toe. They stung and itched so much that all he could do was sit in a corner with a broken piece of pottery and use it to scrape his skin.

When his wife asked why he wasn't cursing God, Job replied, "If we take all the good things God sends, then we should take the bad things too."

Job's friends came to see him. "You must have done something very wrong for God to be punishing you like this!" they said. "Tell him you're sorry and ask for forgiveness!"

They were trying to help, but they only made it worse. Job knew he hadn't done anything wrong, but their words troubled him, and at last he broke out in frustration. "Curse the day that I was born! It would have been better to have died than suffer like this! Oh, God, what have I done to make you so angry with me? How can you do this to me?"

PRAYER
Dear Lord God, please help me not to be cross when things don't go the way that I would like.
Amen

GOD TALKS TO JOB

Another of Job's friends said, "I kept quiet up till now, because I'm younger and I thought you would all be wiser than me. But wisdom clearly comes from God—not from old age! Job, you have no right to criticize God. Think of how great and powerful he is. You cannot begin to understand his ways. God is always just and merciful. Think of all the wonderful things he has done!"

Just then, a dreadful storm began to rage. Lightning filled the sky, and thunder filled their ears. Then out of the storm came the voice of God: "Job, who are you to question me? Were you there when I made the world? Can you command the day to dawn or the rain to fall on the land? How can you dare to question my wisdom?"

Then Job was ashamed. "Oh Lord," he said, "I'm foolish and ignorant. Please forgive me!"

God was pleased with Job. He healed him and blessed the last part of his life even more than the first. Job had many more children and lived happily for many more years.

PRAYER

Dear Lord God, I know that you have all wisdom and knowledge. Help me to praise your greatness when I see the wonders of creation all around me.
Amen

ISAAC IS BORN

Now when Abraham's wife, Sarah, was ninety years old, she gave birth to a baby boy, Isaac, just as God had promised. Abraham and Sarah were overjoyed, but Sarah believed her maidservant Hagar was making fun of her. She was so angry with her that she made Abraham send her away, along with her son, Ishmael, who was also Abraham's son.

Abraham was sad, but God told him things would work out for Ishmael, so he handed Hagar some food and water and sent her and Ishmael into the desert.

Soon all the water was gone, and they began to weep in despair. But an angel called to Hagar from heaven and said, "Don't be afraid, Hagar. God has heard the boy crying. Lift him up and take him by the hand, for he will be the father of a great nation." Then God opened her eyes and she saw a well of water!

God was with the boy as he grew up. Ishmael lived in the desert and became an archer.

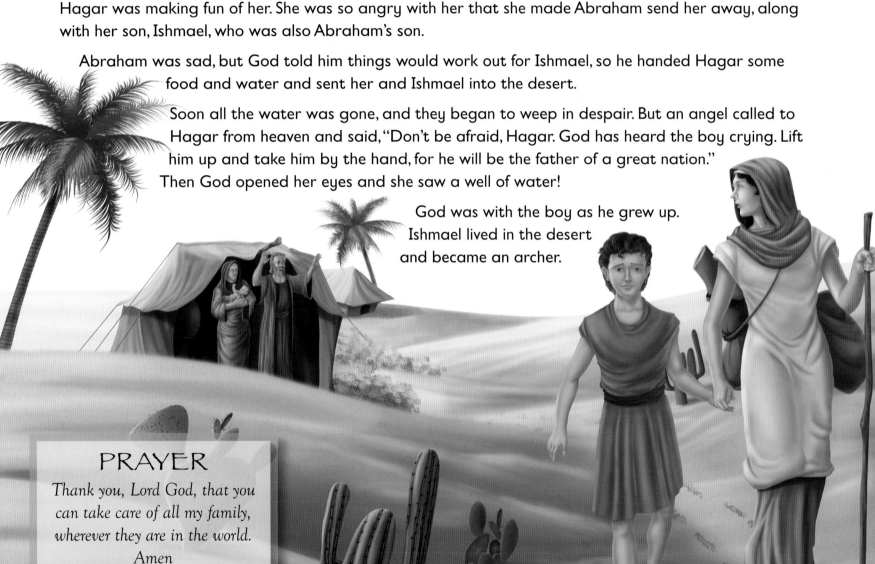

PRAYER

Thank you, Lord God, that you can take care of all my family, wherever they are in the world.
Amen

ABRAHAM IS TESTED

Isaac grew up to be a fine young boy, and his father and mother were very proud of him and thankful to God. But one day, God decided to test Abraham's faith. He told Abraham that he must offer the boy as a sacrifice!

Abraham was heartbroken, but his faith in God was absolute, and so he prepared everything just as he had been commanded. But as he lifted up his knife, suddenly an angel spoke to him. "Abraham, Abraham! Don't harm the boy! I know now that you love the Lord your God with all your heart, for you would be willing to give up your own son."

God sent a ram to be sacrificed in the boy's place, and the angel told Abraham that God would truly bless him and his descendants because of his faith.

PRAYER
Dear Lord God, please help me to love you with all my heart and strength, above everything else.
Amen

A WIFE FOR ISAAC

When Isaac had grown into a young man, Abraham asked his most trusted servant to go back to his homeland and find a wife there for his son. This was a difficult task, and when the servant reached his master's hometown, he prayed to God to send him a sign: "Let it be whoever comes to offer water not just to me, but to my camels also."

Before he had finished praying, beautiful Rebekah came out to draw water from the well. When the servant asked her if he might have a drink, she immediately offered him her jar and then hurried to draw water for his camels too.

The servant thanked God for listening to his prayer. He then explained his mission to Rebekah, and when her father was asked, it was agreed that she should become Isaac's wife. When she traveled back to Canaan to meet her new husband, Isaac fell in love with her instantly, and she with him!

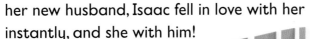

PRAYER

*Dear Lord God, teach
me to talk to you
about things I need
and then to listen for
your answers.*
Amen

THE BOWL OF STEW

Rebekah was old before she became pregnant, and when she did, it was with twins. They seemed to kick and push so much inside her that she was worried, but God told her that the two boys would one day be the fathers of two nations. The firstborn was a hairy boy, whom they named Esau, and his brother was called Jacob. When they grew up, Esau became a great hunter, while Jacob was quieter and spent more time at home. Isaac loved Esau, but Rebekah was especially fond of Jacob.

One day, Jacob was preparing a delicious stew when his brother came in, ravenous after a long trip. When he demanded some of the stew, Jacob told him that he could only have a plate of stew in exchange for his birthright as the firstborn son. Esau was so hungry and impatient that he agreed! He had shown how little he cared about his rights as the firstborn son if he was prepared to sell them for a simple meal!

PRAYER

Dear Lord God, help me to value properly the things that are most important in life and always to keep first things first.
Amen

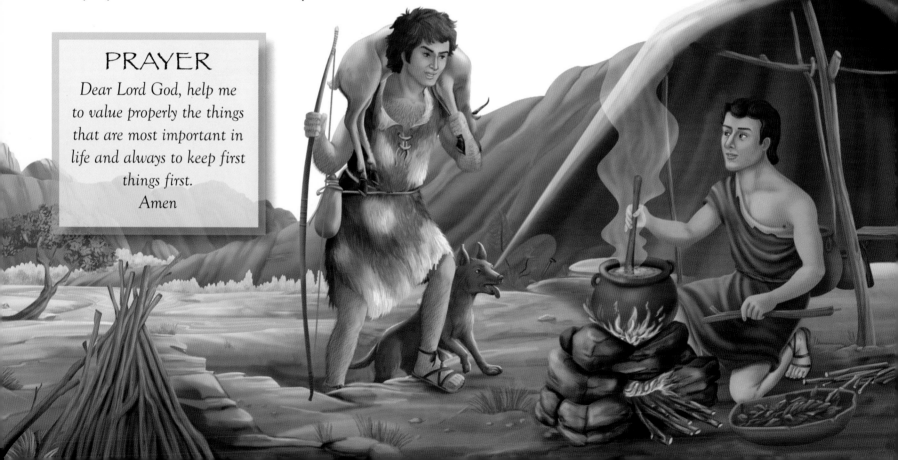

TRICKERY

In later years, Jacob cheated Esau out of his father's blessing too. When Isaac was very old and nearly blind, he prepared to give his blessing to his eldest son. He told Esau to go kill an animal and prepare it for him to eat, and then he would bless him.

But Rebekah overheard their conversation and was determined that it would be her favorite son, Jacob, who would receive the blessing. She told Jacob to fetch two young goats, which she prepared for Isaac. Then, with the help of his mother, Jacob disguised himself as Esau. He wore goatskins around his arms so that he would be hairy like his brother, and then he took in the food.

Jacob didn't sound like his brother, but he felt like him, and so Isaac gave him his blessing to be in charge of the family when he died.

When Esau found out what had happened, he was so angry that he wanted to kill his younger brother! Rebekah sent Jacob away from home to keep him safe.

PRAYER
*Dear Lord God, please help
me to be honest and true,
especially with my close family.*
Amen

JACOB'S DREAM

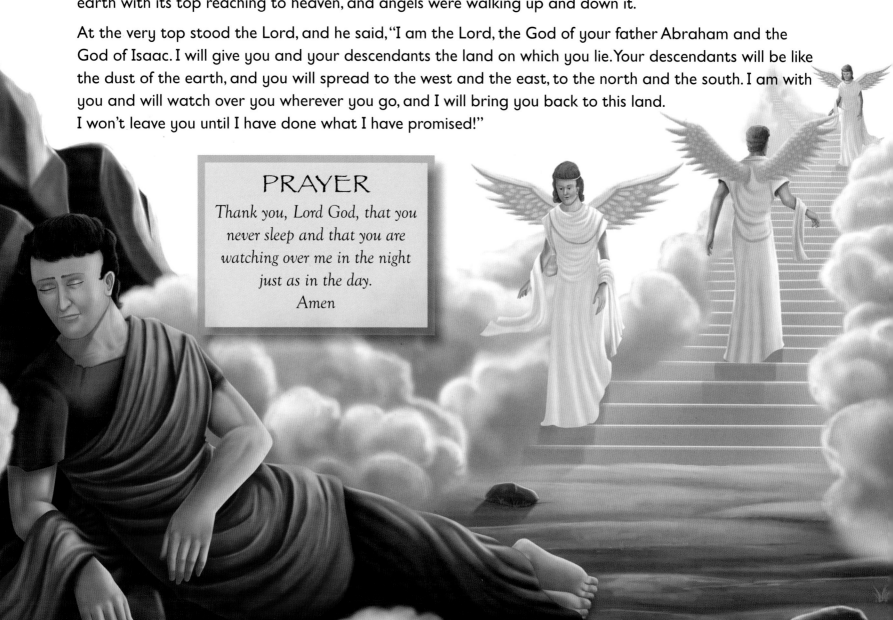

Jacob traveled to the house of his uncle Laban. On the way he stopped for the night. Using a hard stone as a pillow, he lay down to sleep. That night he had a dream. He saw a stairway resting on the earth with its top reaching to heaven, and angels were walking up and down it.

At the very top stood the Lord, and he said, "I am the Lord, the God of your father Abraham and the God of Isaac. I will give you and your descendants the land on which you lie. Your descendants will be like the dust of the earth, and you will spread to the west and the east, to the north and the south. I am with you and will watch over you wherever you go, and I will bring you back to this land.
I won't leave you until I have done what I have promised!"

PRAYER

*Thank you, Lord God, that you
never sleep and that you are
watching over me in the night
just as in the day.*
Amen

TRICKED INTO MARRIAGE

Jacob worked in the house of his uncle Laban, and he fell in love with Laban's younger daughter, Rachel. His uncle agreed that if he worked for him for seven years, he could then marry Rachel. After seven years, the marriage took place, but when Jacob lifted the veil from his wife's face, it was not Rachel standing before him, but her elder sister Leah! He had been tricked!

Laban told him that it was the custom that the oldest daughter marry first, but he said that if Jacob would promise to work for him for another seven years, then he could marry his beloved Rachel. Jacob loved her so much that he agreed.

Rachel was always his favorite wife, but God took pity on Leah and blessed her with six strong sons. It was many years before Rachel had a son.

PRAYER

Dear Lord God, teach me to love my family and friends with a deep, strong love that will never fade away.
Amen

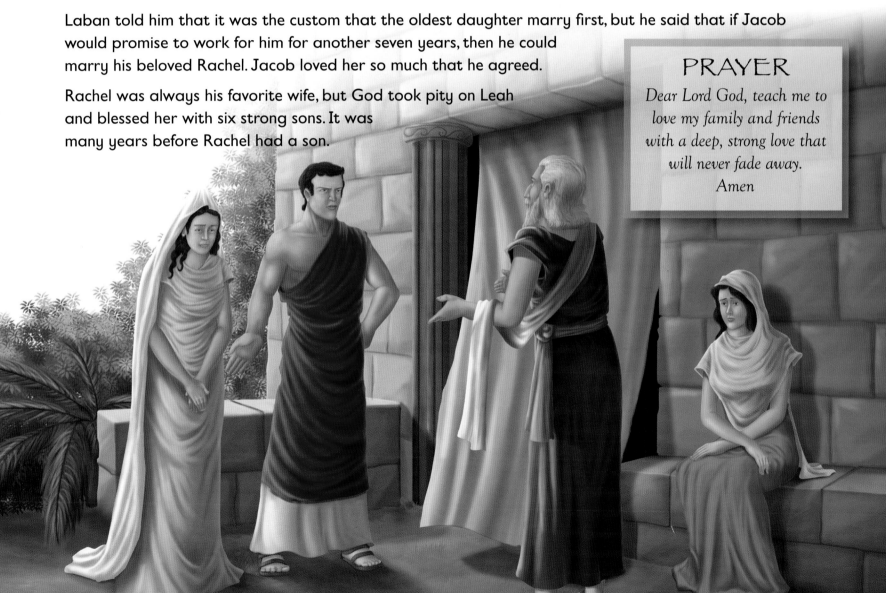

PARTING WAYS

Although Jacob felt it was time to return home, his uncle wanted him to stay. He agreed to give him, as his wages, all the marked or speckled animals in the herds. But then he tried to cheat Jacob by rounding up any marked animals and sending them away with his sons so that all the new animals would be born without marks!

But God told Jacob to place some freshly peeled branches in the animals' water troughs when the strong, healthy animals came to drink, and all the new animals that were born to them were marked or speckled. In this way all the strong animals went to Jacob, and all the weak animals went to Laban.

Jacob knew that his uncle would continue to cheat him, so one day he set off for home, along with all his family, servants, and animals. Laban chased after him, but in the end he let him go.

PRAYER

Dear Lord God, help me to be fair in my work and play, never trying to gain advantage by cheating.

Amen

WRESTLING WITH GOD

Jacob was worried as he returned home with his family, for he didn't know how his brother Esau would greet him. When a messenger said that Esau was coming to meet him with four hundred men, Jacob feared the worst. He sent some of his servants ahead with gifts for his brother to help make peace. Then he sent his family and everything he owned across the river. Jacob himself stayed behind alone to pray.

Suddenly a man appeared, and the two of them wrestled together until daybreak. When the man saw that he could not overpower him, he touched Jacob's hip so that it was wrenched. He cried out to Jacob to let him go, but Jacob replied, "Not unless you bless me!"

Then the man said, "Your name will no longer be Jacob, but Israel, because you have struggled with God and with men and have overcome."

When Jacob asked his name, he would give no reply. But he blessed Jacob, and Jacob understood that he had wrestled with God himself!

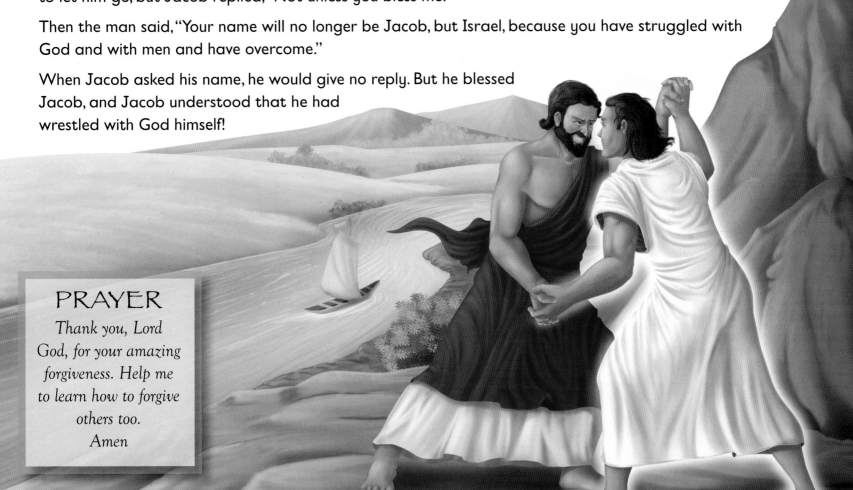

PRAYER

*Thank you, Lord
God, for your amazing
forgiveness. Help me
to learn how to forgive
others too.
Amen*

RETURNING TO BETHEL

God spoke to Jacob and told him to go to Bethel. So Jacob traveled with his family and servants to Bethel, where he built an altar to God to thank him for his mercy.

When they left Bethel, Rachel, who was pregnant for the second time, went into labor, but things didn't go smoothly. Before she breathed her last breath, Rachel saw her lovely baby boy. She named him Ben-Oni, which means "son of my sorrow," although his father called him Benjamin, "son of my right hand." Jacob was heartbroken and built a pillar over her tomb.

Now Jacob had twelve sons. The sons of Leah were Reuben, Simeon, Levi, Judah, Issachar and Zebulun. Joseph and Benjamin were the sons of Rachel. Dan and Naphtali were the sons of Rachel's maidservant, and Gad and Asher were the sons of Leah's maidservant.

PRAYER

Dear Lord God, I pray for all children who do not have a mother. Please provide wonderful people to meet their needs.

Amen

THE WONDERFUL COAT

Jacob lived in Canaan. He had twelve sons, but Joseph was his favorite. He had been born when Jacob was already very old, and, of course, he was the first son of Rachel, whom Jacob had loved above all his other wives. To show Joseph just how much he loved him, Jacob had a wonderful coat made for him, a long-sleeved robe covered with colorful embroidery.

When Joseph's brothers saw that their father loved Joseph more than he loved them, they couldn't help hating their brother. The beautiful coat was fit for royalty—not for working in the fields with sheep and goats, which is what they spent their days doing. They must have felt that Joseph thought he was truly better than them.

PRAYER

Thank you, Lord God, for placing me in my family. Please help all fathers and mothers to care for their children without having favorites.

Amen

JOSEPH'S DREAMS

Joseph's brothers were jealous of him, but they really got angry when he began telling them about his dreams: "Last night I dreamed that we were collecting sheaves of grain, when suddenly my sheaf stood up straight and yours all bowed down before it."

"What are you saying?" growled the brothers. "That you're going to rule over us someday? Get lost!"

Joseph had another dream. "This time the sun and moon and eleven stars were bowing down to me," he told his family. Even Jacob became quite cross when he heard about Joseph's latest dream. "Do you really believe that your mother and I and all your brothers are going to bow down before you? Don't get too big for your boots!" Jacob wondered to himself what the dream might mean.

PRAYER

Dear Lord God, please be near and protect children in families where things have gone wrong and there is anger and hurt.

Amen

THROWN INTO A WELL

Joseph's brothers had had enough. What with the fabulous coat, and now these dreadful dreams, they felt the time had come to get rid of their annoying brother.

One day when they were out in the fields and saw Joseph coming toward them, the brothers said to one another, "Here comes the dreamer! Let's kill him now while we have the chance and throw his body into a well!" But Reuben persuaded them not to kill Joseph, but to throw him in the well without hurting him. He secretly intended to save him later.

The jealous brothers grabbed young Joseph, tore off his precious multicolored coat, and threw him in a deep pit. Then they sat down nearby to eat, deaf to his cries for help.

PRAYER
Dear Lord God, please be near today to people who are wrongly accused and badly treated. Help those who stand up for justice.
Amen

DAY
34

BROTHER FOR SALE

As the brothers were callously eating, they saw a caravan of Ishmaelite traders passing by on their camels on their way to Egypt, and quick as a flash they decided to sell Joseph to the traders. That would be far more profitable to them than killing Joseph and hiding his body! So off to Egypt with the traders went Joseph in chains, sold for twenty pieces of silver!

Then the wicked brothers took his beautiful coat, ripped it into pieces, and smeared it with the blood of a goat. Afterward, they trudged home with long faces and showed the coat to their father, implying that Joseph had been killed by a wild animal.

Jacob was heartbroken at the death of his beloved son.

PRAYER

Dear Lord God, please watch over people today who are cruelly forced to go where they do not want to go. Please send them help and rescue them.

Amen

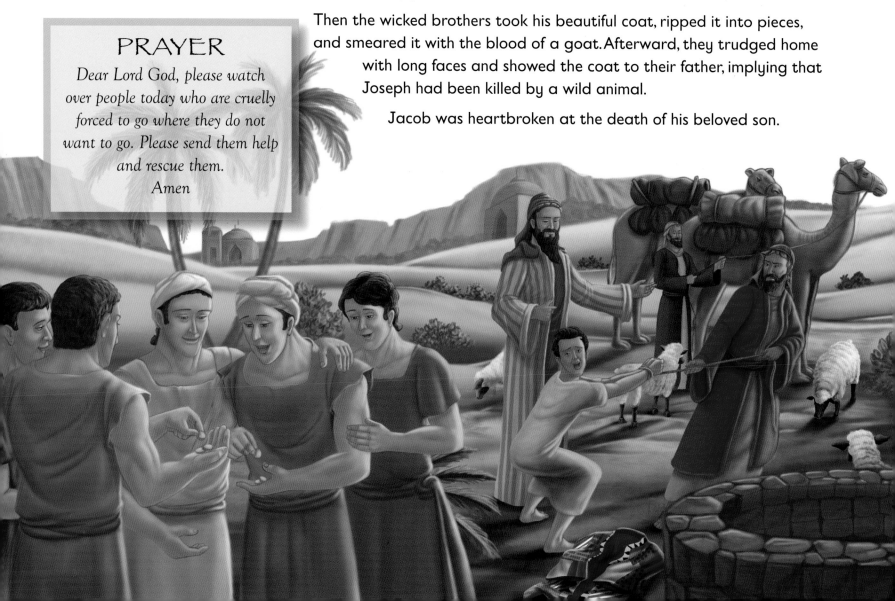

POTIPHAR'S WIFE

Joseph had been sold to one of Pharaoh's officials, a man named Potiphar, but God was still looking after him. He was clever and hardworking, and soon Potiphar decided to place him in charge of his whole household. But the peaceful times didn't last, for Potiphar's wife took a liking to Joseph, who was a handsome and strong young man. Joseph would have nothing to do with her advances, but one day when he pulled away from her, in his haste he left his coat behind. When her husband came back, she showed him the coat and told him that Joseph had come to her bedroom to try to take advantage of her, but had run away when she screamed.

Potiphar was furious and threw poor Joseph into jail!

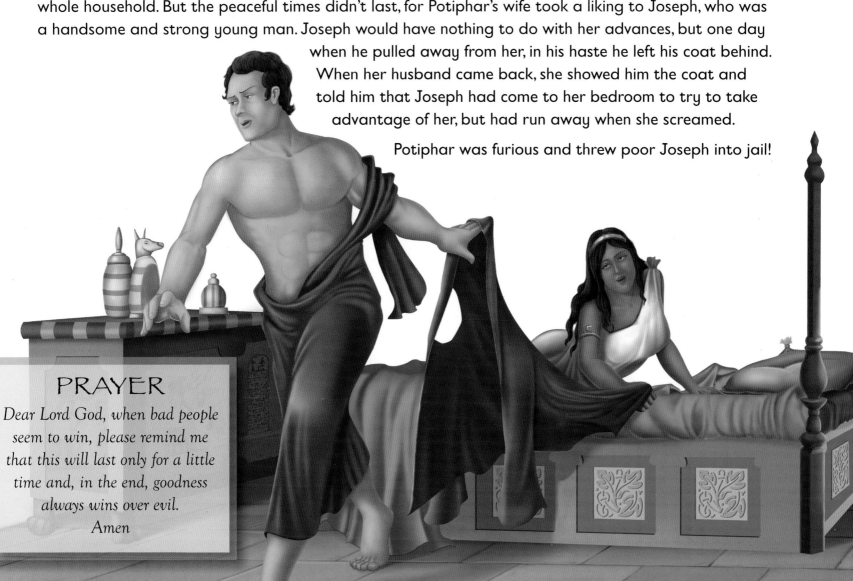

PRAYER

Dear Lord God, when bad people seem to win, please remind me that this will last only for a little time and, in the end, goodness always wins over evil.
Amen

THE WINE STEWARD AND THE BAKER

Some time later, both Pharaoh's wine steward and his chief baker angered Pharaoh and were thrown into prison. One night, both men had strange dreams and were puzzled. Joseph said to them, "My God will be able to help. Tell me your dreams."

The wine steward went first. "In my dream I saw a vine, with three branches covered in grapes. I took the grapes and squeezed them into Pharaoh's cup."

Joseph told him that within three days, Pharaoh would pardon him and take him back—and he asked the steward to remember him.

Now the baker was anxious to tell his dream too. "On my head were three baskets of bread," he said, "but birds were eating Pharaoh's pastries."

Joseph was sad. "Within three days Pharaoh will cut off your head, and the birds will eat your flesh."

Things turned out just as Joseph foretold, for in three days it was Pharaoh's birthday, and on that day he pardoned the wine steward and gave him back his job, but he hanged the chief baker and cut off his head.

PRAYER
Dear Lord God, help me to always speak of your goodness to anyone I meet who needs you.
Amen

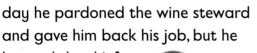

PHARAOH'S DREAMS

Joseph asked the wine bearer to remember him when he got out of prison, but two years passed before the Hebrew slave crossed his thoughts, and it happened like this:

One night, Pharaoh had a strange dream. He was standing by the Nile when out of the river came seven cows, healthy and fat, and they grazed among the reeds. After them, seven other cows, ugly and thin, came up out of the Nile and stood beside them. Then the thin cows ate up the fat cows and yet looked just as thin and sickly as before!

Pharaoh had another dream. Seven healthy heads of grain were growing on a single stalk. Then seven more heads of grain sprouted, and these were thin and scorched by the wind. The thin heads of grain swallowed up the seven healthy, full heads.

In the morning, Pharaoh felt worried. He sent for all the magicians and wise men of Egypt, but no one could interpret the dreams.

PRAYER

Dear Lord God, please give your wisdom to the leaders of my country so that they will make good laws.

Amen

WHAT CAN IT MEAN?

Just then the wine bearer remembered Joseph, and the slave was brought before mighty Pharaoh, who asked him to explain his dream. "I cannot do it," Joseph replied, "but God will be able to explain."

Once Pharaoh had told his dream, Joseph replied, "These two dreams are really one and the same. The seven cows and the seven heads of grain are seven years. The land will be blessed with seven years of healthy crops and bumper harvests, but they will be followed by seven years of dreadful famine. You will need to plan carefully to prepare for what lies ahead."

Pharaoh spoke to his advisors and then turned to Joseph, saying, "It is clear to me that you are the man we need. Since God has made all this known to you, I will put you in charge of my land. You will be second only to me in all of Egypt."

And with that, Pharaoh put his own signet ring on Joseph's finger, put a gold chain around his neck, and dressed him in fine clothes!

PRAYER

Thank you, Lord God, that you already know what will happen in the future, and so I need never be afraid.
Amen

A WISE LEADER

Joseph was thirty years old when he entered the service of Pharaoh, King of Egypt. Riding in a fine chariot, he traveled throughout the land making sure that food was put aside for the times of hardship ahead of them. Just as he had foretold, the country was blessed with seven years of bumper crops, and so much grain was stored in the cities that he gave up counting it.

After seven years, the famine began. When the people of Egypt began to run out of food, Pharaoh told them to go to Joseph.

Now Joseph opened up the storehouses and sold the corn that had been put away so carefully. No one in Egypt went hungry. In fact, there was so much food in Egypt that people from other countries traveled there to buy food, for the famine was severe throughout the world.

PRAYER

Dear Lord God, help those who have plenty to share with those in our world who are in need. Please be close to children in places of desperate poverty and famine.
Amen

THE BROTHERS BUY GRAIN

In Canaan, the famine had hit Joseph's family hard too. Jacob decided to send his sons to buy corn in Egypt. Only Benjamin stayed behind, for Jacob could not bear to lose his youngest son. When they reached Egypt, the brothers bowed down before Joseph. With his golden chain and fine clothes, they didn't recognize him, but Joseph could see his dreams becoming reality as they bowed their heads low and begged to buy food.

Joseph wanted to see if his brothers had changed at all, and so he planned to test their honesty and loyalty. He accused them of being spies. The brothers frantically denied it, so he agreed to let them go back to Canaan with corn—but only if they returned with their youngest brother.

Jacob didn't want to let Benjamin go, but in the end he had to agree, and so the brothers returned with more money to pay for the grain. (When they had opened their sacks, they had been horrified to find that the money they had taken with them to Egypt the first time to pay for the grain was still in them!)

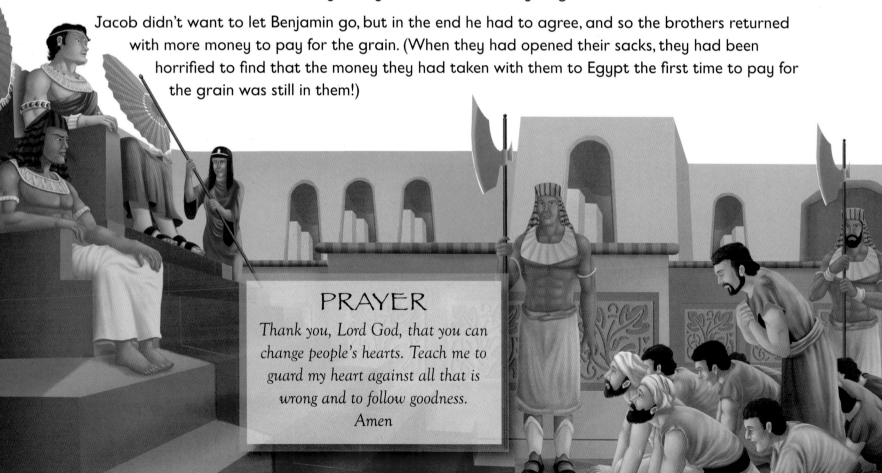

PRAYER

Thank you, Lord God, that you can change people's hearts. Teach me to guard my heart against all that is wrong and to follow goodness.

Amen

TREACHERY

Joseph was so overcome when he saw Benjamin that he had to hide his face. He had his servants feed the brothers and then sent them on their way with more corn, but not before hiding a silver cup in Benjamin's sack. The brothers were traveling home when guards came upon them and dragged them back to the palace.

"Thieves!" shouted Joseph. "I treated you with kindness and you repay me by stealing!"

"There must be some mistake!" cried the brothers, but when the guards checked, there was the silver cup in Benjamin's sack.

The horrified brothers fell to their knees. "My lord!" they cried, "take any one of us, but do not take Benjamin, for his father's heart would break!"

PRAYER

Dear Lord God, thank you that in your plan, people with very hard hearts can become people who care. Please keep working in my heart.
Amen

THE LONG-LOST BROTHER

At this, Joseph knew that his brothers really had changed. They cared so much for their little brother and for how upset their father would be, that any one of them would have given himself up to save Benjamin. Crying tears of joy, Joseph went to hug them, and to their joy and amazement, told them who he really was. He told them not to feel too bad about what had happened, for it had all been part of God's plan. "I was sent to rule in Egypt so that you would not starve in Canaan!" he said.

At first, they could hardly believe that this great and important man was really their long-lost brother, but when they did, they were filled with joy, for they had had many years to feel sorry for what they had done.

PRAYER

Dear Lord God, thank you that you care for families. Where there has been bitterness, please bring families together in peace again.
Amen

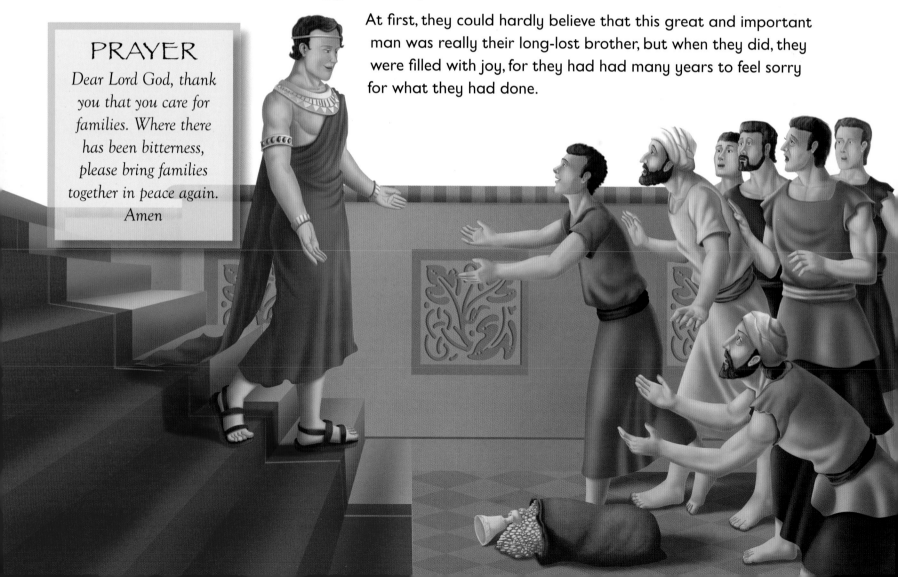

MOVING TO EGYPT

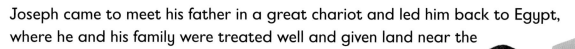

Now it was time to tell Jacob the good news. When the brothers returned, saying that his beloved son Joseph was not only alive and well, but governor of all Egypt, Jacob could hardly believe his ears! But when he saw all the fine gifts that Joseph had sent him, he had to believe his eyes!

Jacob gathered up all his belongings, his herds and flocks, and traveled to Egypt with his family. God reassured him, telling him that he would lead them out of Egypt once again when the time was right.

Joseph came to meet his father in a great chariot and led him back to Egypt, where he and his family were treated well and given land near the Canaan border to tend their animals.

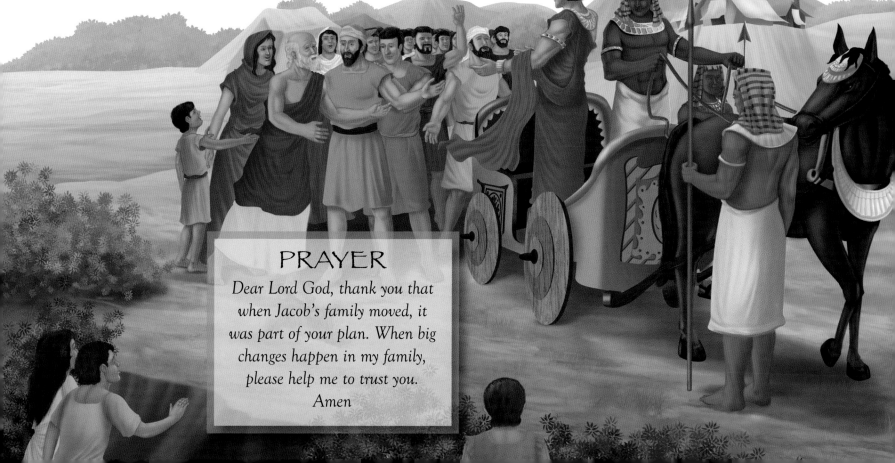

PRAYER

Dear Lord God, thank you that when Jacob's family moved, it was part of your plan. When big changes happen in my family, please help me to trust you.

Amen

THE DEATH OF JACOB

Now Jacob was growing old. Before he died, he called all his sons together to give them each a special blessing, for they were to form the twelve tribes of Israel, and he named Joseph a "prince among his brothers."

He made Joseph promise to bury him in Canaan, in the spot where he had buried his wife Leah, and where Isaac and Rebecca were buried before her, and Abraham and Sarah before them. When Jacob had breathed his last breath, with Pharaoh's permission, all Jacob's family, except the children and those who tended the animals, set off to Canaan, where they buried their father Jacob, also known as Israel.

PRAYER

I know, Lord God, that death is part of life. I know that the old people I love will not always be with me. Help me to value them and give time to them now.

Amen

SLAVES!

The years passed. Joseph and his brothers were long dead, but their families continued to grow, and by now there were many, many Hebrews in Egypt. The new king believed that there were too many of them in his country, and he feared that they would become too strong, so the Egyptians put guards over the Hebrews and turned them into slaves. They forced them to work the land and build for them.

The Hebrews were badly treated, yet still their numbers grew, for the women were blessed by God. Now the new king ordered that any girls born to the Hebrews could live, but any boys must be killed. When the Hebrew midwives failed to do as he asked, he gave a dreadful and cruel new order: "All baby boys must be drowned in the river Nile!"

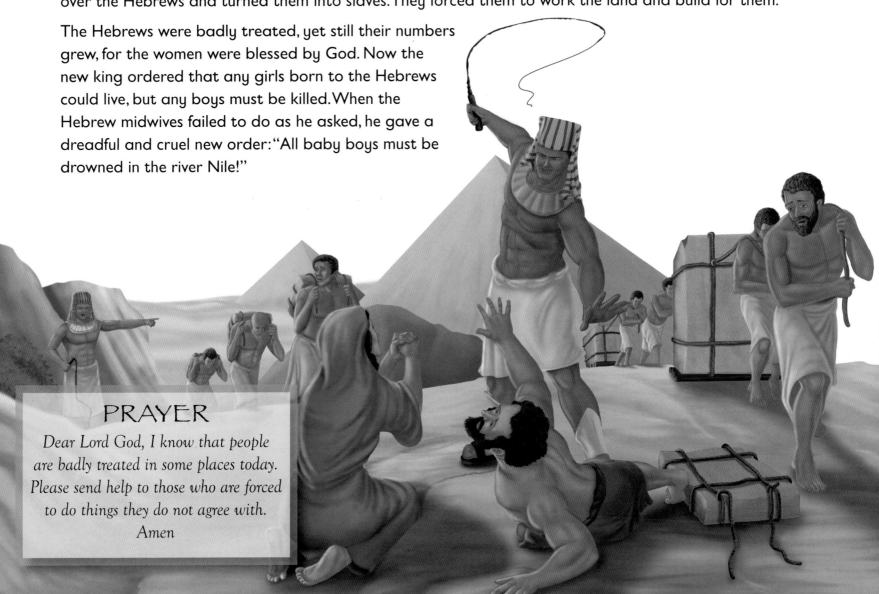

PRAYER

Dear Lord God, I know that people are badly treated in some places today. Please send help to those who are forced to do things they do not agree with.
Amen

A BABY IN THE REEDS

Moses was a beautiful baby boy. His mother loved him dearly, but she knew that if the king found out about him, he would be killed. So she made a basket out of reeds, wrapped her baby in a shawl, and placed him in it tenderly. Then she lowered him into the water among the reeds and rushes.

After a while, the king's daughter came down to the river. She heard a strange gurgling noise and pulled back the reeds to see a lovely baby boy crying. She picked him up and held him gently in her arms. "This must be one of the Hebrew babies," she said softly.

Moses' sister Miriam was secretly watching from nearby. Now she bravely stepped forward and offered to fetch someone to nurse the baby. When the princess nodded, Miriam darted off to find her own mother, and so it was that Miriam's mother looked after her own son until he was old enough for the princess to take him to the palace.

PRAYER

Thank you, Lord God, for all those who work hard to rescue babies and children today. Help me care about protecting those who cannot speak for themselves.
Amen

PRINCE OF EGYPT

Moses grew up among the riches of the royal palace in Egypt. But when he was older, he was shocked to see how the Egyptians treated his fellow Hebrews. One day when he saw an Egyptian brutally beating a Hebrew slave, he became angry and killed him and buried his body in the sand! But word got out of the murder, and so Moses fled the country and traveled to Midian.

There, Moses stopped to drink at a well. As he watched, he saw some nasty shepherds chasing away a group of girls who were trying to get water for their animals. Moses stood up. He hated bullying! The man who had been brought up in a palace chased away the shepherds and then helped the girls get water for their flock.

When the girls returned to their father, a priest, and told him of Moses' bravery and kindness, he insisted that they return to the well right away and bring the man to their house to eat with them. Moses ended up marrying one of the priest's lovely daughters and working as a shepherd in a foreign land!

All this time, the Israelites were suffering at the hands of the Egyptians. God heard their cries and knew that it would soon be time to help them.

PRAYER
Dear Lord God, help me to really care about injustice but always to be peaceable and not get angry.
Amen

THE BURNING BUSH

One day, while Moses was tending his sheep, he noticed that a nearby bush was on fire, yet the leaves of the bush were not burning! As he stepped closer, he heard God's voice say, "Take off your sandals, Moses, for this is holy ground. I am the God of your father, the God of Abraham, of Isaac, and of Jacob." Moses hid his face in fear.

The Lord said, "I have come to rescue my people and bring them up out of Egypt into the Promised Land. You must go to Pharaoh and demand that he free them."

Moses was terrified at the thought of speaking to mighty Pharaoh, but God told him that he would be with him and that he should tell him that it was God who sent him. He promised that he would perform many miracles so that in the end Pharaoh would let the Hebrews go.

Moses was scared, but God would not listen to his excuses and sent him back to Egypt. God also sent Moses' brother Aaron to help him.

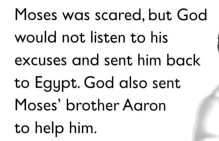

PRAYER

Thank you, Lord God, for giving Moses such a powerful vision, which helped him to be bold in going to Pharaoh. When I have to do hard things, help me to remember your power.

Amen

PHARAOH SAYS NO!

When Moses and Aaron came before Pharaoh and said, "The God of Israel asks that you let his people go so that they may hold a festival to him in the desert," Pharaoh could not believe their nerve. "Who is this God of Israel? I don't know him, and I won't let the Hebrews go!" He was so angry that he made the slaves work even harder.

So Moses and Aaron went back to Pharaoh, who demanded some proof of their God. This time Aaron threw down his staff on the ground, and it was instantly transformed into a fearsome snake! But the king's magicians huddled together and performed sorcery, and when they threw their staffs on the ground, they too turned into snakes. Even though Aaron's snake swallowed them all up, the king's heart was hardened, and he would not let the Hebrews go.

PRAYER

Thank you, Lord God, that you rule over the most powerful governors on earth—even those who say no to you. Thank you that one day, every king or queen or ruler will bow before you.

Amen

PLAGUES!

Then the Lord sent a series of plagues upon the Egyptians, each more terrible than the one before. First he changed the waters of the Nile into blood, so all the fish died and the air stank. He sent a plague of frogs to cover the countryside and fill the houses. Next, the very dust on the ground was turned into gnats, and everything was covered with them. After that came a swarm of flies—so many that the air turned black!

He sent a plague among the livestock of the land but spared those belonging to the Hebrews. Then the Egyptians were afflicted with horrible boils.

But still Pharaoh wouldn't change his mind!

PRAYER

Dear Lord God, please help me never to make my heart hard against you. I hope you never have to send strong warnings to make me listen to your word. Help me to have a heart that is willing to follow your ways.

Amen

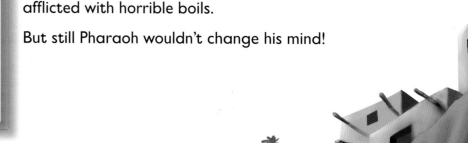

HAIL AND FIRE

Next, God sent a terrible hailstorm that stripped the land while lightning struck again and again, and fires blazed. When this wasn't enough to persuade Pharaoh to change his mind, those plants that had managed to survive were consumed by a swarm of locusts. Nothing green remained in all the land of Egypt! After this, God sent total darkness to cover Egypt for three whole days.

Each time, Pharaoh pretended that he would relent, yet each time, once the plague was lifted, he refused to let the Hebrews go. The Lord hardened his heart to teach Pharaoh a lesson, to show his true power, and to make sure the story was told throughout the world.

But now the time had come for the most dreadful plague of all ...

PRAYER

Lord God, I know that you are all powerful and you can use many ways of speaking to people. I am glad that I am not living in the time of Moses and that today you speak to me through the Bible.
Amen

THE PASSOVER

Moses warned Pharaoh that God would pass through the country at midnight and every firstborn son in the land would die, from the son of Pharaoh himself to the son of the lowliest slave girl, and even the firstborn of the animals as well. But Pharaoh would not listen.

Moses told the Israelites what God wanted them to do to be spared. Each household was to kill a lamb, smear some of the blood on the doorframe, and eat the meat in a special way. That night God passed throughout Egypt, and the next day the land was filled with the sound of mourning, for all the firstborn sons had died—even the son of mighty Pharaoh—but the Hebrews were spared.

Now the Egyptians couldn't get rid of the Hebrews quick enough, and so they prepared to leave.

PRAYER

Thank you, Lord God, that the families who followed your instructions were safe from judgment. Thank you that Jesus is my Passover Lamb and I am safe when I trust in him.

Amen

THE EXODUS

The Hebrews traveled southward across the desert toward the Red Sea. By day, God sent a great column of cloud to guide them, and by night they followed a pillar of fire. Yet their troubles were far from over, for Pharaoh was regretting his decision to let them go and had set off with his army to bring them back.

All those flying hooves and grinding wheels set off a huge cloud of dust that the Hebrews could see coming from miles away, and they panicked, for now their way was barred by the waters of the Red Sea. "Why did you bring us all this way, just to have us killed or dragged back into slavery?" cried the terrified Hebrews to Moses. "It would have been better for us to serve the Egyptians than to die in the desert!"

PRAYER

Dear Lord God, help me to trust you when things seem to be going wrong around me. Help me to look forward and not backward.

Amen

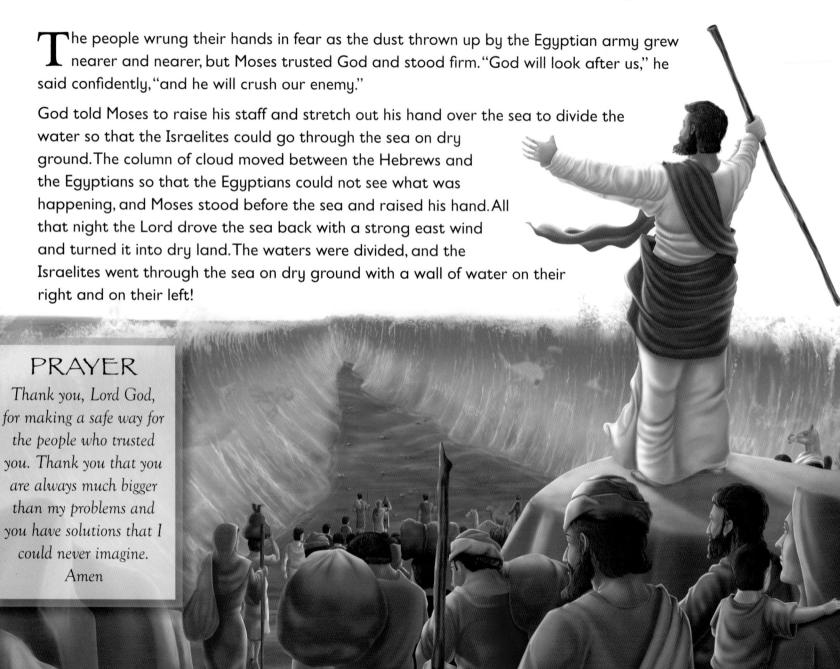

CROSSING THE RED SEA

The people wrung their hands in fear as the dust thrown up by the Egyptian army grew nearer and nearer, but Moses trusted God and stood firm. "God will look after us," he said confidently, "and he will crush our enemy."

God told Moses to raise his staff and stretch out his hand over the sea to divide the water so that the Israelites could go through the sea on dry ground. The column of cloud moved between the Hebrews and the Egyptians so that the Egyptians could not see what was happening, and Moses stood before the sea and raised his hand. All that night the Lord drove the sea back with a strong east wind and turned it into dry land. The waters were divided, and the Israelites went through the sea on dry ground with a wall of water on their right and on their left!

PRAYER

Thank you, Lord God, for making a safe way for the people who trusted you. Thank you that you are always much bigger than my problems and you have solutions that I could never imagine.

Amen

DROWNED!

The Egyptians were hard on the heels of the Hebrews and, without hesitation, followed them into the sea, along the path God had made. But God struck them with confusion so that the wheels of the chariots came off and everything was in chaos. Then he closed the waters together, and the Egyptians were swept under the sea. Of all that mighty army, there were no survivors—not one horse, not one soldier!

And the people of Israel, safe on the other shore of the Red Sea, were filled with gratitude and relief, and sang and danced in their joy. They knew that their God was both mighty and merciful, and they praised him greatly.

PRAYER

Dear Lord God, you did amazing miracles for Moses and the people of Israel. Help me to learn from these stories to trust in your justice and to rejoice in your great salvation.

Amen

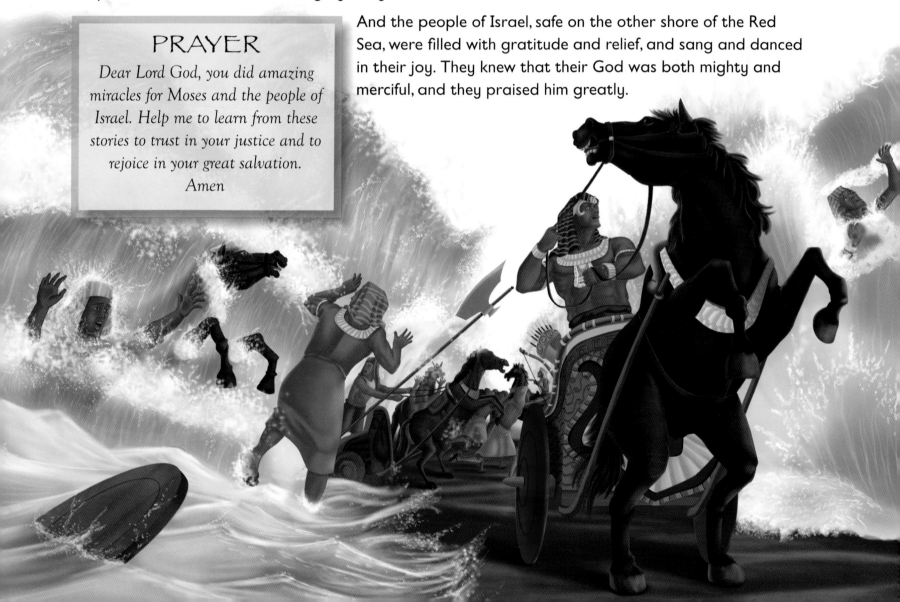

BITTER WATER

Moses led his people into the hot, dry desert. For three days they didn't find a drop of water, and when at last they did, in a place named Marah, it was too bitter to drink. The Israelites forgot what God had done for them and began to complain angrily.

Moses spoke to the Lord and asked for his help. God told him to take a large piece of wood that lay nearby, and when Moses threw it into the bitter water, it became good to drink, and the people eagerly rushed to quench their thirst.

But the Israelites couldn't stay at Marah. They had to travel onward, and soon they began to complain again. "Either we shall die of thirst or of starvation!" they wailed. "Why did you bring us out of Egypt to die?" Their gratitude to God for saving them from their suffering in Egypt only lasted as long as they were not thirsty or hungry!

PRAYER

Dear Lord God, I have so much to be grateful for. Please help me to always remember to say thank you to you and to people who give me so much and not to complain or moan.

Amen

FOOD AND WATER IN THE DESERT

The Israelites wouldn't stop moaning to Moses about how hungry they were. They were wretched and ungrateful. Once again God helped his people. Each day he sent them food from the sky: In the evenings, quail would come into the camp, and every morning, the ground would be covered with white flakes that tasted like wafers made with honey. They called this manna. Each day the people gathered enough for their needs for that day. They were to keep nothing, for if they did it would spoil. But each Friday they gathered twice as much so that the Sabbath could be a special day of rest to honor the Lord. And the extra food that they collected on Friday did not spoil.

For all the time that they were in the desert, God provided quail and manna for them. When they needed water, God told Moses to take his staff and strike a rock, and from the rock flowed good, clear, fresh drinking water.

The people of Israel wandered through the desert for many, many years, and all that time the Lord looked after them and gave them food and water.

PRAYER

Dear Lord God, I have so much food and water every day, and sometimes I take this for granted. Please be with all people today who are working hard to give food and clean water to those who desperately need it.

Amen

HANDS UP!

Hunger and thirst were not the only enemies that the Israelites faced. When a tribe of nomads called the Amalekites confronted them in the desert, the Israelites found themselves under attack!

Moses told Joshua, one of his most trusted warriors, to choose some men to take into battle the next day. "I'll stand on the top of the hill and will watch you," he said. "I'll be holding the staff that God gave me."

The next day, the battle was fierce and terrible. Moses stood at the top of the hill, along with his brother Aaron and another man named Hur. When he held his hands up in the air, his men would start winning the fight, but when he lowered his hands, the battle would swing the other way!

Moses kept his hands held high for as long as he could, but time passed and his arms grew tired. At last, it seemed he could hold them up no longer. But Aaron and Hur found a large rock for Moses to sit on, and then they each took one of his arms and held them up for him in the air until the sun dropped below the horizon.

And so, with God's help, Joshua and his men defeated the Amalekites.

PRAYER

Thank you, Lord God, for those who care for me and stay by me to help me when I am tired and struggling. In return, help me to be a strong supporter and encourager of others in need.

Amen

THE TEN COMMANDMENTS
LOVING GOD

Moses led the people to Mount Sinai. There, the Lord spoke to Moses and told him that if the people would honor and obey him, he would always be with them. The elders agreed to do everything God had told them. Then God told Moses that in three days he would appear to them on Mount Sinai.

On the morning of the third day there was thunder and lightning, a thick cloud over the mountain, and a loud trumpet blast. The people trembled and waited at the foot of the mountain. Then God called Moses to the top of it and spoke to him alone. He gave Moses many laws that would help the Israelites live happily together. Some of those laws were especially important to the people at that time, while others are important to people everywhere. The most famous of these are the Ten Commandments.

The first four of these commandments teach us how to love and respect God:

YOU SHALL HAVE NO OTHER GODS BEFORE ME.

YOU SHALL NOT MAKE ANY FALSE IDOLS.

YOU SHALL NOT MISUSE MY NAME.

REMEMBER THE SABBATH AND KEEP IT HOLY.

We must put God first and love and honor him with all our heart and soul.

PRAYER

Lord God, you are worthy of all my love and worship. I do want to put you first and honor you with my whole heart and soul. May it become the pattern of my life to praise you.
Amen

THE TEN COMMANDMENTS
LOVING OTHERS

While the first four commandments are about loving and respecting God, the next six show us how to love and respect other people. God continued with these commands:

HONOR YOUR FATHER AND YOUR MOTHER.

YOU SHALL NOT MURDER.

YOU SHALL NOT COMMIT ADULTERY.

YOU SHALL NOT STEAL.

YOU SHALL NOT TELL LIES.

YOU SHALL NOT ENVY ANYTHING THAT
BELONGS TO YOUR NEIGHBOR.

All these laws encouraged the Israelites to think about those around them and to treat them with respect and kindness.

When God finished instructing Moses, he told him that he would give him two stone tablets with these commandments engraved on them so that the people would know that they were God's laws.

PRAYER

Thank you, Lord God, for my parents and close family. Please help me to love and honor them always. Help me to respect all people and to live as you have commanded.

Amen

A PLACE TO WORSHIP

Moses spent many days on Mount Sinai. God gave him laws for the people to follow so that they could all live in peace and honor God properly—rules about food, cleanliness, sacrifices, punishment, and many other things. But most important of all were the Ten Commandments written upon two large stone tablets.

God told Moses that the Israelites must build a special place to keep these tablets. They were to be kept inside a wooden chest covered with the purest gold, known as the Ark of the Covenant. This was to be kept inside an inner shrine, in a large tent known as the Tabernacle. The Tabernacle would travel with the Israelites wherever they went, and so they carried the presence of the Lord with them on their travels through the desert.

PRAYER

Thank you, Lord God, that you are everywhere and I can worship you at any time. Thank you too for special worship times with other believers at home, at school, and in my church. Help me to truly worship you today.

Amen

THE GOLDEN CALF

Moses was up on the mountain for such a long time that the people began to believe he would never come back down. They asked Aaron to make them gods to lead them, and Aaron told them all to gather their gold jewelry and used it to make a beautiful golden calf, which he placed on an altar. The people gathered round and began to worship it.

God was angry with them and vowed to destroy them, but Moses pleaded with him to forgive them, and God relented.

When Moses went down from the mountain with the tablets and saw the people singing and dancing around the golden calf, he was so furious that he threw the tablets to the ground, where they shattered. Next, he burned the calf and ground it to powder. God punished those who had sinned with a plague.

PRAYER

Dear Lord God, I pray that I will always honor you and keep close to your ways and never give first place in my heart to anything but you.

Amen

GOD SHOWS HIS GLORY

God told Moses that he and his people must now travel to the land he had promised them, and that he would send an angel to guide them. But Moses begged him to be with them so that the world could see that they were his people, and God promised that he would.

The Ten Commandments were placed on two new stone tablets, and when Moses brought them down from Mount Sinai, his face shone so brightly that everyone was scared to come near him. But he called to them and gave them all the commands the Lord had given him.

Now they worked hard on preparing the holy tent and the special place for the tablets. Everyone did what they could and brought anything precious that they owned. When all the work was complete and everything had been laid out just as God had commanded, a cloud covered the Tent of Meeting, and the glory of the Lord filled the Tabernacle, and at night it looked like fire.

And in all the travels of the Israelites, whenever the cloud lifted from above the Tabernacle, this was the sign for them to set out.

PRAYER

Dear Lord God, I need you to be always with me through each day and night. I need to have your light with me to guide me. Thank you for writing down your commandments for me. Please help me to follow them.
Amen

THE DAY OF ATONEMENT

God gave Moses special instructions for Aaron. Aaron was to make sacrifices to offer atonement for his own sins and for those of his family and servants. Then he was to take two goats from the people. One was to be sacrificed to God, and the other was to take on all the sins of the Israelites and then to be sent away into the desert. It was a "scapegoat" to carry away the sins of all the people.

This ceremony was to take place each year, on the tenth day of the seventh month, and was to be known as the Day of Atonement. It wasn't to be a joyful occasion like many of the other festivals, but was to be serious and somber, a day of rest to be spent in prayer and thought. It was to be a day to seek forgiveness from God. God commanded the people to fast on the Day of Atonement, which meant that they were not to eat any food or drink any water for one whole day.

"All this you shall do," said God, "because on this day atonement will be made for you. Then you will be clean from all your sins in my sight."

PRAYER

Thank you, Lord God, that today I don't need animal sacrifices, because Jesus died for me. Sometimes I need to stop and think quietly about why Jesus died. Thank you that I am clean through Jesus.
Amen

THE PEOPLE COMPLAIN

Once again the people began to complain to Moses. They were tired of the hardships and fed up with eating the same food day after day. "It's not fair!" they moaned. "In Egypt we had cucumbers, melons and onions—we're fed up with manna!"

Moses had had enough of their moaning and grumbling. He went to speak to God. "My Lord," he said, "Why do I have to listen to their wailing all the time? Why is it always me?"

God took pity on him and gave some of the Spirit that he had given to Moses to seventy of the elders. "That way," said God, "they will help you carry the burden of the people."

Now Miriam and Aaron began to complain that Moses wasn't the only important one around. "Hasn't God spoken through us, too?" they grumbled. God was angry and told them sternly, "When a prophet of the Lord is among you, I reveal myself to him in visions and speak to him in dreams. But with Moses I speak face-to-face. He sees my true form. How can you dare then to speak against my servant Moses?" He was so furious that he punished Miriam with leprosy for seven days.

PRAYER

Dear Lord God, I am sorry for the times I have grumbled. Please help me to be glad for all the good things you have provided for me and not to compare them with what others have.

Amen

THE TWELVE SPIES

God told Moses to send some men to explore Canaan, the land he intended for the Israelites. Moses chose twelve men, one from each of the tribes that came from the sons of Jacob, and he sent them to find out what the land was like. They came back loaded with delicious, juicy fruit. "The land really does flow with milk and honey, just as God promised!" they enthused. But they also said that there were too many people living there and that the cities were well defended. Only two of them, Caleb and Joshua, were brave enough and trusted God enough to believe they could take the land that God had promised them.

God was furious with the Israelites for not trusting him. He told them that not one of those who had doubted him would ever set foot in the Promised Land, and he struck down those men who had been sent to explore Canaan and who had doubted him and spread their fear among the people of Israel. Then he cursed the rest of the doubting Israelites to wander the desert for another forty years!

PRAYER

Dear Lord God, please help me to be courageous like those two men who believed what you had promised and stood up for what they believed even though there were only two of them and everyone else doubted.
Amen

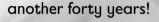

REBELLION!

Some of the leaders began to rise up against Moses and Aaron. They gathered with the rest of the elders at the entrance to the Tent of Meeting. God told Moses and Aaron to stand aside so he could put an end to them.

But Moses and Aaron begged him not to punish the whole assembly, and so God had the rest of the elders move away from the tents of those who had spoken against Moses and Aaron, and when they had done so, the ground beneath those tents split apart and the earth opened its mouth and swallowed the tents, the rebellious leaders, their families, and all their possessions too!

That night, God told the twelve leaders to each leave a staff in the Tent of Meeting. In the morning, Moses entered to find that Aaron's staff had sprouted leaves, budded and blossomed, and even produced almonds! God told Moses, "Put Aaron's staff back in the tent, to be kept as a sign to the rebellious." From now on, only the members of Aaron's tribe, the Levites, could go near the Tent.

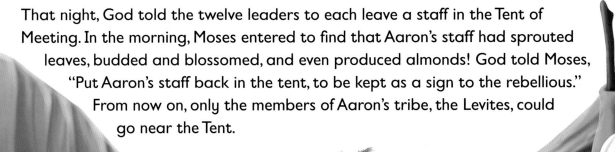

PRAYER

Lord God, I know you are holy and you hate sin. I also know you are kind and merciful. Thank you for your kindness to me and your great forgiveness that saves me from your judgment.

Amen

WATER FROM THE ROCK

Even if the question of leadership was settled, it didn't stop the people grumbling, for they were still in the desert and were without water and thirsty. Moses and Aaron asked God to help once more, and he told them to take the staff and gather everyone before a large rock. "Speak to that rock before their eyes, and it will pour out its water," he commanded them.

Moses and Aaron gathered the people. "Listen, you rebels, must we bring you water out of this rock?" Moses said, and then he struck the rock twice with his staff. Water gushed out, and everyone was able to drink.

But God was disappointed because Moses hadn't followed his instructions, nor had he given the credit to God. So God told the brothers that they would never enter the Promised Land.

PRAYER

Dear Lord God, please help me to listen to what you say and obey exactly. Thank you for your great kindness in caring even for people who are against you. You send the sunshine and rain on both good and evil people.
Amen

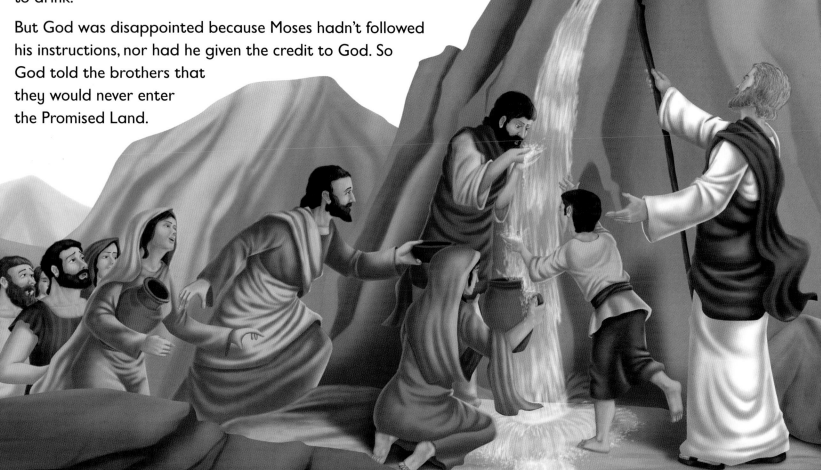

THE BRONZE SNAKE

The Israelites had to travel far in the desert. God helped them to overcome the people and cities that stood in their way, but still the people complained. They spoke against God and against Moses, moaning, "Why have you brought us out of Egypt to die in the desert? There is no bread and hardly any water! And we're sick and tired of this miserable food!"

God was fed up with their ingratitude. He sent venomous snakes into their camp, and many Israelites died. The people came to Moses and said, "It was wrong of us to speak against God. Please ask him to take the snakes away!" So Moses prayed.

Then God said to him, "Make a snake and put it up on a pole. Anyone who is bitten can look at it and live." So Moses made a bronze snake and put it up on a pole. When anyone was bitten and looked at the bronze snake, he lived.

PRAYER

Dear Lord God, I am really sad that sometimes I moan and grumble. Please help me to have a spirit of contentment and thankfulness.
Amen

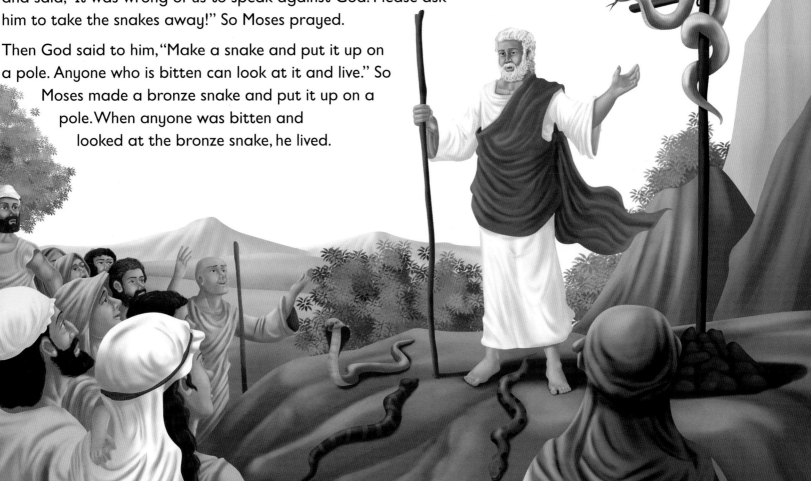

THE DONKEY AND THE ANGEL

The Moabites were worried. They feared that the Israelites would destroy them. Their king, Balak, sent word to a prophet named Balaam that he would pay him to place a curse on the Israelites. When the messenger came, Balaam asked God what to do. God said that he must not curse the Israelites, for they were blessed by him, so Balaam sent the messenger away. Balak sent more messengers and offered more money. Balaam said that he would speak again to God—even though God had already said no!

That night, God told Balaam to go but to say exactly what he was told. So the next morning Balaam set off on his donkey. Along the way, the donkey suddenly veered off the road, for an angel stood blocking the way. Balaam could not see it and tried to force the donkey to go on. When it lay down, he began beating it. Then God made the donkey speak. "Why are you beating me?" it asked, and Balaam replied, startled, "Because you are making a fool out of me!"

Then God opened his eyes so that he could see the angel. Balaam fell to his knees in fright. God told him to go the king and to speak only the words he put in his mouth. In Moab, to the king's horror, Balaam blessed the Israelites instead of cursing them and warned that Israel's enemies would be conquered and Moab crushed!

PRAYER

Thank you, Lord God, for your blessing on my life, which is more valuable than anything I could buy. Thank you for the security of being in your family.
Amen

TIME FOR CHANGE

God told Moses that it would soon be time to leave his people. God said he would let him see the land promised to the Israelites but would not let him enter it. Moses asked God to choose someone to lead the people after his death, and the Lord chose Joshua, who had already shown his faith in God.

Now, the Reubenites and Gadites had very large herds of cattle. They asked if they could stay on the east side of the River Jordan, for the land was good for grazing. Moses agreed that if all their men helped in the fight to conquer Canaan, then after their victory they could come back and claim this land.

God told the Israelites they must drive out the inhabitants of the land before them and destroy all their carved images and idols and temples. God was not giving the Israelites the land because they were good, but because those who lived there were wicked.

PRAYER

Lord God, when it's time for change in my life, help me to be calm. When I start new studies and have new teachers, or when things change at home, please help me to adapt to new circumstances.
Amen

CHOOSE LIFE

Moses gathered the people to him, for God wanted them to renew the covenant that he had made with them. Moses reminded them of all that God had done for them and that God would be angry if they ever turned away from him and went off to worship other gods. But if they obeyed God with all their heart and soul, and kept his commandments, then he would look after them wherever they were. He would bring them to the land promised to their fathers, and they would be wealthy and successful.

"Today, I set before you a choice between life and death. If you truly love the Lord and obey all his commands, then you and your children will live happily in the Promised Land. But if you don't obey God, if you worship other gods, then you will be destroyed. So choose life, for the Lord is your life, and he will be with you in the land you have been promised!"

PRAYER

Dear Lord God, please direct me when I have to make choices. Most of all, please give me the strength to always choose to honor and worship you.
Amen

JOSHUA—ISRAEL'S NEW LEADER

Moses was now very old. He called the people of Israel to him. "God has told me that I may not enter the Promised Land. Joshua will lead you there. You must be brave and strong, for God won't leave you." And he said to Joshua in front of all the people, "Be strong and brave, for you must lead these people into the Promised Land and divide it among them. The Lord himself goes before you and will be with you. He will never leave you nor forsake you, so don't be afraid or discouraged."

God spoke to Moses and Joshua alone outside the Tent of Meeting and told Moses what to say to the people, for he knew that they would soon turn away from him. Then Moses addressed the people. "You have been stubborn and rebellious with me as your leader. How much worse will you be after I die?" And he spoke of what had happened and what would happen. "Take my words to heart," he said. "These words are your life—if you obey the words of the law, then God will be with you and your children."

God had some special words for Joshua. "You will lead the people into the land I have promised them. Don't be afraid, Joshua, for I will always be with you."

PRAYER

Thank you, Lord God, that you will always be with me and so I need never be afraid. When I have to be a team leader or face new responsibilities, please make me strong but kind and gentle.

Amen

MOSES SEES THE PROMISED LAND

It was time for Moses to leave his people. Before he went, he gathered them together and said, "You are truly blessed! Who is like you, a people saved by the Lord? He is your shield and helper and your glorious sword. Your enemies will cower before you, and you will trample down their high places."

Moses climbed Mount Nebo, and the Lord showed him the whole land of Canaan in the distance, the plains and the valleys, the cities and the villages, all the way to the sea. Then Moses died. He was a hundred and twenty years old when he passed away, yet his eyes were not weak, nor was his strength gone. The people mourned for thirty days. They knew that there would never be another prophet like him, who had spoken with the Lord face-to-face.

PRAYER

Thank you, Lord God, that I am among the people who are truly blessed because you are my God and you have given me your Holy Spirit to be my helper always. Thank you that you are my shield and no one can harm my soul.

Amen

SPIES!

God had promised the land of Canaan to the Israelites. For many years they had wandered in the harsh desert, but now it was time to cross the River Jordan into the Promised Land, where food and water were plentiful and the land green and lush.

Joshua sent two spies into the city of Jericho, on the far banks of the river. They spent the night in the home of a woman named Rahab, but the king heard there were spies in his city and sent soldiers to search for them. Kind Rahab hid the men on her roof, and when the soldiers came knocking, she sent them off on a wild goose chase. Then she gave the spies some rope so they could lower themselves down, for the house was part of the city wall. "The people of Jericho live in fear of your coming," she told them, "for we have heard how powerful your God is. Please spare me and my family when you attack Jericho!"

The spies told Rahab to tie a piece of red cord to the window and to make sure all her family were inside her house when the Israelites attacked. But they warned her not to speak a word about them, for if she did she would be shown no mercy.

PRAYER

Dear Lord God, thank you that you call all kinds of people to have faith. Thank you that through Rahab came the family line of Jesus. Please be with your followers today who are in places of danger or battle.
Amen

CROSSING THE RIVER

The River Jordan was in flood. The swift-flowing waters were treacherous, and there was no bridge or ford. Yet God had told the people that today they would cross into the Promised Land!

Joshua told everyone to gather their belongings and then sent the priests ahead, carrying the Ark of the Covenant. As soon as their feet touched the water it stopped flowing and made a huge wall, and a dry path stretched before them! The priests made their way to the middle of the riverbed, and then the people of Israel began to cross safely over. Not a drop of water touched them!

There were so many of them that it took all day to cross, but by nightfall the children of Israel had finally arrived in the land promised to them by God for so many years.

Before the priests finished crossing the river, Joshua had one man from each of the twelve tribes of Israel lift a stone from the middle of the riverbed where the priests had been standing. As soon as the priests stepped onto the shore, the river came crashing down once more. Joshua collected the twelve stones and built them up into a mound as a reminder to the people of how the waters of the river had stopped before the Ark of the Covenant, and how God had brought them safely across it and into the Promised Land.

PRAYER

Thank you, Lord God, that nothing is too difficult for you and your promises always come true—even though it may seem truly impossible. Please give me faith in you.
Amen

THE WALLS OF JERICHO

The Israelites laid siege to Jericho. No one went out and no one went in, and the people were terrified. Then God told Joshua, "March around the city once with all the armed men. Do this for six days. Have seven priests carry trumpets in front of the Ark. On the seventh day, march around the city seven times, with the priests blowing the trumpets. When you hear them sound a long blast on the trumpets, have all the people give a loud shout; then the walls of the city will collapse and Jericho will be yours."

For six days the Israelites marched around the city, and on the seventh day, they marched around Jericho seven times. On the last time, when the priests sounded the trumpet blast, Joshua commanded the people, "Now shout! For the Lord has given you the city!"

When the trumpets sounded, the people raised a mighty cry, and the city walls trembled and collapsed! The soldiers charged in and took the city. Only Rahab and her family were spared, for the city and everything in it was burned, except for the silver, gold, bronze, and iron.

And the story of how the Lord had helped Joshua take Jericho spread throughout the land!

PRAYER

Dear Lord God, help me to trust and obey you when there are big walls in the way of my plans and people around me can seem like enemies. I am so glad that you are in control of everything.
Amen

THE PEACE TREATY

When the people of the nearby town of Gibeon heard how Jericho had fallen, they feared for their own lives. They decided to trick the Israelites into signing a peace treaty with them, by pretending they came from a far-off land.

They sent messengers dressed in ragged clothes, with stale bread and leaking waterskins. When Joshua asked who they were, they answered, "We have traveled a long way. This bread was fresh out of our ovens when we started. Now it is stale. And our shoes are almost worn through from walking!"

Joshua and his men were taken in by the trickery and didn't stop to ask for God's advice. Instead, Joshua drew up a peace treaty with the men of Gibeon on the spot, and he swore an oath to keep it.

Soon enough the Israelites learned the truth, and they were furious, but they had sworn an oath in God's name and could not go back on their word.

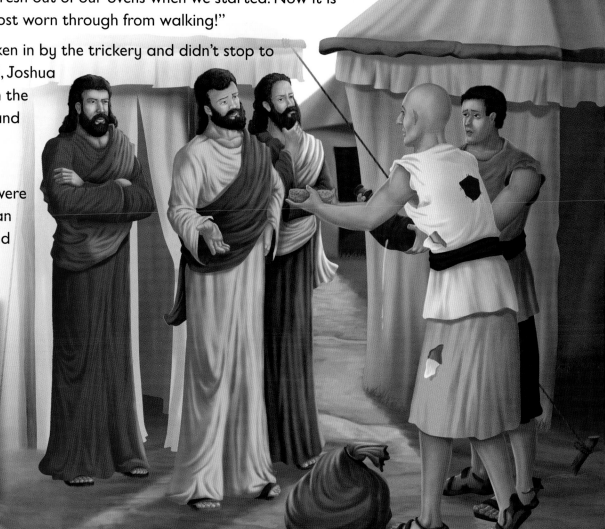

PRAYER

Dear Lord God, I know that bad people use tricks and deceit. Help me always to be honest and truthful. Please protect and deliver me from evil of all kinds.
Amen

THE SUN AND THE MOON

Shortly afterward, Gibeon found itself under attack. The people sent word to Joshua, begging for help, and the Israelites came to their aid, for Joshua was a good and honorable man. God had not been pleased with his rashness in signing the treaty, but he was pleased that he was keeping his word.

Joshua and his army marched all through the night to get to Gibeon, and their enemies were caught by surprise. Throughout the battle God was on their side. He sent great hailstones to fall on the enemy, and soon Joshua knew that the Israelites were winning—but he also knew that night would fall before they could finish the battle!

Then Joshua called out, "Sun, stand still over Gibeon, and you, moon, over the Valley of Aijalon!" God listened to Joshua and made the sun and the moon stand still until Joshua and his men had won the battle!

The people of Israel had many more battles to fight but, with God's help, the land was finally theirs.

PRAYER

Dear Lord God, help me not to make foolish promises. But when I make a good promise, help me to keep it. Thank you for the security I have in the promises given to me by you and my family and friends.
Amen

DEBORAH AND BARAK

Many years passed. The people turned away from God and fell into wicked ways. God was angry and allowed their enemy, King Jabin, and the commander of his armies, General Sisera, to conquer them. When the people called out once again to God to help them, he spoke to Deborah, a wise woman whom he had sent to be a judge over Israel. God told Deborah what to do.

She sent for a soldier named Barak and told him to gather an army of ten thousand men on Mount Tabor. She said she would deliver Sisera and all his soldiers into his hands. Barak agreed to go, but only if Deborah went too! She told him that because he didn't trust God, the final victory would be given to a woman.

The Israelites met Sisera and his chariots on the slopes of Mount Tabor, and because the Lord was with them, not a single one of the enemy soldiers was left standing—every last one was killed!

PRAYER

Thank you, Lord God, that you can use anyone who trusts you. Please help me always to be among those you can use to bring about your plans.
Amen

JAEL AND SISERA

The Israelites had won a great battle, yet in the confusion, General Sisera had managed to escape. The commander came to the tent of one of the king's allies, where a woman named Jael invited him in. She gave him a drink and a place to rest, and before he lay down he told her to guard the entrance to the tent and send anyone away should they come searching.

But Jael secretly hated Sisera and his army, and as soon as he fell asleep, she killed him! When Barak came looking for his enemy, Jael told him what she had done, and he took her back to the Israelite army, where the people praised her. But Deborah and Barak reminded the Israelites that it was God who had won the war for them.

PRAYER

Dear Lord God, please help me always to give you the honor when things go well for me and not to look for personal praise. Help me to do what is right because I want to please you.
Amen

GOD CALLS GIDEON

In time, the Israelites fell back into their wicked ways, so when the terrible Midianites came to take their land, God didn't help them. For seven long years the Israelites were forced to hide in the mountains while the Midianites took their crops and animals. In desperation, the people cried out to God, who sent a messenger to Gideon to tell him that he had been chosen to strike down the Midianites. Gideon was shocked and could hardly believe it, but God told him to tear down an altar to Baal in the village and to build a new one to God.

Gideon did the deed with a few servants in the dark of night. When the villagers found out, they wanted to kill him, but his father told them, "If Baal truly is a god, he can defend himself when someone breaks his altar!" and so they left Gideon alone.

PRAYER

Lord God, please help me to stay close to you always so that I am in a place where you bless me and help me.
Amen

THE FLEECE

Israel's enemies had joined together to fight against them. Gideon gathered together his own army so that he could face them in battle. Yet he was still not convinced he was the right man for the job.

Gideon asked God for a special sign. "I'll leave this fleece on the ground. If, in the morning, it's wet, but the ground around it's dry, then I'll know that you are going to use me to save Israel."

In the morning the fleece was soaking, but the ground was dry. When Gideon wrung the sheepskin out, it filled a whole bowl with water!

Still Gideon begged for one last sign. "Please don't be angry with me, Lord. Let me ask just one more thing. This time, let the fleece be dry but the ground be wet." And the next morning, the sheepskin was dry, but the ground around it was wet with dew. Now Gideon was convinced!

PRAYER

Lord God, thank you that you are patient and kind with people who truly want to choose your way. At special times in my life when I have to make choices, please show me clearly your will.

Amen

GIDEON AND THE THREE HUNDRED

Gideon and the men who had rallied to him looked down on the tents of the Midianites. They stretched as far as the eye could see, covering the ground like a swarm of killer ants! But even so, God said to Gideon, "You have too many men. I don't want the Israelites to think they've won because of their own strength. Tell anyone who is afraid that he can go home."

After Gideon had spoken to his army, over two-thirds of the men went home—only ten thousand remained! But God said, "You still have too many men. Tell them to go and drink from the water, and take with you only those who cup the water in their hands to drink, not those who lap it." After this, only three hundred men were left!

God told Gideon, "With these three hundred men I will save you and deliver the Midianites into your hands."

PRAYER

Thank you, Lord God, that you are the mighty, strong one and you do not need a big human army to bring about your plans. Help me always to remember this.
Amen

IN THE DARK

That night, Gideon looked down on the sea of tents. How could they ever win? God knew he was anxious and told him to creep down to the enemy camp, where he overheard the soldiers recounting bad dreams: "I dreamed that a round loaf of bread came tumbling into the camp and knocked into the tent and completely flattened it!" exclaimed one Midianite soldier to another.

"That will be the sword of Gideon!" wailed the second soldier. "God must have given the whole camp over into his hands!"

Gideon returned full of confidence and roused his men, giving them all trumpets and empty jars with torches inside.

The men reached the edge of the camp and, following Gideon's signal, they blew their trumpets, smashed the jars, and shouted out loud. The harsh noise and sudden light startled the Midianites so much that the camp fell into confusion, and the soldiers fled in terror, even turning on one another in their fright!

In this way, Gideon and God defeated the Midianites with just three hundred men!

PRAYER
Thank you, Lord God, that you have many ways of working, and they are often so different from what people expect! I am excited to know that you can do wonderful things in my life.
Amen

FAITHFUL RUTH

Naomi was moving back to Bethlehem. Many years ago she and her husband and their two sons had come to Moab when there had been a poor harvest in their own country. Her husband had died, but when her sons grew older, they married two lovely girls from Moab and brought them home to live. But now both her sons had died too, and poor Naomi was left in a foreign land without her husband or her sons.

Naomi wanted to go home. She dearly loved her two daughters-in-law, Orpah and Ruth, but she begged them to stay behind, for she was penniless and she knew her life would be hard and uncertain.

Orpah and Ruth both cared very much for Naomi and didn't want to stay behind without her, but finally Orpah agreed to go home to her own mother. Loyal Ruth, however, said, "Don't ask me to leave! I'll go wherever you go. Your people will be my people, and your God will be my God."

PRAYER

Dear Lord God, thank you for people in my wider family circle. Please help me to love them and keep in touch, even if they are far away and I don't see them often.

Amen

DAY
87

RUTH'S REWARD

So it was that Ruth and Naomi came to Bethlehem. Soon they had no food left, and brave Ruth went out into the fields where workers were harvesting the crops. She asked the owner if she could pick up any of the barley that his workers left behind.

This man was Boaz. He kindly let Ruth work in his fields and told his servants to share their food with her. When Ruth returned with a full basket of food, Naomi knew that the Lord was looking after them, for it turned out that Boaz was a relation of hers.

In time, Ruth married him, and when they had a son, there was no happier woman in all of Bethlehem than Naomi!

PRAYER

Thank you, Lord God, for those in charge of workers who are kind and generous to them. Thank you for good employment laws that help to bring fairness for everyone.
Amen

JEPHTHAH'S PROMISE

Once again, the people of Israel were under attack. This time, their leader was a brave and honorable man named Jephthah. Before he led his people into battle, Jephthah spoke to God. "O God, if you deliver the Ammonites into my hands, I solemnly swear that on my return I shall sacrifice to you the very first thing that comes out of the door of my house to greet me!" Then Jephthah went out to fight his enemy, and because God was with him, he won.

But on his return home, who should come out to meet him but his lovely daughter, his beloved only child! When he saw her, he tore his clothes and cried out in despair as he told her of his promise to God. She replied sadly but gravely, "My father, you have given your word to the Lord, and you must keep your promise. Grant me just one request," she asked. "Give me two months to grieve."

And so for two months Jephthah's daughter went into the hills with her friends and wept for the life she would not have. But at the end of the two months, she returned to her father and he kept his promise to God.

PRAYER

Dear Lord God, May I follow the words of Jesus who taught, 'Do not swear, but let your 'Yes' mean 'Yes' and your 'No' mean 'No'. May I always keep my word.
Amen

SAMSON THE STRONG

All too soon, the Israelites returned to their wicked ways, and now the Lord delivered them into the hands of the Philistines. For forty years the Israelites had been enslaved by their enemies. One day God sent a message to a man called Manoah and his wife, who lived in Zorah: "You will have a son who will grow up to deliver you from the Philistines."

Now Manoah and his wife had been trying to have a baby for years without any success, so they were amazed and thrilled at this news. When their son was born, they named him Samson, and they never once cut his hair. It was a sign that he belonged to God in a very special way.

One day when Samson was older, he was attacked by one of the fierce lions that roamed the land of Canaan. Samson was filled with the Spirit of the Lord, and he became so strong that he was able to kill the beast with his bare hands!

PRAYER

Dear Lord God, please prepare special leaders today who are full of your Spirit to teach your word faithfully and to inspire many of your disciples.

Amen

SAMSON AND DELILAH

Samson was a thorn in the side of the Philistines. They both hated and feared him. Although he never led an army, he carried out many attacks against them. But when he fell in love with Delilah, a beautiful Philistine woman, they bribed her to find out the secret of Samson's strength.

Night after night, Delilah would plead with Samson to tell her his secret. In the end, she wore him down, and he said, "If anyone were to cut my hair off, then I would lose all my strength."

When Samson awoke, it was to discover that the Philistines had come into his room and cut off his hair. Now he was powerless as they bound and blinded him and threw him into prison!

PRAYER

Dear Lord God, please help me as I grow up to understand the power of attraction between boys and girls and to judge when this is good or bad. Please keep me pure in my thinking and behavior to all in my social group.

Amen

RETRIBUTION

Over time, Samson's hair grew back. One day, the Philistine rulers were all gathered for a feast in a crowded temple. Samson was brought out to be made fun of. He was chained between the two central pillars of the temple.

Then Samson prayed to God with all his heart, "Give me strength just one more time, my Lord, so that I can take revenge upon my enemies!"

Once more Samson was filled with strength. He pushed against the pillars with all his might, and they toppled. The temple crashed down, killing everyone inside. Samson killed more of his enemies with this final act than he had killed in all of his life!

PRAYER

Dear Lord God, thank you that you are the fair judge. Sometimes, when things look unfair, help me not to fret, but to leave that in your care.
Amen

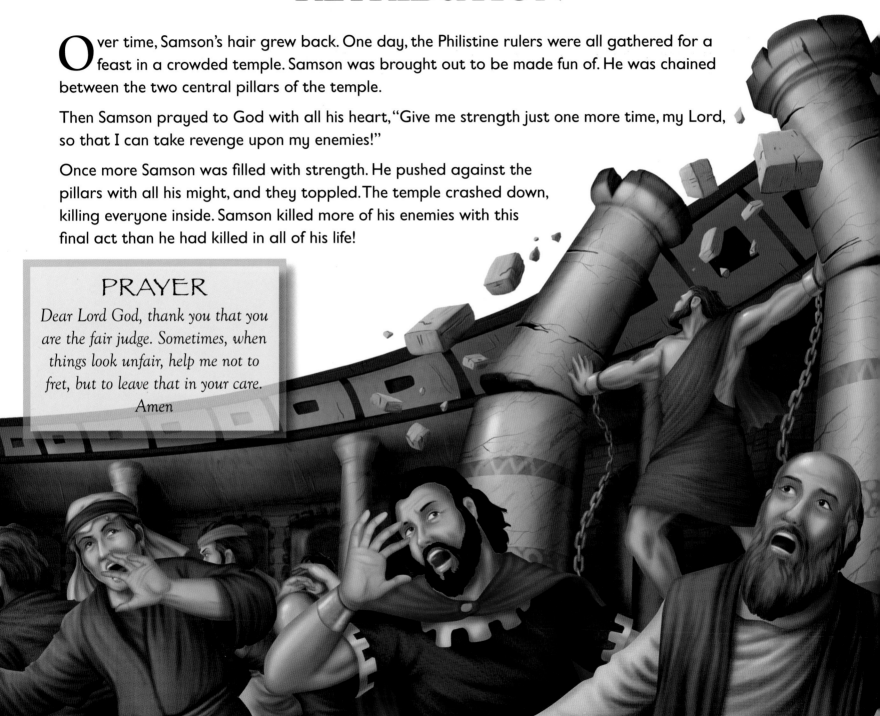

GOD HEARS HANNAH'S PRAYER

1 Samuel 1-2

PRAYER

Thank you Lord God, that you are really listening when I speak to you. Thank you that you care about the things that really worry me and I can talk to you about anything at any time.

Amen

Hannah longed to have a child. She could think of nothing else. One day when she was visiting the tabernacle at Shiloh, she went to the door of the holy tent and, weeping bitterly, began to pray. "Dear Lord, please give me a child, for I'm so unhappy," she begged. "I swear that if you do, I'll give him back to you to serve for all his life!" When Eli, the priest, saw Hannah and learned of her troubles, he sent her on her way gently, saying, "May God answer your prayer."

Hannah left, feeling as if a great weight had left her shoulders. She had spoken to God—now he would decide what was best for her. And how thrilled she was when, some time later, she gave birth to a beautiful baby boy named Samuel!

She didn't forget her promise to God, for when the boy was old enough, she took him to the tabernacle, knowing he would be well looked after by the kind priest. Each year she visited him, and God, knowing how difficult it had been for her to give up her son, blessed her with more children to love and cherish at home.

A VOICE IN THE NIGHT

Eli grew fond of Samuel, for he was a good boy. One night Samuel awoke with a start when he heard his name called. He rushed through to Eli's room, but the priest sent him back to bed with a yawn, saying, "Go back to bed. I didn't call you, child."

Samuel had barely pulled the covers back over him when he heard his name called again. As before, he rushed through, but once more Eli grumpily sent him away. The third time the boy came to his room, Eli realized who was really calling Samuel—God!

So Samuel returned to bed, and when God spoke to him again, he answered. God told him that he had decided to judge Eli's family, for his sons were wicked, and Eli had not stopped them. In the morning, Samuel could hardly bring himself to tell the priest what God had said, but when he did, Eli sighed in resignation, "He is the Lord. Let him do what is right in his eyes."

As Samuel grew up, God often spoke to him, and in time people began to listen to what Samuel had to say.

PRAYER

Dear Lord God, thank you that you know my name and everything about me. Thank you that you speak to me through the Bible. Help me to listen for your voice.

Amen

THE ARK IS CAPTURED!

The Israelites were once more at war with the Philistines. Things were not going well, so they decided to take the Ark of the Covenant into battle. They hoped that it would bring them victory, believing that God would then be with them. But the Philistines fought so fiercely that they slaughtered all the Israelites and stole the Ark of the Covenant!

In triumph, the Philistines placed the Ark inside the temple of their god. In the morning they found the statue had fallen over! They lifted it up again, but the next morning they found it smashed to pieces! When the people of the city were struck down by a strange illness, they became really scared and moved the Ark to a different city. But everywhere it went, the plague followed it!

The terrified Philistines loaded the Ark and an offering of gold onto a cart pulled by two cows and let them go wherever they would. The cows took the cart straight back to Israel, where the people rejoiced to see the Ark returned safely to them!

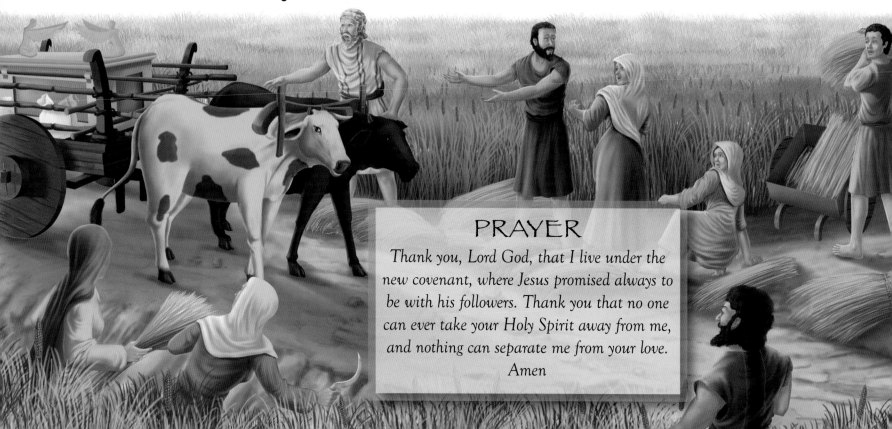

PRAYER
Thank you, Lord God, that I live under the new covenant, where Jesus promised always to be with his followers. Thank you that no one can ever take your Holy Spirit away from me, and nothing can separate me from your love.
Amen

ISRAEL DEMANDS A KING

Samuel led Israel wisely for many years and brought the people back to God. He was fair and honest, and during this time Israel was strong against the Philistines. But when Samuel grew old, the people began to worry about what would happen after he died, and they began to call out for a king.

Samuel knew that they should be happy with God as their King, and he tried to warn them that a king might treat them badly, but the people simply wouldn't listen. They wanted a king in fine clothes to lead their armies, just like all the other nations around. In the end, Samuel agreed to their demands.

The man God chose was the son of a farmer from the tribe of Benjamin. Saul was a tall, handsome young man. He was shocked when Samuel anointed him, but God sent some special signs so he would know that it was the truth.

When Samuel tried to show Saul to the people, the young man was so scared that he hid! When he was found, Samuel announced, "Here is your new king!" and the people cheered and shouted with joy.

PRAYER

Thank you, Lord God, that you are the one true king. Please help me to honor you and worship you as you deserve and to know that your words are above those of any person.
Amen

SAUL IS IMPATIENT

Saul became a mighty king and had many victories over the Philistines. To begin with, he was good and brave, but over time, Saul became proud and obstinate, and he didn't always obey God.

Saul and his army were waiting at Gilgal. They were preparing to fight a great battle against the Philistines and were dreadfully outnumbered. Samuel had promised to meet them there within seven days to offer a sacrifice before going to war. But Saul and his soldiers were quaking with fear, and day after day Samuel didn't come.

One by one, Saul's soldiers fled into the hills and caves, and finally Saul decided that he couldn't wait for Samuel any longer—he would make the offering himself!

Just as he finished, Samuel arrived. When he saw what had happened, he was sad and angry. "You have been very foolish, Saul," he scolded the king. "You have disobeyed God. If you had kept his command, he would have made sure that you and your family ruled over Israel for all time. But as it is, he will choose another man—one who will obey him."

Saul's impatience had cost him dearly.

PRAYER

Dear Lord God, please help me to learn patience. Thank you that all your good plans for me will surely happen, though sometimes I will have to learn to wait.
Amen

TWO BRAVE MEN

The Israelites had a problem—they had no weapons! Over the years the Philistines had killed all their blacksmiths so that they could not make swords or spears, and during peacetime the Israelites had been forced to go to the Philistines to have their axes and scythes sharpened. Of course, now that they were at war, the Philistine blacksmiths wouldn't sharpen their enemy's weapons!

In all of Saul's army, only the king himself and his son Jonathan had good swords. The Israelites knew they could not defend themselves, and more and more left their camp every day in fear and despair.

One day, Jonathan had had enough. Along with his armor bearer, he crept out of the camp, and they made their way up to a Philistine outpost in the hills. They walked up the pass in plain sight of the enemy soldiers. The Philistines laughed at them. "Come up here, and we'll soon teach you a lesson!" they jeered.

Jonathan looked at his companion—that was their sign from God that he would deliver their enemies into their hands. The two brave men climbed up the cliff, and between them they killed about twenty of the Philistine soldiers and took control of the pass!

Then panic filled the entire Philistine army. Thinking this must be the start of a massive attack, they took to their heels and fled. When Saul saw what was happening, he and his men gave chase, and they drove their enemy away.

PRAYER

Dear Lord God, please be with those who have to go bravely into difficult places to help others. Give them courage and physical strength to do what is right.
Amen

SAUL DISOBEYS GOD

Some years later, God told Saul to attack the Amalekites, who had once treated the Israelites badly. God ordered him to destroy Amalek and everything in it—every man, every woman, every child, and even all the sheep and cattle and donkeys. Saul attacked the city and killed all the people, but he spared the best of the animals and brought back the king as a hostage.

Samuel knew that God was furious with Saul. When he asked the king why he had disobeyed God, Saul told him that he was planning to sacrifice the animals to the Lord.

"God wants you to obey him!" said Samuel. "He didn't ask for sacrifices!" And he turned his back on the disobedient king.

Saul begged for forgiveness and grabbed hold of Samuel's robe to stop him from leaving. A corner of it tore off in his hands! Samuel told him that just as Saul had torn his cloak, the Lord would tear the kingdom away from Saul, for he regretted that he had ever made him king over Israel. Samuel parted from Saul sadly and never saw him again.

PRAYER

Dear Lord God, when I hear your instructions, please help me never to reinterpret them to suit myself. Please make me strong against all temptation.
Amen

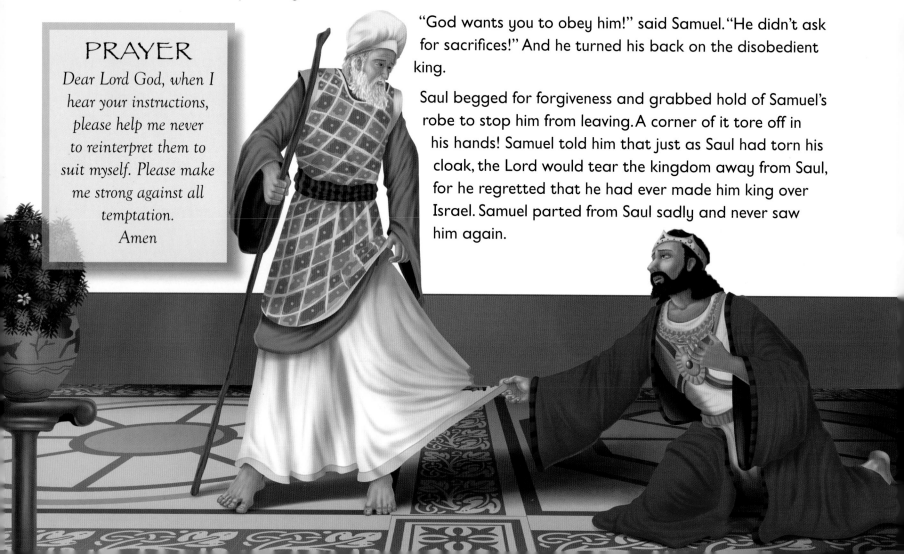

THE SHEPHERD BOY

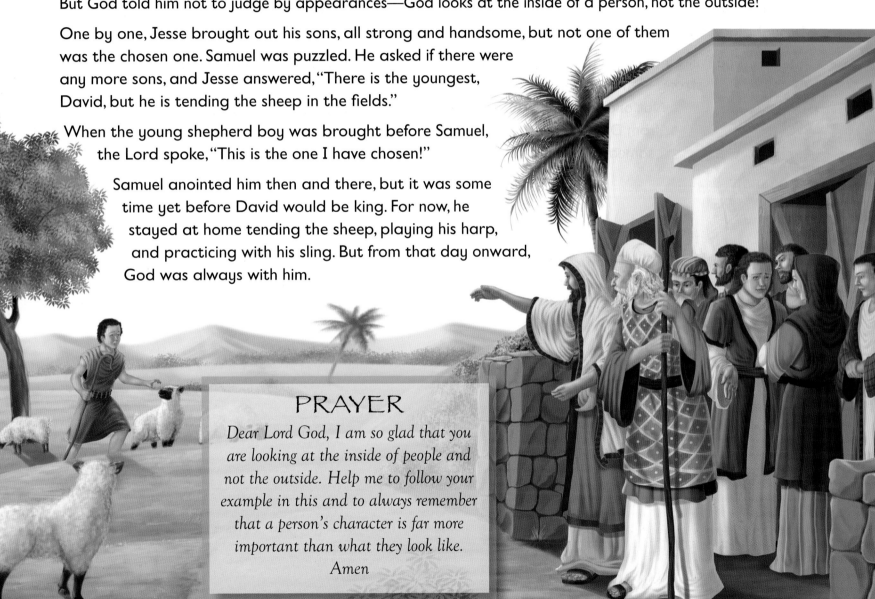

Samuel went to the house of Jesse in Bethlehem, for God had chosen one of his sons to be king of Israel. When he saw Jesse's eldest, a fine-looking young man, he thought, "This must be the one God has chosen." But God told him not to judge by appearances—God looks at the inside of a person, not the outside!

One by one, Jesse brought out his sons, all strong and handsome, but not one of them was the chosen one. Samuel was puzzled. He asked if there were any more sons, and Jesse answered, "There is the youngest, David, but he is tending the sheep in the fields."

When the young shepherd boy was brought before Samuel, the Lord spoke, "This is the one I have chosen!"

Samuel anointed him then and there, but it was some time yet before David would be king. For now, he stayed at home tending the sheep, playing his harp, and practicing with his sling. But from that day onward, God was always with him.

PRAYER

Dear Lord God, I am so glad that you are looking at the inside of people and not the outside. Help me to follow your example in this and to always remember that a person's character is far more important than what they look like.
Amen

DAVID IN THE ARMY CAMP

David was just a shepherd boy. He was the youngest of his family, and he had many brothers who were older and stronger than he was. But God had chosen him as the future leader of Israel!

The Israelites were at war with the Philistines, and the two armies had gathered to do battle. David had brought food to his brothers who were fighting in the army.

The Philistines had a mighty champion. His name was Goliath, and he was powerful and strong—and ten feet tall! Goliath had challenged the Israelite soldiers to single combat. Not one of them had dared to fight this terrible warrior. No one, that is, apart from David, for courage has nothing to do with size, and David knew that he had someone very special on his side—the Lord!

PRAYER

Thank you, Lord God, for the wonderful confidence that David had in you. Please keep reminding me that I need never fear with you at my side.

Amen

A STONE IN A SLING

Young David stood before Goliath. Mighty Goliath was so big and powerful that he was practically a giant! No one else had dared to fight him, but David did! God had been with him when he had protected his sheep from lions and bears, and David knew that God would be with him now.

The king gave David his own armor and weapons, but they were too big and heavy for the boy. So David stood before Goliath with nothing but his staff, a sling, and five smooth stones from a nearby stream.

Goliath laughed when he saw the young shepherd boy, but David fearlessly ran toward him, putting a stone in his sling and flinging it with all his might. It hit Goliath right in the middle of his forehead, and when he fell to the ground, David raced up and, drawing out Goliath's own sword, cut his head from his body with one strike!

The Philistines were so shocked when they saw their champion killed that they turned and fled!

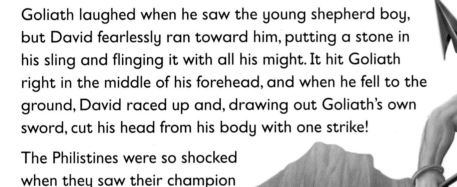

PRAYER
Lord God, how I love this story! I am so glad you used a young boy to defeat a big evil. I know you still want to use young people today. Please use me.
Amen

TEMPER TANTRUM

David was a hero! He came to live in the palace with Saul and his son, Jonathan, who became as fond of him as if he were his own brother. David would go to fight wherever Saul sent him, and wherever he went he seemed to win, so Saul put David in charge of his soldiers.

But soon Saul became jealous. When David returned from a battle, the people would rush out into the street to sing his praises, and Saul's wins seemed to pale in comparison. Saul became angry and upset, for the people seemed to love David more than him.

One day, David was playing his harp when evil spirits came upon the king and he threw his spear at David! When it missed, he tried again, and when David leaped out of the way a second time, Saul became fearful, for he saw that God had left him and was with David.

PRAYER

Dear Lord God, I know that sometimes people may dislike me just because I follow you. Thank you that you have promised to protect me always, so nothing can harm me.

Amen

SAUL IS JEALOUS

Saul tried again and again to have David killed, and in the end David had to flee the palace. Jonathan hoped to persuade his father to forgive David, so they agreed on a sign that would show whether it was safe for David to return. "I'll go with my servant and fire three arrows," said Jonathan. "Then I'll send the boy to fetch them. If I say to him, 'Look, the arrows are on this side of you. Bring them here,' then it is safe to come home. But if I say, 'Look, the arrows are beyond you,' then go, for your life is in danger!"

Jonathan tried to speak to the king, but Saul became furious, and his son realized he would never change his mind. The next day, Jonathan went to the woods where David lay hidden and fired his arrows. As his servant ran to fetch them, he called out, "Isn't the arrow beyond you? Be quick!" and David was filled with sorrow. Jonathan sent the boy back to the palace, and the two friends hugged and said a sad farewell.

PRAYER

Thank you, Lord God, for special friends I know I can trust. Please help me always to be a loyal and true friend to those who love me.
Amen

BREAD AND A SWORD

David and his loyal officers were outlaws now. He had no food and no weapons, but he didn't dare to go back to the palace. Instead, he went to the house of a priest and there asked for bread for himself and his men. He didn't tell the priest that he was hiding from the king, but let him believe that he was on a secret mission.

The priest told him that he had no bread except the holy bread used in ceremonies, but he was welcome to take it. David asked the priest if there was any weapon to be found in the place, for he had left in such a hurry that he had not brought his sword. The priest answered, "The only sword here is the sword of Goliath that you took from him when you killed him! You may take it if you want," and so David left the priest's house with holy bread and Goliath's sword!

But Saul's head shepherd, Doeg, happened to be at the priest's house when David was there and saw what happened. Doeg went straight to the king and told him that the priest had helped David. Saul was furious and ordered the priest and his family killed. One son survived and went straight to David, who felt awful about what had happened. He told the young man to stay with him from then on and promised to look after him.

PRAYER

Lord God, please help me to always tell the truth but not to be a gossiper passing on information that could harm others.
Amen

DAVID SPARES SAUL

Saul did not forget his hatred of David and searched for him throughout the land. A day came when David held Saul's life in his hands. He and his men were hiding in a cave when Saul himself came in, needing to go to the toilet! David managed to creep up and cut off a corner of Saul's robe. His soldiers whispered to him that God had delivered his enemy into his hands, but David didn't want to harm Saul. As Saul left the cave, David called after him and showed him the piece of his robe.

PRAYER

Lord God, may the Spirit of Jesus in me help me to show kindness to people who don't like me and may even hurt me. May I never wish harm to anyone.

Amen

"You see?" he called to Saul. "You shouldn't believe those who tell you I'm a danger to you or that I want your throne. I would never harm you!"

Saul felt humbled by David's goodness and mercy, and asked David to forgive him. For a while there was peace between them. But it didn't last long!

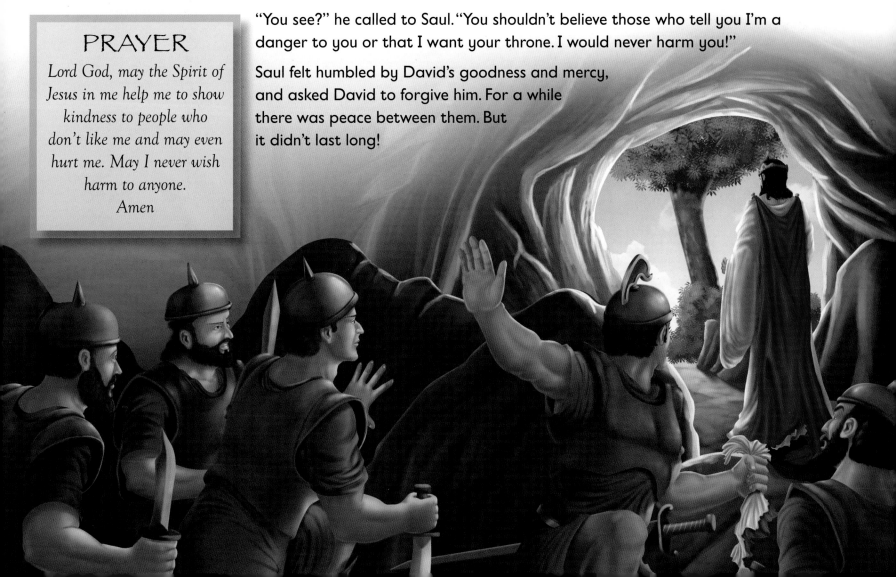

DAVID AND ABIGAIL

One day, David and his men were in the lands of a rich man named Nabal. His wife Abigail was beautiful and wise, but Nabal was evil and selfish. David sent messengers to ask for food and to promise that they meant no harm, but Nabal replied rudely, "Why should I give food to this David?"

David was furious at this and marched toward Nabal's house. But when Abigail learned of Nabal's rudeness, she gathered together some food and rushed to meet David, begging him to forgive her husband and to accept the food she had brought.

David was moved by her plea and promised there would be no fighting. When Nabal learned what had happened, he was overcome with shock and died soon afterward. Then David sent messengers to Abigail, asking her to marry him, which she did with joy.

PRAYER

Dear Lord God, may I always be willing to share what I have with those in need. Please help me to be a peacemaker, bringing calm and comfort to troubled situations.
Amen

SAUL AND THE WITCH OF ENDOR

The years passed, and Samuel died an old man. When the Philistines once again prepared to attack Israel, Saul felt terrified and helpless. He called out to God to guide him, but he received no answer, for God had turned from him. In desperation, he disguised himself and traveled to see a witch living in Endor who could call up the spirits of the dead.

At first the witch didn't want to help, but when Saul swore that she would not be harmed, she agreed. Saul asked her to call up Samuel. Silently the woman began her rites. When she saw the spirit of Samuel, she was frightened, for she guessed now who her visitor was. When Saul realized that the spirit was Samuel, he cried out, "What am I to do? The Philistines are about to attack, and God won't tell me what to do!"

"If God won't answer you, then you shouldn't be talking to me," replied Samuel sternly. "You have disobeyed him, and you will be punished. Tomorrow, you and your sons will be dead."

The next day, the army of Israel was utterly defeated. One by one, Saul's soldiers were killed or deserted, and by nightfall, Saul and his sons were dead!

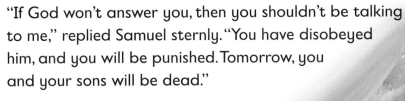

PRAYER

Dear Lord God, please help me to be aware when people are dabbling in evil and witchcraft and any of the things you have forbidden. Please protect me and help me to run from those things.
Amen

DAVID BECOMES KING

David was filled with sorrow when he learned of the deaths of Saul and Jonathan, and things went from bad to worse. David returned to Hebron in the south of Israel, where the people of Judah made him their king, but Saul's only remaining son, Ishbosheth, was proclaimed king over all the northern part of Israel by Saul's general, Abner.

For some time there were two kings in Israel. The conflict was bitter and the fighting fierce, but gradually Ishbosheth's side weakened, and David's side began to win more of the battles. Ishbosheth's general, Abner, eventually changed sides and promised David that he would bring all of Israel to him. David trusted him, but his army leader, Joab, hated Abner bitterly, for in the fighting Abner had killed Joab's brother.

The battles may have been over, but the killing was not. On the very day that David was proclaimed king over all Israel, Joab tricked Abner into a secret meeting and then stabbed him to death! Not long after this, two soldiers came upon Ishbosheth in his sleep and beheaded him!

David was distraught. He ordered the execution of Ishbosheth's murderers and cursed Joab and his family. This was not the way he had wanted his reign to start, but from now on, things would be better.

PRAYER

Thank you, Lord God, that your promises always come true. Thank you that David became king even though it was many years after you had chosen him as a boy. Teach me to be patient in waiting for your timing.
Amen

THE WATER TUNNEL

As one of his first acts as king, David decided to make the fortress city of Jerusalem his new capital, for he knew that the enemies of Israel were always waiting to pounce.

When David marched his army to Jerusalem, which was still held by a Canaanite tribe, the people there laughed at him, believing that they would be safe behind their high walls. Hills surrounded the city on three sides, and on the fourth it was protected by the huge city gates. "You'll never get inside," they taunted. "The blind and the lame could defend us!"

But David had God's blessing. He discovered that a water tunnel ran up through the hill to the city. His men climbed up the water shaft, right into the heart of the city, and unlocked the gates from the inside. So the mighty fortress fell to David and his soldiers!

PRAYER

Dear Lord God, when life gets tough and there seems no way ahead, please remind me that you have amazing plans that overcome obstacles!
Amen

THE ARK IS BROUGHT TO JERUSALEM

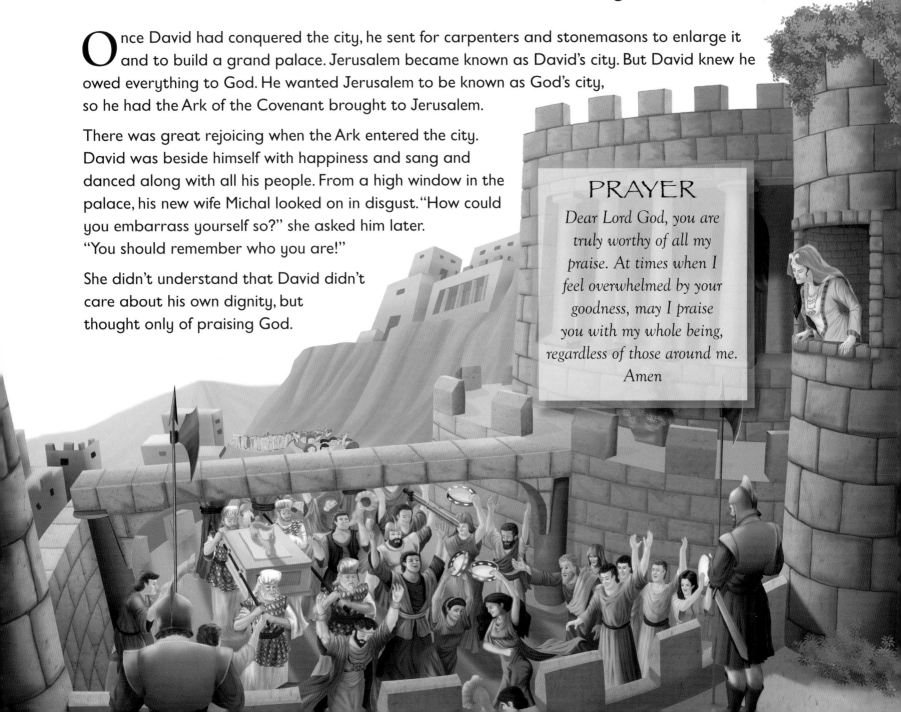

Once David had conquered the city, he sent for carpenters and stonemasons to enlarge it and to build a grand palace. Jerusalem became known as David's city. But David knew he owed everything to God. He wanted Jerusalem to be known as God's city, so he had the Ark of the Covenant brought to Jerusalem.

There was great rejoicing when the Ark entered the city. David was beside himself with happiness and sang and danced along with all his people. From a high window in the palace, his new wife Michal looked on in disgust. "How could you embarrass yourself so?" she asked him later. "You should remember who you are!"

She didn't understand that David didn't care about his own dignity, but thought only of praising God.

PRAYER

Dear Lord God, you are truly worthy of all my praise. At times when I feel overwhelmed by your goodness, may I praise you with my whole being, regardless of those around me.

Amen

GOD'S PROMISE TO DAVID

One day David said to Nathan, the prophet, "It doesn't seem right that I'm living in such a splendid palace while God's covenant chest is in a makeshift tent. I want to build a fine temple for it!"

That night God spoke to Nathan, and in the morning, the prophet told the king, "God has always traveled with his people in a tent, to be with them wherever they went. He doesn't want you to build him a temple."

David was bitterly disappointed, but Nathan continued, "God doesn't want you to build him a house, for it is he who will build a house for you. It is because of him that you left your sheep and fields to become king of all Israel. He promises that he will be with you and help you overcome your enemies. With his guidance you will become the greatest king on earth, and your sons will be kings of Israel after you forevermore."

David was filled with gratitude. When Nathan had gone, David gave his thanks to God in a heartfelt prayer. He had wanted to do something for God, but God had done something wonderful for him, a simple shepherd boy, instead.

PRAYER

Dear Lord God, sometimes I feel I want to give something to you, yet I know that everything is already yours. There is nothing I can give you except the love and adoration of my heart, shown in what I do for other people.

Amen

DAVID IS KIND

Even though he was now king, David didn't forget his dear friend Jonathan. He asked his advisors to find out if any of Jonathan's family were still living, for he wanted to do something for them if he could. At last they found a servant who told them that a son of Jonathan was still living, but that he was crippled in both feet. His name was Mephibosheth.

David sent for Mephibosheth, and when he was brought before the king, he bowed down low. "Don't be afraid," said David to Mephibosheth. "I'll make sure that all the land that belonged to your grandfather Saul is given back to you, and you will always eat at my table."

Mephibosheth asked in amazement, "Who am I that you should honor me?"

"You are the son of Jonathan, who was my dearest friend," replied David, and so Mephibosheth moved to Jerusalem and was always welcome at David's table.

PRAYER

Please fill me, Lord God, with your Holy Spirit of compassion and generosity so that I may look for opportunities to do good to those in need.
Amen

DAVID AND BATHSHEBA

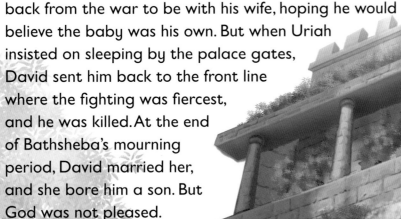

It was early evening in Jerusalem, and David was walking on the palace roof when his eyes were drawn to a beautiful woman bathing. His guards told him it was Bathsheba, the wife of one of his soldiers, Uriah, who was away fighting the Ammonites. David was filled with love for Bathsheba and had her brought to the palace that night. Soon afterward he learned that she was expecting his child!

David didn't know what to do. Uriah would be furious if he learned the truth, so David brought him back from the war to be with his wife, hoping he would believe the baby was his own. But when Uriah insisted on sleeping by the palace gates, David sent him back to the front line where the fighting was fiercest, and he was killed. At the end of Bathsheba's mourning period, David married her, and she bore him a son. But God was not pleased.

PRAYER

Dear Lord God, please help me to stand against the tide of impurity that is all around me and to wait for the joys of marriage in their proper time and place.

Amen

THE PRECIOUS LAMB

God was not pleased with David. He sent his prophet Nathan to tell the king a story about two men, one rich and one poor. The rich man had many sheep and cattle, but the poor man had just one lamb. This lamb used to live in the house with the poor man. It ate the same food and drank from his cup. It was like a child to him.

One day the rich man held a feast, and instead of using his own animals, he killed the one lamb that the poor man owned, and gave it to his guests.

"Such a man deserves to die!" exclaimed David in disgust.

But Nathan said sternly, "That man is you. You have everything you could wish for, yet you took that which was not yours!"

David fell to his knees with his head bent. He realized now how wicked he had been. But God forgave him, and although that child didn't live, in time Bathsheba gave David another child, a son named Solomon, and Solomon was loved by God.

PRAYER

Dear Lord God, please help me to be sensitive to your Holy Spirit so that I quickly repent when I have failed and disappointed you. Thank you for your great forgiveness.
Amen

ABSALOM REBELS

David had many sons, and there was often fighting among them. One of his favorite sons was Absalom, a fine young man with long, thick, curly hair. But Absalom plotted against his own father, for he wanted the throne for himself. He spent his time among the people, gaining their support. When he felt the time was right, he fled to Hebron, had himself proclaimed king, and raised an army.

David gathered his soldiers to him, and the two armies met in a forest. There was a dreadful battle, but in the end it was clear that David's side would be the victors. Absalom tried to flee, but as his horse passed under a low branch, his long, curly hair caught in the twisted branches, and he found himself hanging there, helpless!

David's soldiers found him dangling there and killed him. When David learned of the death of Absalom, he was filled with anguish and wished that he himself had died instead of his beloved, treacherous son.

PRAYER

Dear Lord God, please bring peace to families where there is discord and bitterness. Help me to learn from other people's mistakes so that I can avoid such pain.

Amen

DAVID MAKES WAY FOR SOLOMON

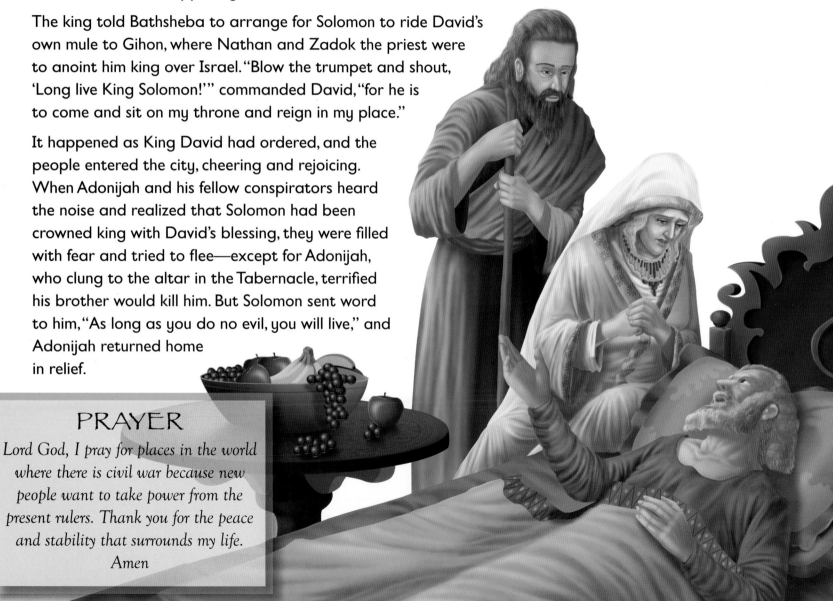

David was old and on his deathbed, and his sons were still fighting over the throne. He had promised it to Solomon, but another of his sons, Adonijah, tried to claim the throne. The prophet Nathan learned what was happening, and he and Bathsheba went to tell David the news.

The king told Bathsheba to arrange for Solomon to ride David's own mule to Gihon, where Nathan and Zadok the priest were to anoint him king over Israel. "Blow the trumpet and shout, 'Long live King Solomon!'" commanded David, "for he is to come and sit on my throne and reign in my place."

It happened as King David had ordered, and the people entered the city, cheering and rejoicing. When Adonijah and his fellow conspirators heard the noise and realized that Solomon had been crowned king with David's blessing, they were filled with fear and tried to flee—except for Adonijah, who clung to the altar in the Tabernacle, terrified his brother would kill him. But Solomon sent word to him, "As long as you do no evil, you will live," and Adonijah returned home in relief.

PRAYER

Lord God, I pray for places in the world where there is civil war because new people want to take power from the present rulers. Thank you for the peace and stability that surrounds my life.
Amen

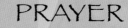

GOD SPEAKS TO SOLOMON

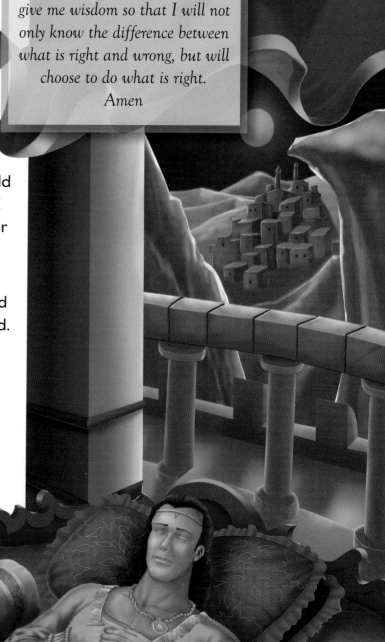

PRAYER

Dear Lord God, I ask you to give me wisdom so that I will not only know the difference between what is right and wrong, but will choose to do what is right.

Amen

Soon after Solomon had been crowned king, God spoke to him in a dream. "What would you like me to give you, Solomon?" he said. "Ask for whatever you want, and it shall be yours."

Solomon thought for a moment and then answered humbly, "I'm young and have no experience of ruling a nation. I would like to be a great king like my father, but I don't know how. I would ask you to give me wisdom that I might rule over your people wisely and do as you would have me do. Help me to distinguish between what is right and what is wrong."

God was pleased with Solomon's answer. "Most people would have asked for wealth, or long life, or great victories," he said. "You have asked only to be wise. I will give you wisdom. But I will also give you those things you did not ask for. You will be rich and respected, and if you follow in my ways, you will live a long and good life."

When Solomon awoke, he felt comforted and strengthened knowing that God was by his side.

THE WISDOM OF SOLOMON

Two women came before Solomon holding a baby between them. "Pardon me, my lord," said one. "This woman and I live in the same house, and we both bore babies within a few days of one another. But her baby died in the night, and she took my son from my side and replaced him with her dead son!"

The other woman said, "No! You are lying! The living one is my son; the dead one is yours." And so they argued before the king.

Then the king said, "Bring me a sword." So they brought a sword for the king. He then gave an order: "Cut the child in two and give half to one woman and half to the other."

The woman whose child it really was, cried out in horror, "No! No, my lord! Give her the baby! Don't kill him! I would rather she looked after him than he died!"

But the other said coldly, "No, we should do as the king says. Then neither of us will have him. That will be fair."

Then the king gave his ruling: "Give the baby to the first woman. Don't kill him; she is his true mother."

When all Israel heard the verdict the king had given, they saw how wise and clever God had made him.

PRAYER

Thank you, Lord God, that you give me your Holy Spirit of wisdom and understanding. Please develop true wisdom within me. Thank you for wise leaders who bring truth and justice.

Amen

BUILDING THE TEMPLE

Solomon soon began to build the temple that his father David had once dreamed of building. He sent for the finest cedar wood, and the stones were cut at the quarry so that hammers and chisels would not be heard on the holy site. The temple was wide and long and tall, with many chambers, and the most sacred of all was the inner temple. Here, the fine cedar was sculpted into beautiful shapes and forms, and the doors were exquisitely carved and covered in fine gold.

The temple took thousands of men seven years to build, and when it was finished, King Solomon filled it with fine treasures. But the finest treasure of all was the chest of the Covenant, containing the two stone tablets. It was brought to lie in the inner temple, where it rested under the wings of two cherubim made of olive wood and covered in gold, each fifteen feet high, their wings touching in the middle of the room.

The cloud of God's presence filled the temple, and the people were full of wonder and thankfulness. Then Solomon thanked God. "I know that you who created heaven and earth would never live in a building made by man, but I pray that here we can be close to you and hear your word."

God told him that he had heard his prayer, that his heart and eyes would be in the temple, and that as long as the king walked in God's ways and kept his laws, he would be with him.

PRAYER

Dear Lord God, I worship you because you are great and holy. You are the Creator of everything. Help me to worship you, not only in church buildings but wherever I am. Help me to worship you with words and also in deeds.

Amen

THE QUEEN OF SHEBA

Solomon grew very rich. After he had built the sacred temple, he built magnificent palaces for himself and one of his wives, the daughter of the Egyptian pharaoh. He ate off gold plates using gold cutlery and drank from a golden goblet. Even the clothes he wore were threaded with gold.

The stories of his wealth and wisdom traveled far and wide. The Queen of Sheba came to visit him from her kingdom far away. She arrived with a long caravan of camels carrying rare spices, gold, and precious stones as gifts.

She asked Solomon many questions, and every question was answered wisely and clearly. "Everything I heard was true!" she told the king. "I thought that people were exaggerating, but now I know they were not. Your people must be proud to have you as their ruler, and it is a sign of your God's love for them that he has made you their king, to rule them with justice and wisdom."

PRAYER

Lord God, you have given me an inquiring mind so that I want to find things out for myself. As I learn more about science and geography and history, help me to see that everything in this world demonstrates your love and power.

Amen

TURNING FROM GOD

King Solomon was greater and richer and wiser than any other king, yet when he grew old, he turned away from God. He had married many foreign princesses, and as the years passed, they turned his heart to the strange gods they worshipped. God was angry and sad. For the sake of David, he didn't want to take the kingdom in Solomon's own lifetime, but he let his enemies rise up against him.

One day, when Jeroboam, one of the king's officials, was out walking in the country, the prophet Ahijah came to him with a message from God. Ahijah took off the new cloak he was wearing and tore it into twelve pieces. He gave ten to Jeroboam, saying, "These are like the twelve tribes of Israel. I have given you ten pieces, because soon God will take away ten tribes from Solomon and give them to you. God will punish Solomon and Israel because they have forsaken him, but he won't take away all the kingdom from David's children; he will give them the tribes of Judah and Benjamin. And if, when you are king, you serve God truly, he will give your kingdom to your sons after you."

When Solomon learned what Ahijah had said, he was afraid and tried to kill Jeroboam. But Jeroboam escaped to Egypt, where he stayed in safety until Solomon died, and then the kingdom of Israel split in two. In the south, the tribes of Judah and Benjamin stayed loyal to Solomon's son, King Rehoboam, but the ten northern tribes broke away and made Jeroboam their king.

PRAYER

Dear Lord God, please hold on to me so that I do not turn away from you. I hope that in my future days I will always use my free will to choose your ways.

Amen

ISRAEL IS DIVIDED

In the south, King Rehoboam ruled over Jerusalem and the tribes of Judah and Benjamin. In the north, Jeroboam was king. Israel was divided, and the fighting between the tribes was fierce.

Despite Ahijah's message, Jeroboam didn't follow God's laws. He had two calves made out of gold for the people to worship, for he was worried that if they traveled to Jerusalem to worship at the holy temple there, they might go back to King Rehoboam.

Things went from bad to worse, and so God sent a holy man to deliver a message. He came to the king at one of the altars and told him God would send a sign: The altar would split open and ashes rain down. Jeroboam was furious. He stretched out his hand to tell his guards to seize the man, and as he did so his hand shrivelled up, the altar was split apart, and its ashes poured out. Yet even after this dire warning, Jeroboam still didn't change his ways!

Nor was King Rehoboam in the south much better, for he too had let his people return to the wicked ways of the tribes who had lived in this land before them.

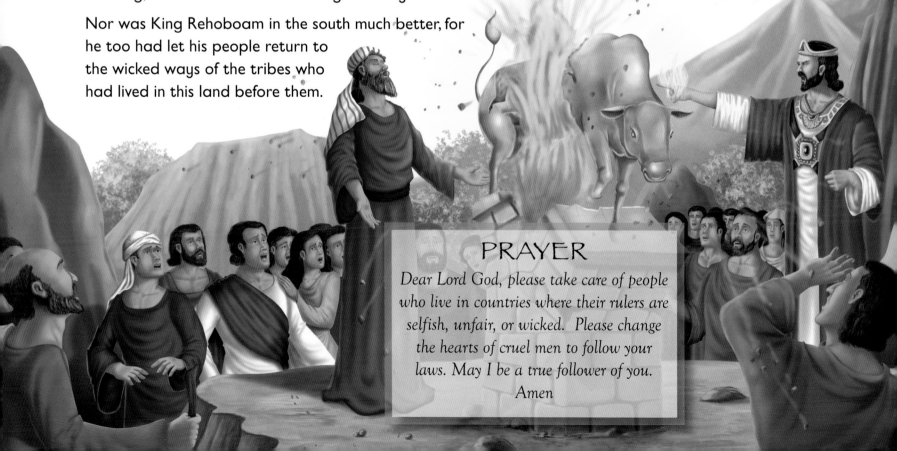

PRAYER

Dear Lord God, please take care of people who live in countries where their rulers are selfish, unfair, or wicked. Please change the hearts of cruel men to follow your laws. May I be a true follower of you.

Amen

ELIJAH AND THE RAVENS

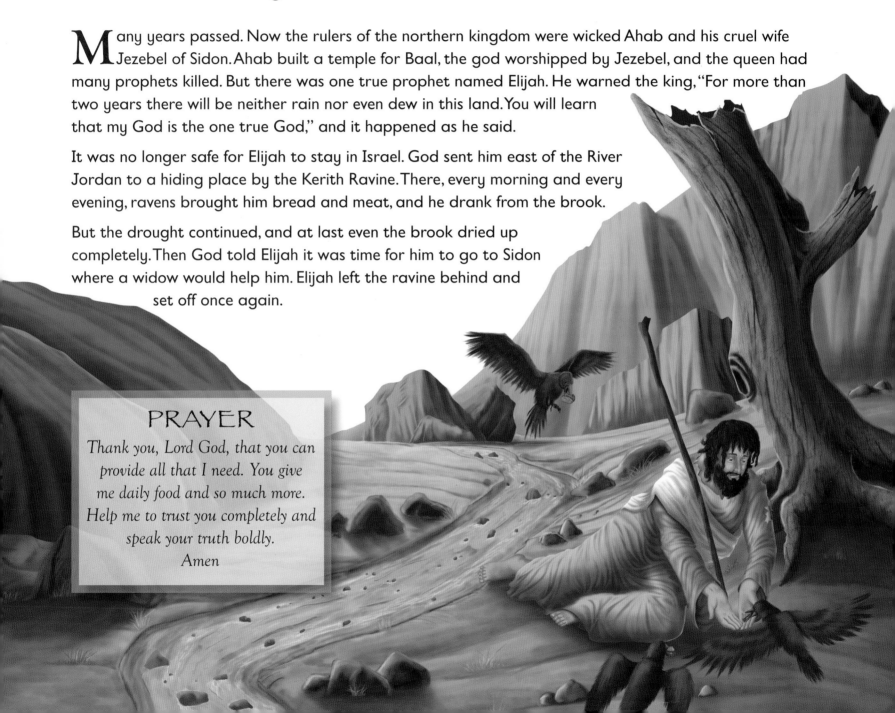

Many years passed. Now the rulers of the northern kingdom were wicked Ahab and his cruel wife Jezebel of Sidon. Ahab built a temple for Baal, the god worshipped by Jezebel, and the queen had many prophets killed. But there was one true prophet named Elijah. He warned the king, "For more than two years there will be neither rain nor even dew in this land. You will learn that my God is the one true God," and it happened as he said.

It was no longer safe for Elijah to stay in Israel. God sent him east of the River Jordan to a hiding place by the Kerith Ravine. There, every morning and every evening, ravens brought him bread and meat, and he drank from the brook.

But the drought continued, and at last even the brook dried up completely. Then God told Elijah it was time for him to go to Sidon where a widow would help him. Elijah left the ravine behind and set off once again.

PRAYER

Thank you, Lord God, that you can provide all that I need. You give me daily food and so much more. Help me to trust you completely and speak your truth boldly.

Amen

DAY
124

1 Kings 17

FLOUR AND OIL

When Elijah reached the city gates of Sidon, he met a woman gathering firewood and asked her for a drink of water. The kind widow went to fetch him a jar of water even though water was scarce. As she was going, Elijah asked her for some bread.

"I'm afraid I have no bread," she sighed. "I have only a handful of flour in a jar and a little olive oil in a jug. I'm gathering a few sticks to take home and make one last meal for myself and my son, that we may eat it—and die."

Elijah told her not to worry, but to go home and make a small loaf of bread for him first and then one for herself and her son, for God had promised that the flour and oil would not run out until the day that rain fell on the land.

The kind widow did as Elijah had asked and found that when she had made one loaf, she still had enough flour and oil to make another. And so it went on, day after day, and there was always enough food for Elijah and for the widow and her young son.

PRAYER

Dear Lord God, thank you for the wonderful lessons in the Bible. I really need to learn to trust you more every day so that when I am an adult I will know how to live.
Amen

THE WIDOW'S SON

Elijah and the widow and her son didn't go hungry, but one day the boy became ill. Day by day he grew worse, and finally he stopped breathing. Beside herself with sorrow, the widow cried out to Elijah, "Why did you come here? Did you come to punish me and kill my son?"

"Give me your son," Elijah replied calmly, and he took the boy to his room and laid him on the bed. Then he cried out to God, "O Lord, my God, why have you brought tragedy on this widow when she has been so good to me?" Then Elijah stretched himself out on the boy three times and cried, "O Lord, let this boy's life return to him!"

God heard Elijah's cry, and the boy's life returned to him. Elijah carried him from the room and gave him to his mother, saying, "Look, your son is alive!"

The woman fell to her knees in gratitude. "Now I know that you are truly a man of God and that the word you preach is the truth!"

PRAYER

Dear Lord God, when terrible things happen among my family and friends, help me still to trust you and know that you are in control of everything—even sickness and death.
Amen

THE GREAT CONTEST

Three years passed without rain, and King Ahab was desperate. Elijah told him to gather the people of Israel and the prophets of Baal at Mount Carmel. "It is time for you to learn who is the true God of Israel!" he said, and he proposed a test. Both he and the prophets of Baal would prepare a bull for sacrifice. Then each would call upon their god to answer with fire! There were four hundred and fifty prophets of Baal, but Elijah was the only one of the Lord's prophets still alive! No one believed that he could possibly win the contest, but Elijah had no fear in his heart, for he knew that he was the prophet of the one true God.

Everyone watched eagerly as the many priests of Baal prepared their bull and then called upon their god to send fire. They prayed and prayed, but nothing happened. They danced frantically around the altar calling Baal's name, but nothing happened. They tore their clothes and slashed themselves with swords and spears, but still nothing happened.

"Perhaps Baal hasn't heard you," mocked Elijah. "Maybe he is asleep! Try harder!"

But try as they might, there was no answer or sign, and at last they fell to the ground in exhaustion.

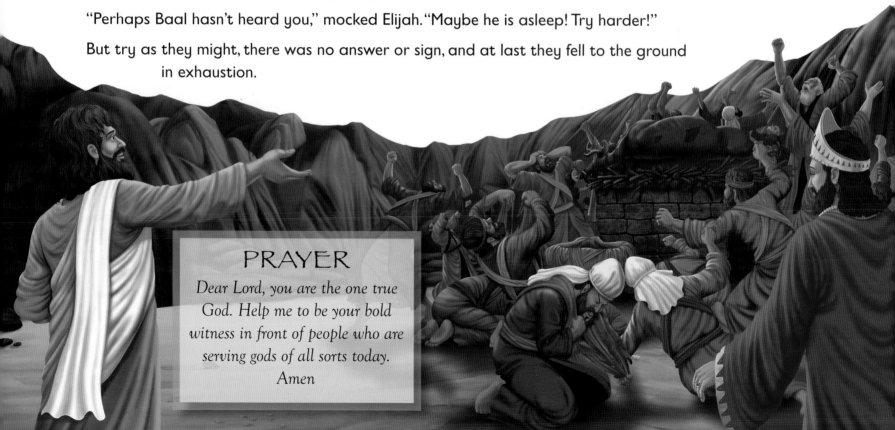

PRAYER
Dear Lord, you are the one true God. Help me to be your bold witness in front of people who are serving gods of all sorts today.
Amen

FIRE!

Now Elijah went to the broken altar of the Lord and used twelve stones, one for each of the tribes, to build an altar, around which he dug a deep trench. He prepared the bull and laid it on the wood. Then he told the people to fill four large jars with water and pour it on the sacrifice and the wood. When they had done this, he told them to do it again, and then he told them to do it a third time, until the altar was drenched and the water filled the trench.

Then Elijah stepped forward and prayed: "Lord, the God of Abraham, Isaac, and Israel, let it be known today that you are God in Israel and that I have done these things at your command."

Then the fire of the Lord fell and burned up the sacrifice, the wood, the stones, and even the water!

The people fell to their knees. "It's true!" they cried. "The Lord is God!"

PRAYER
Lord God, you are the all-powerful one. Thank you that you not only show yourself in power and judgment, but also in quiet humility and grace. I long for many more people to honor and recognize you.
Amen

THE FAST RUNNER

The people were amazed at what Elijah had done in the name of the Lord. They could hardly believe their eyes! Elijah made sure that the prophets of Baal didn't escape in the confusion, but were seized and slain.

Then the prophet told Ahab to go and find something to eat and drink, for the rains were coming. He himself climbed to the top of Mount Carmel and lowered his head in prayer.

"Go and look toward the sea," he told his servant, but his servant returned saying that there was nothing to be seen.

"Go and look again," said Elijah.

Seven times this happened, and when the servant returned the seventh time, he told Elijah that he had seen a tiny cloud in the sky. Then Elijah sent him to tell Ahab to get his chariot ready quickly if he wanted to get back before the rains stopped him.

Soon the sky darkened and grew black with clouds. The wind picked up, and drops of rain fell from the sky—softly at first but quickly becoming a fierce thunderstorm.

Then Elijah was filled with God's power, and tucking his robes into his belt, he began to run. And although the palace at Jezreel was many, many miles away, Elijah ran the whole way, ahead of Ahab in his fine chariot!

PRAYER

Thank you, Lord God, for the blessings of the rain and sunshine that you send. Thank you that I live in a country where crops grow well and there is more than enough for everyone.

Amen

NABOTH'S VINEYARD

From his elegant palace, King Ahab could see a fine plot of land which his neighbor, Naboth, had made into a vineyard. King Ahab thought that this would make a wonderful vegetable garden for the palace. He offered to buy the land, but Naboth didn't want to sell. "This land was given to my ancestors by God. It would not be right to sell it, however much you paid me."

Ahab was used to getting his own way, and he sulked dreadfully. When his wife Jezebel learned what was making him cross, she simply decided to get rid of Naboth, and paid a couple of scoundrels to make up false charges against him. Naboth was put on trial, found guilty, and stoned to death! And so Ahab got his precious vegetable garden.

PRAYER

Dear Lord God, help me to see how selfishness makes a person so ugly. Please help me to guard my heart against wanting my own way and instead to look for what will be good for others.

Amen

CONSEQUENCES

God was not pleased with Ahab and his wife, and he sent Elijah to speak to the king. "Here comes my old enemy!" moaned the king when he saw Elijah before him.

"It is you who have made an enemy of God with your actions!" replied Elijah. "How could you have had an innocent man killed just so that you could have something that didn't belong to you? God is angry and will punish you, and the throne will be taken from you and your family!"

When Elijah had gone, Ahab felt very ashamed. He took off all his fine clothes and ate only plain food. He did everything he could to show that he was sorry.

God said to Elijah, "It looks as if Ahab really is sorry for what has happened. Because of this, I will not bring disaster on his family now, but will do it in the time of his sons, for they are not fit to be kings of Israel."

PRAYER

Dear Lord God, I can see how evil it is to want what belongs to someone else, and how this can lead to dreadful actions. Teach me to be content with what you have given me and not to be envious of others.
Amen

TAKEN TO HEAVEN

Elijah and Elisha were walking together by the River Jordan. Elijah was old now, and he knew it was time to hand over his work to Elisha. He took off his cloak and struck the water with it, and a path opened up before him. The two men walked across. Then Elijah turned to his companion, saying, "Soon, I shall leave you. Is there anything you would ask of me before I go?"

Elisha thought carefully. "I should like to inherit your spirit, your greatness and power, to help me carry on your work."

Suddenly a chariot of fire drawn by horses of fire appeared before them. As Elisha looked on in amazement, Elijah was taken up to heaven in a whirlwind!

When the sky was empty once again, Elisha noticed that Elijah's cloak had fallen to the ground. He picked it up and walked to the riverbank. He struck the river with the cloak, and the waters parted before him! When the other prophets saw what happened, they bowed to the ground. "The spirit of Elijah has been passed on to Elisha!" they said in wonder.

PRAYER

Thank you, Lord Jesus, that you trained your disciples so that they in turn could teach others. Help me to be a learner, a teacher of your truth, and a good example for younger children who follow me.
Amen

THE JAR OF OIL

One day a worried woman came to see Elisha. "Sir," she said, "my husband has died and I cannot pay the debts that he left. The man he owes money to has threatened to come to my house and take away my two sons as slaves in payment for his debt. Please help me!"

Elisha wondered what he could do, for he certainly had no money to give her. Then he asked her, "What do you have in your house?"

"Nothing except a small jar of olive oil," replied the woman despondently.

Elisha told her to go and ask all her neighbours for their empty jars—every last one of them! Then she must go inside with her sons and pour the oil into the jars, one by one.

The widow did as she was told, pouring oil into each jar and putting each one to the side when it was full. When all the jars were full, she asked one of her sons to bring her another, but there were no more left. And at that moment, the oil stopped flowing!

When, in awe and wonder, she took the jars to Elisha, he told her to sell the oil and pay her debts. There was enough money left over for her and her sons to live comfortably!

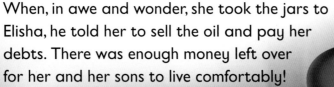

PRAYER

Thank you, Lord God, that your creation is full of abundance. Thank you for your great generosity. Help me to copy your example and be an unselfish giver.
Amen

ELISHA HEALS

Elisha came across some kind people in his travels. One wealthy woman always offered him a meal when he passed by. She even arranged a small room for him on the roof of her house so that he would have somewhere comfortable to sleep. Elisha wanted to do something nice in return. The lady had no son, and her husband was old, but Elisha promised her that within a year she would have a son!

It came to pass just as Elisha had said, and the boy grew up to fill their home with happiness. But one day the boy clutched his head in pain, and within a few hours, he died in his mother's arms. She laid him on the bed set aside for Elisha, closed the door softly, and then, saying nothing about what had happened to anyone at all, got her husband to arrange for a servant and a donkey to take her to Elisha.

When Elisha saw her coming, he sent his servant to ask what was wrong, but she would say nothing until she spoke to the prophet himself. She reproached him bitterly for ever asking God to give her a son. Elisha traveled back with her to the house. There he found the boy lying dead on the bed. He went into the room alone and prayed to God. He lay on the bed beside the boy and warmed his body with his own. Then he paced around the room before again lying on the boy to warm him up.

Suddenly the boy sneezed! He sneezed seven times and then opened his eyes!

Elisha called the woman in, and she took her son in her arms! Her gratitude toward Elisha and God was immeasurable.

PRAYER

Thank you, Lord God, that you are the God of miracles and nothing is too hard for you! Thank you for my parents and their joy when I came into their home. Please watch over husbands and wives who long for a child, and answer their prayers.
Amen

WASHED CLEAN

Naaman, the general of the armies of Syria, was a great soldier, but he was struck with a dreadful skin disease. An Israelite slave girl told him that the wonderful prophet in Samaria might be able to help, so Naaman traveled to Israel.

When Naaman reached Elisha's house, he expected the prophet to come out and perform a spectacular miracle. Instead, Elisha sent his servant out to tell the general to bathe in the River Jordan seven times, and he would be cured.

The general was offended. "Why should I wash in that filthy river?" he shouted. "We have plenty of rivers in Syria!" And he would have left in disgust had not his servant calmed him down.

Realizing that he was being foolish, Naaman went to the river and bathed in it. And sure enough, when he emerged after the seventh time, his skin was soft and smooth.

He went to thank Elisha. "Yours is the true God. From now on I'll worship him too," and he offered Elisha a gift. Elisha would take nothing, but his servant went after the general secretly, saying Elisha had changed his mind. Naaman gave him money, which the servant hid under his bed. But Elisha knew what had happened and was angry. "For your greed and lies you will be punished," he said sternly. "You will suffer from the same disease Naaman had!"

PRAYER

Dear Lord God thank you that your blessings cannot be earned or bought with money. Thank you that you are the great and generous giver of all that is good. Help me to follow you in blessing others.

Amen

THE BLIND ARMY

The king of Aram was at war with Israel, but wherever he planned to set up camp, the Israelites were there before him. His officers told him that the prophet Elisha somehow knew all their secrets and told them to his king.

The king of Aram sent many horses and chariots and soldiers to surround the city where Elisha was staying by night. When Elisha's servant awoke to see a great army surrounding the city, he was dismayed and cried out in fear. But Elisha said calmly, "Don't be afraid. Those who are with us are more than those who are with them." God opened the servant's eyes, and he saw that the hills were filled with horses and chariots of fire.

As the enemy began to approach, Elisha prayed to the Lord to strike them with blindness, and all of a sudden the soldiers couldn't see a thing! Elisha went outside and told them that they were going the wrong way. He led them straight to the king of Israel, who asked if he should kill them. But instead Elisha told him to give them food and water and then send them home. How surprised the terrified soldiers were to be given a feast by their enemies. After that, there were no more raids from Aram!

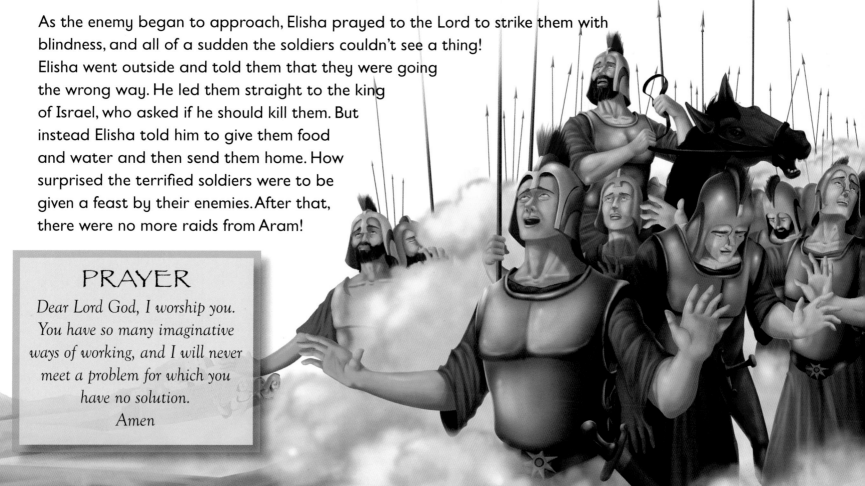

PRAYER

Dear Lord God, I worship you.
You have so many imaginative
ways of working, and I will never
meet a problem for which you
have no solution.
Amen

FAMINE IN SAMARIA

The army of Syria was camped outside Samaria. No one could get in or out and there was almost nothing left to eat. The king stormed to Elisha's house. "This is all God's fault!" he complained. "Why doesn't he help us?"

"By tomorrow, there will be food in Samaria!" promised Elisha. The officer with the king told him that was ridiculous, to which Elisha replied calmly, "Ridiculous or not, it will happen, and you won't live to see it!"

Now, outside the city gates were four men who were even worse off than those inside, for they were lepers and were banned from the city. In desperation, they went to the Syrian camp to beg for some food, but when they got there, they were amazed to find it deserted. They went into one of the empty tents and helped themselves to food and drink eagerly.

Then they looked at one another uncomfortably. "This isn't right," said one. "We can't keep this to ourselves," and they returned to spread the news. When the king sent out scouts, he found that the Syrians had fled, for God had made them hear the sound of chariots and horses in the night and they had thought that a great army was about to attack! Their food stores were brought into the city and the people celebrated in delight.

But the officer who had doubted God was knocked down when the people rushed to buy the food, and was killed instantly!

PRAYER

Thank you, Lord God, that you have given me good news to share. Thank you for the good news that anyone can trust in Jesus for eternal life. Help me not to keep this to myself but freely to pass it on.
Amen

JEHOSHAPHAT TRUSTS GOD

King Jehoshaphat had gathered all the people of Judah to Jerusalem. A vast army was on its way to destroy the land. But Jehoshaphat didn't despair—he knew who to talk to! He had called his people together to pray to God for help.

As he and the people prayed, the Spirit of the Lord came on one of the priests, and he said, "God says, 'Don't be afraid, for this is God's battle, not yours. Go out to face your enemy tomorrow, and the Lord will be with you.'"

So the next morning, the army of Judah set out for the battlefield, singing God's praises as they went. As they marched, God made the different groups of the enemy army fight against themselves. By the time the soldiers of Judah came to the place where they had expected to give battle, all they saw before them was a sea of dead bodies! No one had escaped!

The neighboring kingdoms were filled with fear at this sign of God's power, and for a while, the people of Judah lived in peace.

PRAYER

Help me, Lord God, to always praise you, even when problems look too big and I have no answers. Thank you that you can solve everything when I praise you and trust you.
Amen

THE FALL OF JEZEBEL

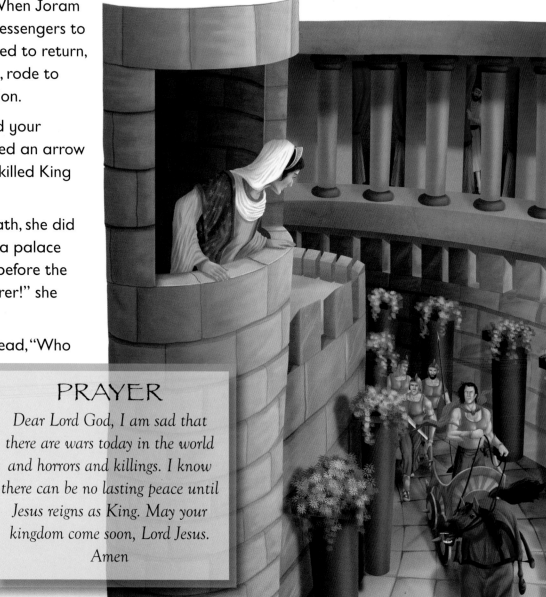

Joram, the son of Ahab and Jezebel, now wore the crown. He was no better than his parents, so God told Elisha that it was time to put a new king on the throne of Israel. Elisha sent one of his followers to the army camp to anoint an officer named Jehu. As soon as Jehu was anointed, he gathered the soldiers and set off for the city in his chariot. When Joram saw the army approaching, he sent messengers to ask if it came in peace. When they failed to return, he and his ally, King Ahaziah of Judah, rode to meet the army to ask the same question.

"There can be no peace while you and your mother rule!" shouted Jehu, and he fired an arrow right through Joram's heart. Then he killed King Ahaziah too!

When Jezebel learned of her son's death, she did her hair carefully and then waited at a palace window. Soon Jehu's chariot drew up before the palace. "You are nothing but a murderer!" she spat.

But Jehu ignored her, shouting up instead, "Who is on my side?" A few faces appeared cautiously in some of the windows. "Throw her down!" ordered Jehu, and they took Jezebel and threw her from the window, and she was killed instantly. And now Jehu ordered Ahab's family and all of the priests of Baal to be killed too!

PRAYER

Dear Lord God, I am sad that there are wars today in the world and horrors and killings. I know there can be no lasting peace until Jesus reigns as King. May your kingdom come soon, Lord Jesus.
Amen

JOASH, THE BOY KING

When King Ahaziah's mother Athaliah learned of his death, she tried to gain the throne for herself and ordered the death of all the royal family. But Ahaziah had left a baby son named Joash, and Joash's aunt hid him in the temple, where he was brought up in secret until he was seven years old. Then the high priest decided it was time for Joash to take the throne and put an end to his wicked grandmother's reign.

Before a great crowd, Joash was brought out of hiding, and the high priest anointed him and placed the crown on his young head. A great cheer went up, so loud that Athaliah heard and hurried to see what was going on. When she saw the young boy with the crown on his head, she was furious. "Treason!" she cried. But not one soldier came to her aid! Instead, she was taken away and put to death, and the people went to the temple of Baal and smashed the altars and tore down the idols. Joash tried to be a good king and to remember God's laws. One of the first things he did was to repair the temple of God.

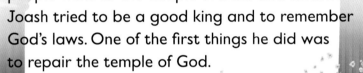

PRAYER

Thank you, Lord God, that you care for children and you have important work for them to do. I know that though I am young, I must respect places of worship and learn your ways.

Amen

GOD CALLS ISAIAH

For a time things were relatively peaceful in Judah and in Israel, but Isaiah knew it wouldn't last. Isaiah was a prophet—one of the greatest that the people of Israel had ever had. He was first called by God in the year that King Uzziah (the grandson of King Joash) died. God sent him an amazing vision.

In his vision, he saw God sitting on a throne. Above him flew winged angels covering their faces and calling to one another, "Holy, holy, holy is the Lord Almighty; the whole earth is full of his glory." The floor shook with the sound of their voices, and the temple was filled with smoke.

At first Isaiah was dismayed, for he knew he was a sinner and had looked upon the Lord. But one of the angels touched his mouth with a live coal taken from the altar, saying, "See, this has touched your lips; your guilt is taken away and your sins are forgiven."

Then he heard the voice of the Lord saying, "Whom can I send? Who will be my messenger?"

Isaiah called out, "Here I am, Lord. Send me!"

Then God gave Isaiah a message for his people. He warned Isaiah that people wouldn't want to listen, that they would close their ears—and their hearts too—but Isaiah was still willing to be God's prophet.

PRAYER

Dear Lord God, help me to understand more of your holiness. May your Holy Spirit teach me how much my sin hurts you and puts me at a distance from you. Thank you that through Jesus, all my sin is forgiven and I can be your messenger.
Amen

CAPTURED BY ASSYRIA

The years passed, and Israel fell into disgrace. Its kings were rotten, and the people had turned from God to worship Baal and other false idols.

God was sad that his people had turned away from him. He had done so much for them—he had saved them from slavery in Egypt and had brought them to this beautiful land, but they had fallen into wicked ways and had not listened to the warnings of the prophets that he had sent them.

So when the great armies of Assyria came, Israel fell, for it was time for God to punish his children. For nearly three years the armies of Assyria laid siege to the city of Samaria, and at last it fell. Then the Israelites were forced to leave their country and made to march to a far-off land, and new people came to live in Samaria, bringing their false gods with them.

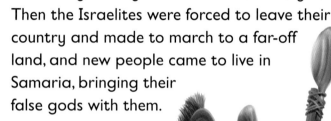

PRAYER

Dear Lord God, please keep me true to you. I really don't want to follow the idols of money and things in the world around me. Please keep me away from the path of your punishment.
Amen

HEZEKIAH'S PRAYER

Farther south, Hezekiah was king of Judah. He was a good man and refused to make an alliance with Assyria, choosing to depend upon God alone for protection. Before long, the mighty army of Assyria came before the walls of Jerusalem and demanded that the city surrender. The people cowered in fear, but Isaiah said, "Don't be afraid. Don't make the same mistake as Israel. Trust in God, for he will save us."

The enemy commander sent another message. "Your God won't save you. He didn't save Samaria! And none of the gods from any of the other countries that we have conquered ever saved their people either! Give up, and I'll be merciful."

Hezekiah went to the temple and prayed. "You are the only true God," he said. "I place all my trust in you. Deliver us from these Assyrians who insult you so that all the kingdoms may know that you alone, Lord, are God."

That night the angel of the Lord passed through the Assyrian camp, and when the sun came up the next morning, it rose on the dead bodies of thousands of Assyrian soldiers. After that, those Assyrians still alive packed up their things and marched home as quickly as they could!

PRAYER

Lord God, I know that you can overcome any problem I face. Please give me a strong trust in you so that I won't be sidetracked by scary stories from people who don't know you.
Amen

CRYING OUT FOR HEALING

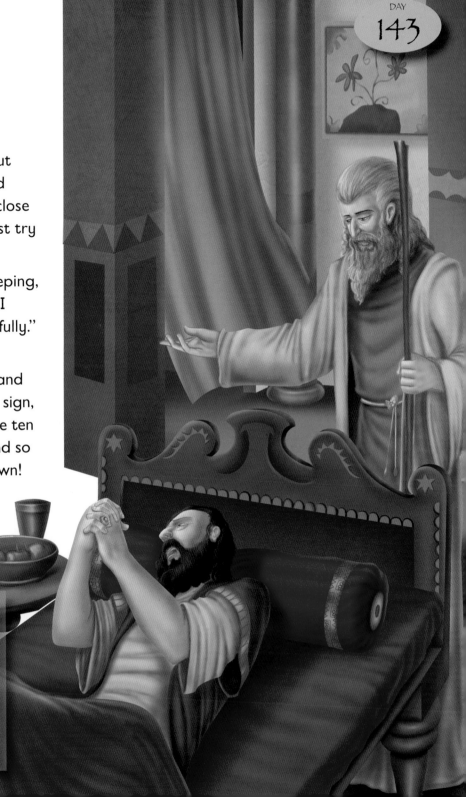

Hezekiah needed to be strong to rule Judah, but instead he became ill. A boil on his skin spread infection through his body like poison until he was close to death. Isaiah told him that God had said he must try to put his affairs in order.

Hezekiah was dismayed. He turned to the wall, weeping, and said a heartfelt prayer. "Remember, Lord, how I have always loved you and tried to serve you faithfully."

Then Isaiah told the king, "The Lord has heard your prayer. He will let you live for another fifteen years, and he will save you from your enemy, Assyria. And as a sign, he will make the shadow cast by the sun go back the ten steps it has gone down on the stairway of Ahaz." And so the sunlight went back the ten steps it had gone down!

Isaiah told the servants to prepare a paste from figs to put on the boil, and by morning, Hezekiah was cured! He promised to spend the rest of his life praising God.

PRAYER

Thank you, Lord God, that you will be with me all of my life and you already know all about the years ahead of me. You are the great Healer; please be with doctors and nurses and others who are working today to heal sick people.

Amen

JOSIAH AND THE BOOK OF LAW

Josiah was only eight years old when he first sat on the throne of Judah, many years later. The land had once again fallen into evil ways, but Josiah was a good king who tried to bring his people back to God's way. He sent men to repair the Lord's temple, for it had been sadly neglected. One of the workmen came across the Book of Law, and a priest took it to the king.

When Josiah began to read God's laws, he was appalled and dismayed. He saw how far the people had fallen and how they had broken their promise to God. He sent for all the people of Judah and Jerusalem and read the Book of Law out loud to them all. They promised to obey God's word. He made them destroy their false idols and drove out the priests of Baal, and he also made sure that they celebrated the Passover properly.

As long as Josiah lived, the people worshipped God and followed his laws. But Josiah died in battle when he was still young, and his son Jehoiakim became king. Under his rule, the people soon slipped back to their old ways.

PRAYER

Dear Lord God, please keep me true to the Bible all of my life. May I always treasure your word. May it never get lost and neglected among the many other things that I need to be busy with.

Amen

JEREMIAH IS CALLED

One of the greatest prophets of the Lord was Jeremiah. He was chosen by God to pass on his message to the kings and people of Judah in a very difficult time. When Jeremiah first heard God speak to him, he thought he was far too young and inexperienced to be a prophet. But God said, "Don't worry. I will be with you, and I will put the words into your mouth."

God wanted to warn his people that a great enemy would come upon them. He showed Jeremiah a large cooking pot over a blazing fire. As Jeremiah watched, the liquid in the pot began to boil, spilling over in a huge rush of steaming liquid.

"In just such a way will an enemy from the north spill over into the lands of Judah and Jerusalem and destroy all that lies in its path," warned God. "You must warn the people so that they turn from their wicked ways, back to my laws, for only then will they be saved."

The people didn't like listening to what Jeremiah had to say. They didn't want to have to obey God's laws to be blessed by him, and so Jeremiah became extremely unpopular! But still he passed on God's messages.

PRAYER

Dear Lord God, you know that sometimes I feel afraid to say anything because I am young. Yet I know that you will always be close to me, and I ask you to give me the words I need to speak at the right time.
Amen

THE POTTER'S CLAY

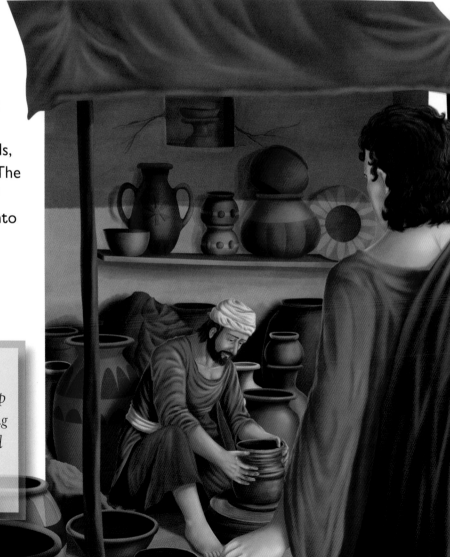

Jeremiah watched a potter mold pieces of rough clay into beautiful vases and useful jugs. Sometimes the clay didn't do what the potter wanted it to, so he would start again and make it into something different. "Israel is like the clay," God said. "If Israel does evil, I will change whatever good thing I had planned for it, but if Israel repents, then I will relent."

God told Jeremiah to warn the people that disaster was coming and that only by being truly sorry could they stop it. But he knew they would not listen. Jeremiah took some priests and elders to the Valley of Ben Hinnom. He warned them that God was going to punish his people for their wrongdoing. Judah and Jerusalem would fall to their enemies' swords, and their bodies would carpet the ground. The place would become known as the Valley of Slaughter. Then Jeremiah broke a clay jar into many pieces and said, "God will smash this nation and this city just like this jar."

The priests were so cross that they threw Jeremiah into prison!

PRAYER

Dear Lord God, my life could be like a lump of clay in your hands. I do want to be willing to let you shape my life into something good and useful and pleasing to you.

Amen

THE SCROLL

For more than twenty years, Jeremiah continued faithfully to warn the people of Judah to turn back to God. God told Jeremiah to write down everything he had said on a scroll. When everything had been written down, Jeremiah asked his friend if he would read from the scroll at the temple, for Jeremiah was not allowed to enter it anymore.

When King Jehoiakim's officials found out, they knew the king would be furious. They brought the scroll to him, and as they read to him from the scroll, his face grew redder and redder with anger. Each time the official read part of the scroll, the hard-hearted king took his knife and cut off the section and threw it into the fire. When the entire scroll was burned, he sent his guards to arrest Jeremiah and his friend, but they were safely hidden.

The king thought that he had gotten rid of God's words, but God simply told Jeremiah to write them out again. He told Jeremiah to tell the king that he and his children and all Judah would be punished.

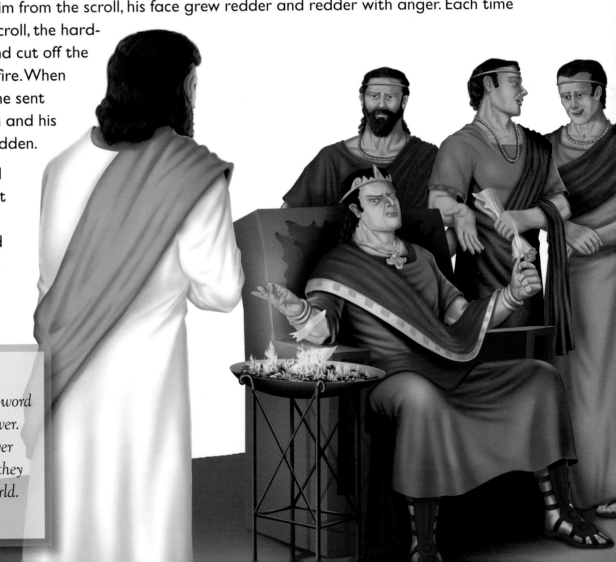

PRAYER

Thank you, Lord God, that your word is living and true and lasts forever. Thank you that no one will ever get rid of what you say, even if they burned all the Bibles in the world.
Amen

CONQUERED!

For too long the people of Judah had ignored God's warnings. It was time for them to be punished. There came a new enemy from the north, more terrifying than before—Babylon! Just as Jeremiah had warned, Jerusalem fell to mighty Nebuchadnezzar and his army, and all the strong, skilled people were sent away to Babylon. Nebuchadnezzar chose his own puppet king to put on the throne and stripped the temple of its treasures.

God knew that the Israelites exiled in Babylon would be in the depths of despair, so Jeremiah, who had stayed behind, wrote a letter to comfort them and give them hope:

"This is what the Lord says: 'When seventy years are completed, I will bring you back to this place. You will pray to me, and I will listen. You will seek me and find me when you seek with all your heart, and I will bring you back from captivity. I will gather you from all the places where I have banished you, and will bring you back to the place from which I carried you into exile.'"

PRAYER

I am so glad, Lord God, that alongside your judgment, there is always mercy. Thank you for your precious promises that always come true.

Amen

GOOD AND BAD FIGS

The people left in the city were feeling rather pleased with themselves. They had been beaten by a foreign ruler, but at least they hadn't been captured and taken away. Jeremiah asked God why he didn't punish them, for they were proud and had not changed their wicked ways.

God showed Jeremiah two baskets of figs and asked him what he saw. Jeremiah replied rather puzzled, "I see one basket full of ripe, tasty-looking figs, and another full of figs so rotten that nobody would ever want to eat them."

"The people of Jerusalem are like those good figs," God told him. "Those already taken from Jerusalem to Babylon have begun to repent and are learning to come back to me. I will look after them, and one day I will bring them back to their own land.

"But the people left in Jerusalem are like the figs in the second basket. They are rotten and will never change their ways. Whether by sword or famine or plague, they shall all be wiped from this land, every last one of them!"

PRAYER

Dear Lord God, thank you that I don't have to be anxious about things that seem unfair. Help me always to remember that you are the great Judge who sees everything, and one day all wrongs will be put right.

Amen

DOWN A WELL

Time after time Jeremiah tried to warn the new king that Judah was not strong enough to rebel against the might of Babylon. For now, they would have to do as Nebuchadnezzar ordered. But King Zedekiah and his officials became angry when Jeremiah tried to tell them things like that.

One day, when he was leaving the city, the guards arrested him, and he was accused of trying to run off to the enemy. They put him in chains and locked him up in prison. But some of the people of the city still came to listen to the prophet, and in frustration, the furious officials threw him into the bottom of an unused cistern, deep and dark and muddy.

But one of the king's officials felt bad about this. He went to ask the king if he could let Jeremiah out, for otherwise he would surely starve, and the king agreed. Taking some men with him, the good official went to the cistern and carefully pulled poor Jeremiah back out into the fresh air.

PRAYER

Dear Lord God, please be near to all today who have been wrongly accused and punished. Please send helpers to encourage them and stand up for them.
Amen

THE FALL OF JERUSALEM

Zedekiah refused to listen to Jeremiah and tried to rebel against Nebuchadnezzar. Then, once again, the mighty forces of Babylon came against Judah and camped outside Jerusalem. Zedekiah was terrified. This time he begged Jeremiah for his advice, and Jeremiah told him, "God says, 'If you surrender, your life will be spared and the city won't be burned down. But if you won't surrender, the city will be given to the Babylonians, they will burn it down, and you won't escape.'"

Even now, Zedekiah would not listen to Jeremiah. Instead, he tried to flee the city with his army in the middle of the night. But the Babylonians cut them down and then destroyed the city utterly. They set fire to the temple, the palace, and all the houses, and the rest of the people were taken away as slaves. They had refused to listen to God, and now they were being punished.

PRAYER

Dear Lord God, help me to take note of the warnings you have given me in the Bible. Help me to live according to your truth, rather than my own ideas and those of other people.
Amen

COMFORT IN DESPAIR

Jerusalem was destroyed. God had punished his disobedient children. But he hadn't stopped loving them. Years before, Isaiah had known this would happen and had a message of hope for the exiles from God: "'Comfort my people,' says your God. 'Speak tenderly to Jerusalem, and tell her she has paid for her sins.'

"A voice calls out, 'Prepare a way in the wilderness for the Lord. His glory will be revealed, and all will see it together. The people are like grass, their faithfulness like flowers. Grass withers and flowers fall, but the word of our God lasts forever.'

"God rules with a mighty arm. He tends his flock like a shepherd. He gathers the lambs and carries them close to his heart. So never believe he doesn't care about you. God gives strength and power to those who need it. Those who place their trust in God will soar on wings like eagles; they will run and not grow tired."

God knew that his children would learn from their lesson. They would once again learn to love and worship him and follow his ways, and then they would return home, with God by their side. But for now, they were slaves in a foreign country.

PRAYER

Dear Lord God, thank you for people who bring your words of comfort to those who need them. Please strengthen today those who are giving up their time to bring comfort in hospitals, refugee camps, war zones, and other places of despair.

Amen

EZEKIEL'S AMAZING VISION

It was five years since Ezekiel had seen his beloved homeland. Now he lived in Babylon among the other captives. At this time, the final fall of Jerusalem and its temple had not yet happened, but most of the skilled people had been forced to leave the city.

Ezekiel was a good man who loved God. One day, he was by the river when an enormous cloud appeared in the sky encircled by brilliant light, and within it Ezekiel saw the most amazing vision.

Within the cloud there appeared four creatures surrounded by fire. Lightning flashed all around. Each had four faces—human, lion, ox, and eagle—and four wings. The sound of the wings was like rushing water. Beside each creature was a wheel, and within that there was another wheel, and the wheels sparkled like topaz and moved with the creatures, which stood under a sparkling vault. Above this was a throne of startling blue lapis lazuli upon which sat a figure like a man, but glowing as if on fire, surrounded by light. Then God spoke to Ezekiel and told him he had been chosen to pass God's message on to his people, however obstinate and rebellious they might be.

PRAYER

Thank you, Lord God, that you speak in many ways: through nature, through dreams and visions, and most of all through the Bible. Thank you for speaking clearly to people in this world. May I always have open ears to your truth.

Amen

EZEKIEL'S WARNING

God told Ezekiel to take a clay brick and draw a picture of Jerusalem on it. Next, he was to lay siege to the city by setting up enemy camps and battering rams around it, and then he was to take an iron pan and place it between himself and the brick like a wall. Finally, he was to lie on his side for many, many days to bear the sins of the people of Israel and Judah, and was to eat only a small loaf of bread, which he was to make each day, and to drink only a little water. God was showing the people that Jerusalem would be under siege once again and that the people would have little to eat or drink.

After this, God told Ezekiel to shave his hair and beard, burn a third of it upon the brick, chop another third with a sword, and throw the rest to the wind, apart from a few strands caught in his clothes (though even some of those were to be thrown on the fire).

God was explaining that some of his people would be killed by famine or plague and some by the sword, while the others would be chased across the land. Yet a few would be saved. They would understand how evil their ways had become, and they would repent and turn back to God.

PRAYER

Dear Lord God, I am glad that to you the future is just like the past. You know everything, and sometimes you reveal the future. Help me never to fear, but to trust in you.
Amen

STRAY SHEEP

As Ezekiel had warned, Nebuchadnezzar's armies once again attacked Jerusalem, and this time they destroyed everything. The walls were razed to the ground, the holy temple was ransacked and burned, and everyone left was killed or taken captive.

Ezekiel told the leaders of those in exile that they had failed their people. They should have been looking after them like shepherds with their sheep, caring for the weak and healing the sick, looking for those who were lost or who had strayed. But instead, they had been harsh and cruel, and the sheep had strayed and become prey for the wild animals that roamed the land.

Now God himself would gather his stray sheep, rescuing them from the dark places they had scattered to and bringing them back to Israel, where he would look after them.

PRAYER

Thank you, Lord God, that you are the Good Shepherd. Thank you that you will always care for me and provide for me. I pray that leaders in nations, churches, schools, and families will be good shepherds to those in their care.

Amen

THE VALLEY OF BONES

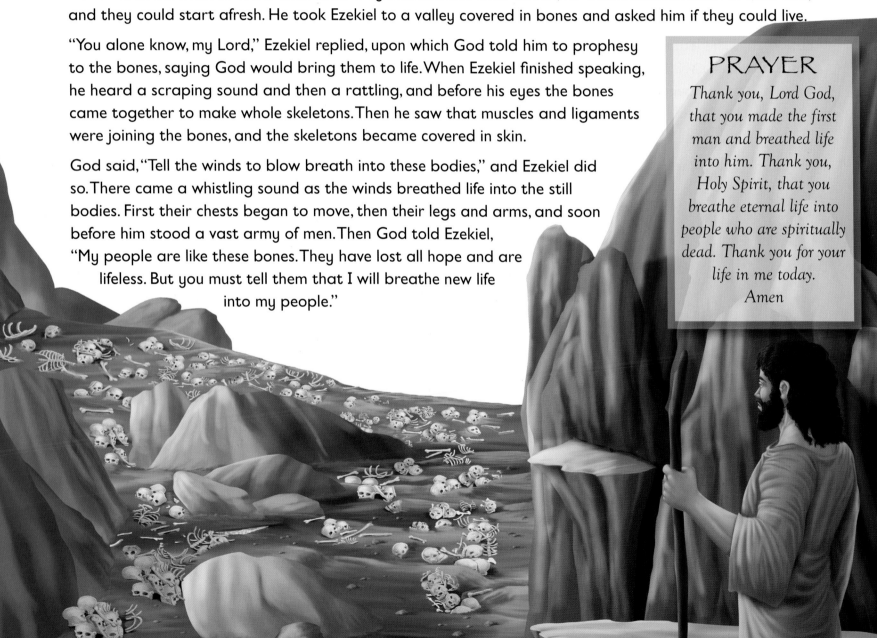

When the exiles learned of the fall of Jerusalem, they believed God had abandoned them. God wanted them to know that once they had learned their lesson, he would cleanse them of their sins, and they could start afresh. He took Ezekiel to a valley covered in bones and asked him if they could live.

"You alone know, my Lord," Ezekiel replied, upon which God told him to prophesy to the bones, saying God would bring them to life. When Ezekiel finished speaking, he heard a scraping sound and then a rattling, and before his eyes the bones came together to make whole skeletons. Then he saw that muscles and ligaments were joining the bones, and the skeletons became covered in skin.

God said, "Tell the winds to blow breath into these bodies," and Ezekiel did so. There came a whistling sound as the winds breathed life into the still bodies. First their chests began to move, then their legs and arms, and soon before him stood a vast army of men. Then God told Ezekiel, "My people are like these bones. They have lost all hope and are lifeless. But you must tell them that I will breathe new life into my people."

PRAYER

Thank you, Lord God, that you made the first man and breathed life into him. Thank you, Holy Spirit, that you breathe eternal life into people who are spiritually dead. Thank you for your life in me today.

Amen

VEGETABLES AND WATER

Daniel was another exile living in Babylon, but because he came from a good family and was clever and strong, he had been chosen to live in the royal palace, where he and his three friends were treated well and taught the language, science, and philosophy of Babylon.

Daniel was unhappy about eating the king's fancy food and wine, for God had forbidden his people to eat certain foods. So he asked if he and his friends might have vegetables and water instead. Worried that they would become weak and ill, the head of the household refused, but Daniel didn't give up. He said to the guard who brought the food, "Give us vegetables and water for ten days and then see how we look!" The guard agreed and after ten days was amazed to see that the friends were actually healthier and fitter than the other young men, and so they were allowed to continue.

For three years, God was with them, and by the end they were the cleverest and wisest of all the students. Daniel could even understand dreams. So it was that they were chosen to be advisors to the king himself.

PRAYER

Dear Lord God, please help me to choose your way for living. Thank you that you are my maker and your commandments lead to life and health. Help me to follow your instructions.

Amen

THE MYSTERIOUS DREAM

Not long after this, the king began having bad dreams. In fact, he had the same horrible dream over and over again. He was so worried and upset about it that he called all his fortune-tellers and wizards to him, saying, "My dream is worrying me. Tell me what it means."

His advisors looked puzzled. They asked him to describe the dream, but the king wanted them to work it out themselves and then tell him the meaning. "No king has ever asked such a thing!" exclaimed the bemused wizards. "What you ask is impossible! Only the gods could do this!"

The king was so furious that he ordered them all executed—and all his advisors, including Daniel and his friends!

PRAYER

Thank you, Lord God, that you speak in many ways—even in dreams! Please speak today to many people who are not even thinking of you. May I always be listening for your voice.

Amen

THE DREAM EXPLAINED

Daniel begged for time to interpret the dream, and then he and his friends prayed to God. That night, the mystery was revealed to him. The next day, he explained to the king that it foretold the future:

"You saw a terrible and massive statue standing before you. Its head was made of shining gold, its chest and arms of silver, its waist and hips of bronze, its legs of iron, and its feet partly of iron and partly of clay. While you watched, a great stone fell, smashing into its feet and shattering them. Then the whole statue crumbled, disappearing into dust blown away by the wind. But the stone grew into a mountain that covered the whole earth.

"This is what it means. The mighty kingdom of Babylon is the gold head, and the other parts of the statue are empires yet to come. There will be another empire, then another, which will rule the whole earth. Then yet another empire will emerge, as strong as iron, crushing all the earlier ones. Yet it will be divided, for the feet were made of iron and of clay. But God will establish another kingdom that will never be conquered and that will destroy all those before it. God's kingdom will never end. That is the stone that will become a mountain."

The impressed king declared that Daniel's God truly was the wisest and greatest, and he made Daniel his chief advisor.

PRAYER

Thank you, Lord God, that when I hear of nations rising and falling, I need never fear. I know that you know the future of the world and its kingdoms. Nothing can take you by surprise.

Amen

THE GOLD STATUE

King Nebuchadnezzar's humility didn't last long. Some time later he decided to have a great statue built out of gold, ninety feet high and nine feet wide. When it was completed, a special ceremony was held. A herald announced in a loud voice:

"People of the Empire! Soon you will hear trumpets and other instruments. You must bow down and worship the statue. If you don't, you will be thrown into a blazing furnace!"

PRAYER

Lord God, you have set rulers in place, and you tell your people to obey them, except when they work against your honor. I want to be strong to honor you first in my life. Please help me.

Amen

As soon as the fanfare sounded, everyone bowed down and worshipped the gold statue. But among the crowd were Daniel's three friends, Shadrach, Meshach, and Abednego, who refused to bow down before the statue, for to do so would be to disobey God's commandment to worship him alone.

THE FIERY FURNACE

When the king learned of the three men's defiance, he was furious. He offered them one more chance to obey, but the young men still refused, saying, "Your Majesty, we won't bow down to anyone but our God. He can save us from the furnace, but even if he doesn't, we will never worship your statue."

The angry king told his guards to tie them up with ropes and to stoke up the furnace until it was seven times hotter than usual. Then they were thrown into the flames. The furnace was so hot that the guards themselves were scorched to death!

Nebuchadnezzar looked on. Suddenly he leaped up in disbelief, for within the furnace he could see four men. Shadrach, Meshach, and Abednego were no longer bound, but walked around freely, and with them was a fourth man who looked like the Son of God!

The king called to the men to come out of the fire, and the friends walked from the flames unharmed. Their skin was not burned, and their clothes were not singed. Nebuchadnezzar was amazed. "Your God is indeed great, for he sent an angel to rescue his servants, who were willing to give up their lives to follow his commands. He should be praised. No other god could do as he has done!"

PRAYER

Lord God, you are wonderful, all-powerful, and amazing! Today, you are right there alongside those Christians who are in torture or prison or persecution for your name. Please let them know your presence.
Amen

THE GREAT TREE

King Nebuchadnezzar had another terrifying dream. None of his advisors could help, so he sent for Daniel, saying, "I know that your God can solve all mysteries. Last night I had a dreadful dream. There stood before me an enormous tree, towering above the land, strong and tall, with its topmost branches touching the sky. It could be seen to the ends of the earth. The leaves were green, and the branches were laden with fruit. Animals sheltered beneath its boughs, and birds lived happily in the branches.

"Then came a messenger from heaven who cried out that it must be cut down and the fruit scattered. The birds and the animals were to flee, but the stump and its roots were to remain. And the messenger said, 'Let him live outside among the animals for seven long years, with the mind of a wild animal, so all will know that God alone controls all kingdoms and chooses their rulers.'"

Daniel hardly knew what to say! "Your Majesty," he replied, "How I wish this dream were not meant for you! You see, you are that tree. Your empire is strong and great and covers the earth. Yet unless you learn to honor God, you will be cut down and become mad and will be forced to live like a wild animal for seven years! But the stump of the tree will remain, and if you lose your pride and worship God, then he will give you back your greatness again. Please do as God wishes, and maybe this will never come to pass!"

PRAYER

I am glad, Lord God, that you don't tell everyone what will happen in their individual life. It is enough for me to know that what I sow is what I will reap in life. Help me to sow good seeds of peace and faith.
Amen

THE WILD MAN

Nebuchadnezzar was shaken at first, but little by little he fell back into his old habits. One day, about a year later, Nebuchadnezzar was walking on the roof of the palace, looking down upon Babylon. He was filled with pride. "All this is my doing!" he said arrogantly. "How powerful and great I am!"

No sooner had he said this than his ears were filled with a great booming sound. "Nebuchadnezzar, this kingdom is no longer yours. You will be forced to leave the places of men and go and live with the wild animals, until you learn that God is in control of all earthly kingdoms and that he chooses their rulers."

Then the king was taken by a terrible madness, and he was forced to flee the city and live in the fields, eating grass like a wild animal. His hair grew long, his fingernails looked like the claws of a bird, and he didn't remember that he had once been a mighty king living in a fine palace.

After seven long years, his mind cleared, and he understood at last that he had nothing to be proud about—everything on earth was given by the goodness of God. God alone was mighty and powerful. Nebuchadnezzar humbly returned to his palace and once again became the ruler of the kingdom.

PRAYER

I pray, Lord God, that you will never have to deal severely with me to make me learn your ways. I pray that you will keep me humble and always acknowledging you as the giver of everything good in my life.
Amen

THE WRITING ON THE WALL

After Nebuchadnezzar, Belshazzar was king. One evening he held a grand banquet, and he sent for the gold and silver goblets taken from the holy temple in Jerusalem so that he and his guests could drink wine out of them as they praised the false idols they had created. Suddenly the fingers of a human hand appeared and began to write on the plaster of the wall. The king turned white with terror and began to shake. He asked his advisors what the strange writing meant, but not one of them had a clue.

At the queen's suggestion he sent for Daniel, who told him that he didn't want any reward but would tell him what the writing meant because of what God showed him.

"King Nebuchadnezzar was mighty and proud, but he learned that God alone rules over this world and chooses who shall be king. You have not learned this lesson. Your heart is hard, and you are full of pride. You don't honor God, who has given you all you have, but use goblets taken from God's holy temple and bow down before false idols.

"This hand was sent by God. He has written, '*Mene, Mene, Tekel, Parsin*,' and this is what it means: *Mene*—the days of your kingdom have been numbered; *Tekel*—you have been weighed on the scales and found wanting; *Parsin*—your kingdom will be divided."

That very night, Belshazzar was killed, and Darius the Mede took over the kingdom.

PRAYER

I praise you, Lord God, that all your ways are perfect and all your words come true. You see not only my actions but also the intentions of my heart. Thank you for your great mercy in Jesus, without whom I would be utterly condemned.
Amen

THE SNEAKY TRAP

Darius was impressed with Daniel, for he was wise and honest, and soon Darius put him in charge of his whole kingdom. The other officials were jealous. They knew Daniel prayed to his God every day at his window, and they came up with a plan.

"Your Majesty," said one of them, "we have written a new law. It states that for the next thirty days, whoever asks anything of any god or any man, except of you, our king, shall be thrown into a den of lions. Please sign your name to the decree so that it is official and cannot be changed." So the king signed his name, for he didn't realize that they were setting a trap for Daniel!

When Daniel heard of the law, he went home and prayed just as he had always done. He would not stop praying to God or even hide what he was doing. When his enemies saw, they rushed to the king and told him that Daniel was breaking the law. Darius' heart sank. He spent the whole day trying to think of some way out, but at sunset, his advisors came to demand that Daniel be thrown to the lions.

Daniel was taken to the pit. "You've been loyal to your God. I hope he can save you," said the king sadly as Daniel was thrown to the lions.

PRAYER

Thank you, Lord God, that you are much more powerful than any number of evil men. Please today intervene where men are plotting terrible things. Please protect innocent people caught up in terrorism and violence.
Amen

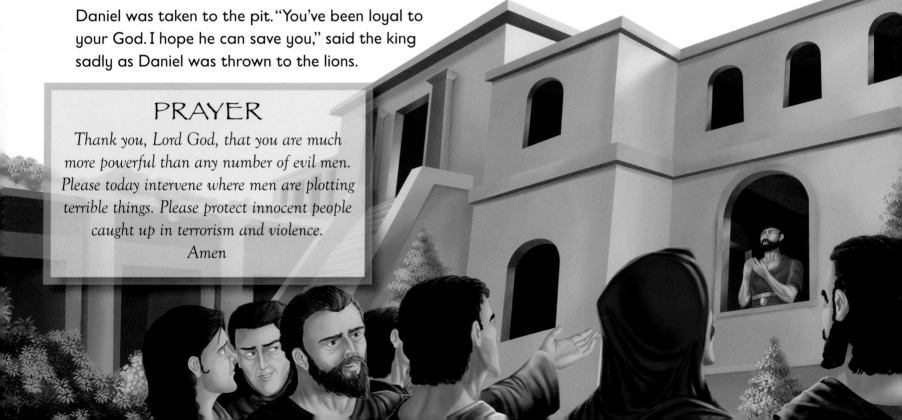

DANIEL IN THE LIONS' DEN

That evening the king didn't sleep a wink. At first light, he rushed down to the pit. "Daniel!" he cried out, more in desperation than hope. "Has your God been able to save you?"

He could not believe his ears when Daniel answered, "My God sent an angel and shut the mouths of the lions. They have not hurt me, for I was found innocent. Nor have I ever wronged you." The king was overjoyed and had Daniel brought out immediately. Then he ordered the men who had tricked him to be thrown into the pit themselves— and this time the lions were ruthless!

After this, Darius ordered his people to respect and honor Daniel's God, "For he can do wonderful things in heaven and on earth, and he rescued Daniel from the power of the lions!"

PRAYER

You, Lord, are the great Creator of everything, and you are above the laws of nature that you have established. I am happy to know you and to be able to trust your great control.
Amen

DANIEL'S VISIONS

Daniel had many visions. They told of the future of the land. In one, he saw the winds of heaven churning up the sea and four great beasts coming forth. He described them: "The first was like a lion with the wings of an eagle; the second was like a bear with three ribs in its mouth; the third was like a leopard with four heads and four wings; while the final beast, with iron teeth and ten horns, was more terrifying than the others. It crushed and devoured its victims and trampled underfoot whatever was left.

"As I looked, the Ancient of Days was seated in a flaming throne, and a river of fire flowed before him. The first three beasts were stripped of their authority yet allowed to live a while longer, but the fourth was slain and thrown into the fire.

"As I watched, there appeared one like the Son of Man. He was given glory and power, and all people and nations worshipped him. His kingdom is everlasting and cannot be destroyed.

"I was told that the four beasts are four kingdoms that will rise up, each conquering the one before, and the fourth will crush the whole earth. Yet in the end, it will be judged, and all the kingdoms under heaven will be handed over to the holy people of the Most High. His kingdom will be everlasting, and all rulers will worship and obey him, and his people will possess his kingdom forever."

PRAYER

Dear Lord God, I would love to grow up to be the kind of person that you trust. Thank you for the great heroes of the Bible to whom you revealed things because they were so close to you.
Amen

RETURN TO JERUSALEM

When Daniel was an old man, King Cyrus took the throne. His Persian empire stretched far and wide, but God touched his heart, and the mighty king issued a decree that the exiles from Judah could at last return home. He also sent for the precious treasures taken from God's temple so many years ago and gave them to the exiles to take back.

Great was the excitement and the rejoicing among the people. They couldn't believe that they were finally going to return home! But not everybody was able to return to Jerusalem. The journey would be long and hard, and it would take time to rebuild the temple and city. Only the strongest and fittest were able to go.

Daniel was one of those who stayed behind. But his heart was filled with joy as he saw his people set out on their way, singing praises to God and laughing and smiling, and he gave thanks to God for allowing his people to return home and start again.

PRAYER

Dear Lord God, help me to rejoice when good things happen to other people, even if I am not included. Help me to see your goodness all around in other families as well as my own.
Amen

THE TASK AHEAD

When the exiles returned to Jerusalem, they were shocked and saddened. The walls and buildings were ruined, and the holy temple was no more than a pile of rubble. Still, everyone pulled together to help and gave whatever they could spare.

It took time to get everyone settled, but they put up an altar where the temple had once stood so they could worship God properly. When the foundations for God's temple were finally laid, people cheered and celebrated, but many also wept, for the eldest among them had seen the wonderful temple that had once stood there so proudly, and they knew it could never be equaled.

PRAYER

Thank you, Lord God, that you are a God of new beginnings and rebirth and rebuilding. Help me to start each new day with worship so that I remember your greatness and don't get anxious even when things look completely broken.

Amen

NASTY NEIGHBORS

When the Israelites had been exiled, new people had come to live on the rich, fertile land. They were known as Samaritans and were not thrilled to see the return of the Jews. However, they offered to help build the temple. "Let us help," they said. "We worship God too!" But Prince Zerubbabel refused, for they also worshipped false idols. God would not want him to accept their help.

This angered them, and now they were determined to make trouble for their new neighbors. They tried to frighten them into stopping work, they bribed officials to work against them, and in the end they sent a letter to the new king of Persia:

"Your Majesty, we thought you should know that the Jews have settled in Jerusalem and are rebuilding that evil city. Jerusalem has always been a rebellious city, and if they manage to rebuild it, then they will surely give you trouble and will stop paying your taxes. As your loyal subjects, we felt obliged to warn you!"

The king of Persia commanded that all work on rebuilding the city was to cease, and for sixteen years, work on the temple stopped altogether.

PRAYER

Lord God, when bad people seem to be winning, and when things I enjoy are stopped, help me to still trust you and know you are in control. Thank you that your plans are always bigger than mine.

Amen

REBUILDING THE TEMPLE

God didn't want his people to give up so easily, so he sent two prophets to speak to them. Zechariah reminded the people that God was with them and would protect them against their enemies. Haggai told them it was wrong to be making their own homes comfortable when God's temple was not finished. Haggai also said that God had promised that the new temple would be so full of his presence that it would be even more glorious than King Solomon's temple!

The Jews began work once more. When the Samaritans questioned them, they replied that they were doing as King Cyrus had commanded. The Samaritans sent yet another letter to Persia telling the king what the Jews had said. But a new king was on the throne, and he checked through the royal records and found the original order. Then he told the Samaritans to stop interfering and to give the Jews whatever they asked for!

Now the Jews were able to work properly on the temple, and when at last it was finished, everyone gave thanks to God.

PRAYER

Dear Lord God, I would like to become an encourager. Thank you for everyone who encourages me at home and in church and in school—especially those who urge me to trust your promises.

Amen

THE SAME MISTAKES

Many years later, when yet another mighty king sat on the throne of Persia, there was a man named Ezra. He was worried that the people in Judah were not obeying God's law as they should, and he asked the king if he might go back to Jerusalem to guide them. Ezra had God's blessing, and the king respected him greatly. He sent him back to Jerusalem and gave him silver and gold for the temple to take with him.

When he got to Jerusalem, Ezra realized that he had been right to worry. The men had married foreign wives who had gods of their own. This was what had gotten his people into trouble before! Ezra felt ashamed that they had made such a stupid mistake when they had been given such a wonderful second chance.

He spoke to the leaders. They agreed that they must put things right, and the foreign wives were sent away. The people promised God that they would try to honor his commandments.

PRAYER

Dear Lord God, you know that I am weak and make the same mistakes time and again. You know that I forget to worship you, I don't always honor my parents, and I get cross and ungrateful. Please help me to learn.

Amen

NEHEMIAH WEEPS

Nehemiah was Emperor Araxerxes' wine steward. He was a Jew in Babylon but was well respected. He learned that although the temple had been rebuilt in Jerusalem, the walls were still ruined, the city was without gates, and people were still struggling. Nehemiah was sad. He sat down and wept. He wanted to be with his people and to help them. He prayed to God to soften the emperor's heart so that he would help.

One day, some time later, when he was serving the emperor his wine, Araxerxes looked closely at him. "You look dreadful," he said. "Is something making you unhappy?"

Servants were not supposed to show any expression, but the emperor looked concerned, and so Nehemiah decided to speak. "Your Majesty," he replied humbly, "how can I not be sad when I learn that my city is still in ruins?" and then he begged for permission to return to his homeland to help rebuild the city.

The emperor looked at him for a moment and then smiled. "Tell me what you need," he said, and Nehemiah thanked God for answering his prayers.

PRAYER

Dear Lord God, please help me to care deeply about people who are in trouble and do what I can to help—joining in fund-raising to send aid and helpers.

Amen

NEHEMIAH IN JERUSALEM

When Nehemiah arrived in Jerusalem, he didn't tell anyone that he was there. He wanted to see what was happening for himself. One night, he took a trip around the walls to see what state they were in. In some places there was so much rubble on the ground that his donkey couldn't pass.

The next morning he went to the leaders of the people and said to them, "This is a disgrace! We need to rebuild the walls and make new gates. God answered my prayers when I wanted to come back here, and he will help us now!" And so work began on the city walls.

PRAYER

Thank you, Lord God, for leaders who see what needs to be done and can get people organized. Help me to value good leadership in my home and school so that everyone can contribute their abilities to good projects and make a difference.
Amen

REBUILDING THE WALLS

Everyone who could helped out on the walls. But even now the Samaritans tried to discourage them. "You'll never be able to rebuild those walls!" they taunted. "You think you can pray to your God and it will all be done overnight! And what sort of a pathetic wall will you be able to build anyway?" But the men of Judah turned their backs and carried on. It was hard work, but they refused to give in.

The Samaritans were worried. They didn't want Jerusalem to be strong and safe, so they plotted an attack. But Nehemiah divided his men into two—half worked, and half stood guard, and those who worked carried weapons—and he told them not to worry, for God was with them.

They worked from first light until the stars came out, always watching for the enemy, and in fifty-two days the walls were finished, and the city was protected!

PRAYER

Thank you, Lord God, for the great things that can happen when people work together. Thank you for charities and hospitals where many people bring their skills together to do good. Please bless their efforts.

Amen

EZRA READS THE LAW

When the walls were completed, the people gathered in the city square and asked Ezra to read from the Book of Law. First Ezra praised God, and everyone knelt in worship. Then Ezra began to read from the scroll in sections, and the priests went among the people, helping them to understand.

Many were upset when they realized how far wrong they had gone, but Nehemiah and Ezra told them not to be sad, but to go home and have a feast and share their food with the poor. "This is a holy day, so be happy. The joy God gives you will make you strong."

For two weeks Ezra taught the leaders more about God's law and then the people gathered once more to make a solemn promise to God that they would obey his laws. At last they understood just how badly they had let him down. Now they planned to honor him and keep their side of the covenant.

PRAYER

Thank you, Lord God, that your rules never change and so I can always come back to them. Thank you that your Holy Spirit in my heart prompts me to want to obey your rules and please you.

Amen

THE ANGRY KING

There was a new king in Persia. Foolish King Xerxes wanted to impress all the princes and nobles of his mighty empire, so he invited them to a fabulous feast. It lasted six months! The guests were served the finest food on gold plates, and they drank the finest wine. He drank rather too much himself and decided to send for his beautiful wife, Queen Vashti, to show her off!

Queen Vashti didn't want to be paraded and refused to come down. The king was furious, and his advisors suggested he should make an example of her. "You should stop her from being queen," they told him. "Otherwise all the women will think it's fine to disobey their husbands!" The king agreed and had a proclamation sent out that every husband should be the master of his home!

PRAYER

Dear Lord God, please help me to recognize what is foolish around me. Help me never to value people by their appearance or outward display of wealth. Help me to avoid self-centeredness and all that it leads to.
Amen

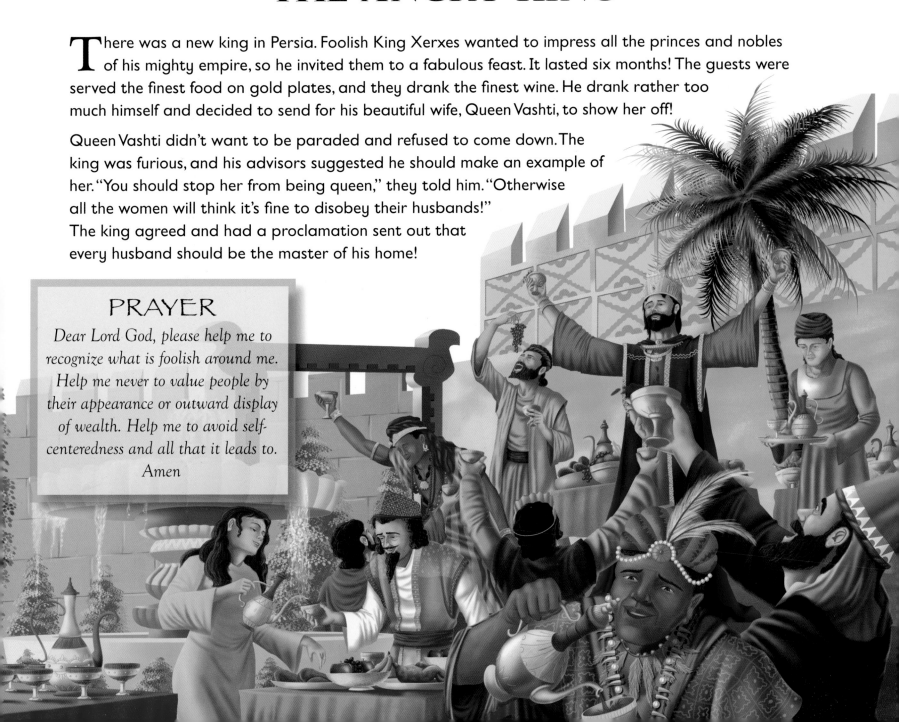

BEAUTIFUL ESTHER

King Xerxes needed a new queen, and so servants were sent out to find all the beautiful young maidens of the land and bring them to the palace. Among them was a lovely young girl named Esther, and as soon as King Xerxes saw her, he declared that she would be his wife. Esther didn't tell him she was a Jew.

When Esther became queen of Persia, her cousin Mordecai was given an administrative position in the king's court, and one day he chanced to overhear a conversation between two of the king's guards who were plotting to kill the king!

Mordecai told Esther to warn Xerxes. The king ordered an investigation, and the treacherous guards were hanged. What had happened and Mordecai's part in it was written down in the official records, but the king forgot to reward the man who had saved his life!

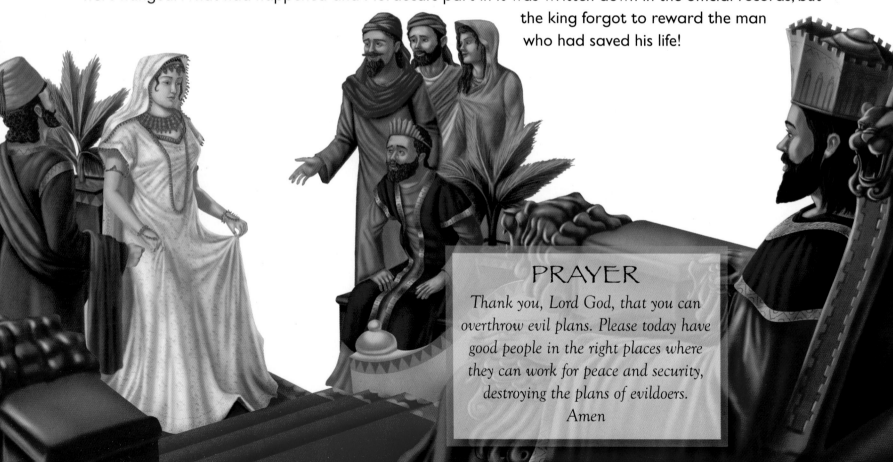

PRAYER
Thank you, Lord God, that you can overthrow evil plans. Please today have good people in the right places where they can work for peace and security, destroying the plans of evildoers.
Amen

HAMAN BEARS A GRUDGE

The king's prime minister, Haman, thought very well of himself. He loved to ride through the streets and see the people bow before him. It made him feel powerful. And it truly annoyed him that Mordecai would never bow before him. When Haman found out that Mordecai was a Jew, he decided to punish not only him, but all the other Jews as well.

Haman was cunning. "Your Majesty," he said to the king. "There is a race of people in your empire that doesn't obey your laws. I would advise you to issue a decree that they be put to death."

The king agreed, and so Haman sent out a decree, stamped with the royal ring, stating that on the thirteenth day of the twelfth month of that year, all Jews—young and old, women and children—were to be killed throughout the empire!

PRAYER

Dear Lord God, help me to always remember that I did not choose my family or nationality, and neither did anyone else. So, help me never to judge someone by the color of their skin or their customs. Thank you that you love and treat all people the same.

Amen

THE BRAVE QUEEN

Never before had the Jewish people faced such annihilation! When Mordecai learned of the decree, he tore his clothes and put on sackcloth and ashes. He sent a message to his cousin, begging that Esther plead their case before the king.

Esther was terrified. To go before the king without a summons was punishable by death! Only if the king held out his scepter would the person be spared. But Mordecai sent another message, saying, "You must help the Jews, or God will be angry. Maybe he made you queen precisely so that you could save his people."

Esther was scared but made up her mind to go to the king. When he saw her, he smiled and held out his golden scepter, saying, "Tell me what you want, and you shall have it—even if it is half my empire!" Esther could not bring herself to ask the king there and then. Instead, she invited him and Haman to a banquet in her rooms.

PRAYER

Thank you, Lord God, for all the brave people in the world. You make people strong to endure war and storms and earthquakes —and you also give courage for exams and operations and times of being separated from loved ones. Thank you.

Amen

MORDECAI IS HONORED

Haman was feeling pleased until he passed in front of Mordecai and the Jew still refused to bow! When his friends saw how furious he was, they suggested that he build a gallows and then ask the king the next morning to have Mordecai hanged.

That same night, the king couldn't sleep, so he sent for the official records of the kingdom—maybe that would help! As he was reading, he came across the account of how Mordecai had saved his life, and his officials confessed that he had never been rewarded. When Haman arrived early at the palace that morning, King Xerxes asked him, "There is someone I wish to honor. What should I do for him?"

Thinking the king was talking about him, Haman replied, "Have the man dressed in one of your royal robes and led through the city on one of your horses, with an official proclaiming, 'This is how the king treats those he wishes to honor.'"

He got a dreadful shock when the king told him to send for Mordecai and he realized that his hated enemy would be the one honored in the very way he had suggested!

PRAYER

Lord God, I know that you have a record of everything. The things in my life that honor Jesus are the things that please you. Help me to be more concerned to hear you say, "Well done," than to hear praise from people around me.
Amen

HAMAN IS PUNISHED

Haman was still seething when he arrived for the queen's banquet. But things were only going to get worse! During the banquet, the king again asked Esther what it was that she wanted. This time the queen was brave enough to ask, "Your Majesty, if I have found favor in your sight, I beg you to save my life and that of my people, for we have been sold for slaughter!"

"Who has dared to do such a thing?" roared the king, and Esther pointed to Haman. The king was so furious that he left the room to calm down. Haman, his face as white as a sheet, flung himself at Esther's feet and begged her to protect him.

When the king returned to find Haman with his hands on the queen's robes, it only made him angrier. Then Haman's fate was sealed as one of the guards said, "Your Majesty, this man built a gallows for Mordecai. He wanted to hang the man who saved your life!"

"Hang Haman on it himself!" ordered Xerxes, and so it was that Haman was hanged on the very gallows that he had built for Mordecai!

PRAYER

Dear Lord God, I know that some people today will face impossible situations full of hatred and anger. You have given people free will, but often it is used badly. Please be with those who desperately need your help.

Amen

ARM YOURSELVES!

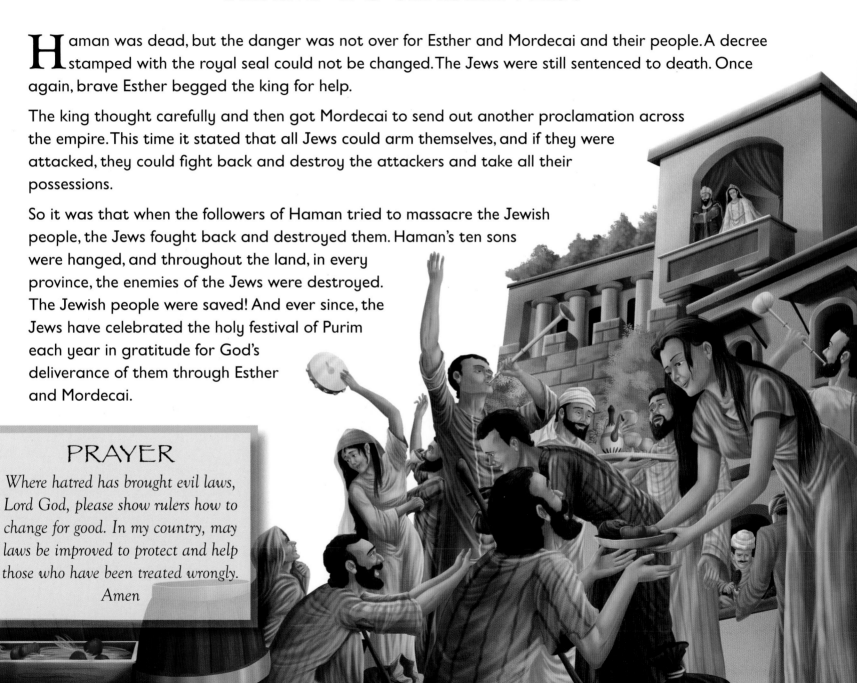

Haman was dead, but the danger was not over for Esther and Mordecai and their people. A decree stamped with the royal seal could not be changed. The Jews were still sentenced to death. Once again, brave Esther begged the king for help.

The king thought carefully and then got Mordecai to send out another proclamation across the empire. This time it stated that all Jews could arm themselves, and if they were attacked, they could fight back and destroy the attackers and take all their possessions.

So it was that when the followers of Haman tried to massacre the Jewish people, the Jews fought back and destroyed them. Haman's ten sons were hanged, and throughout the land, in every province, the enemies of the Jews were destroyed. The Jewish people were saved! And ever since, the Jews have celebrated the holy festival of Purim each year in gratitude for God's deliverance of them through Esther and Mordecai.

PRAYER

Where hatred has brought evil laws, Lord God, please show rulers how to change for good. In my country, may laws be improved to protect and help those who have been treated wrongly.
Amen

JONAH DISOBEYS GOD

Jonah was a prophet. One day God told him to go to Ninevah, many miles away, and tell the people there that unless they turned from their wicked ways, God would destroy their fine city.

Now, the people of Ninevah were enemies of the Jews, and Jonah didn't want to go and warn them just so that God could spare them. He thought they deserved to be punished! So, instead of doing as God had told him, Jonah boarded a ship heading in the opposite direction from Ninevah! He was trying to run away from God, but of course, God is everywhere!

PRAYER

Dear Lord God, please help me to listen to what you say and to know that you are always right and I never know better than you. Help me to want to go your way and never to deliberately do the opposite.

Amen

THE DREADFUL STORM

A dreadful storm sprang up from nowhere. The winds howled, and the waves towered above the ship. The terrified sailors threw their cargo over the side to lighten the ship, and they prayed to their gods. The captain found Jonah asleep in his cabin. He woke him roughly, saying, "How can you sleep when we are in such danger? Pray to your god to save us!"

The sailors drew straws to see which of them had angered the gods. When Jonah picked the short straw, they asked him what he had done. Jonah told them that he was running away from God and that he was being punished. As he spoke, he realized how foolish and wicked he had been. He told them that they must cast him over the side, for God was only angry with him.

The sea became rougher and rougher, and in the end, the sailors lowered Jonah over the side with heavy hearts. Instantly, the sea became calm! The sailors were filled with awe and began to pray to God with all their hearts, to thank him for sparing them, and to promise to worship only him from that day forward.

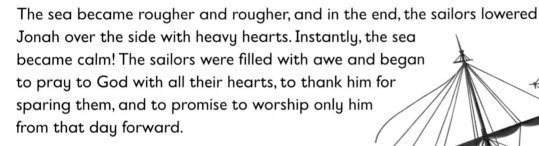

PRAYER

Lord God, you are the great Judge, and you know what is in everyone's heart. You see beyond our actions to our motives. Help me to be honest before you, not trying to hide what you already know, and not trying to impress you when you see everything.

Amen

THE BIG FISH

But what about Jonah? The prophet sank swiftly to the bottom of the sea, certain he was going to die. But before he could take his last breath, God sent an enormous fish. The fish opened its mouth and swallowed Jonah whole, and there inside the fish Jonah could breath once again and was safe.

For three days and nights Jonah sat inside the belly of the fish. He had plenty of time to think about his mistakes and to feel very sorry for having disobeyed God. He prayed to God, thanking him for delivering him from the sea and letting him know how remorseful he felt.

After three days, God commanded the fish to spit Jonah up, unharmed, onto dry land. And when God once again asked him to take his message to Ninevah, Jonah was ready to do his will.

PRAYER

Lord God, you really are amazing!
How wonderful that you could use
a fish to rescue a man! How kind
you are too. Thank you that you give
opportunities for people to turn away
from wrong and be forgiven. I pray that
many people will find forgiveness today.
Amen

GOD'S MERCY

When the people of Ninevah heard Jonah's message, they were appalled and frightened. The king issued a royal proclamation that everyone should fast and wear sackcloth, and the people prayed to God and vowed to give up their evil ways. When God saw how sorry they were, he was filled with compassion and forgave them. The city was spared! But this made Jonah angry, for he felt that the people of Ninevah didn't deserve to be saved, and he went to sulk in the desert!

The desert was hot, and God made a large, leafy plant grow up to protect Jonah from the fierce sun. But the next day, God told a worm to nibble at the plant, and soon it withered and died. Jonah was cross, but God asked him what right he had to be angry.

"Every right!" replied Jonah indignantly. "I might as well die now that the plant has gone!"

Then God answered, "Jonah, you are unhappy about losing that plant even though you didn't plant it yourself or tend it, and even though it was here one day and gone the next!

"Nineveh has more than a hundred and twenty thousand people living there—men, women, and children that I have made and cared about over the years. Do I not have the right to be concerned and to take pity on them?"

PRAYER

Thank you, Lord God, for your great mercy and kindness. Help me to always be glad when you pour your forgiveness on others as well as on me.

Amen

A MESSENGER IS COMING

Years had passed since the Jews had returned to Jerusalem. To start with, they had been full of good intentions, but things had begun to slip. They didn't realize how much they had to be thankful for. Instead, they wanted things to be easier and felt that God had forgotten them. God sent Malachi to speak to them:

"You complain that God isn't blessing you. Yet you have stopped loving him with all your heart. Love and honor him, and then you will receive his full blessing.

"One day he will send a messenger to prepare the way for him. He will be like a scouring soap, a blazing fire that burns away everything impure, leaving behind only those who will worship God properly. For one day, God's judgment will come upon those who do wrong. But those of you who obey him will feel his power shine on you like the warm rays of the sun! Just remember to obey his laws!

"God has also promised that before the Day of the Lord, Elijah will return to earth to bring fathers and children together in order that people might follow in God's ways."

Now the people of Israel knew that one day a mighty messenger would come to prepare the way for the Lord!

PRAYER

Thank you, Lord God, for the Bible. Thank you that I can read your promises to people long ago and how they came true. Thank you that I can trust your promises to me.
Amen

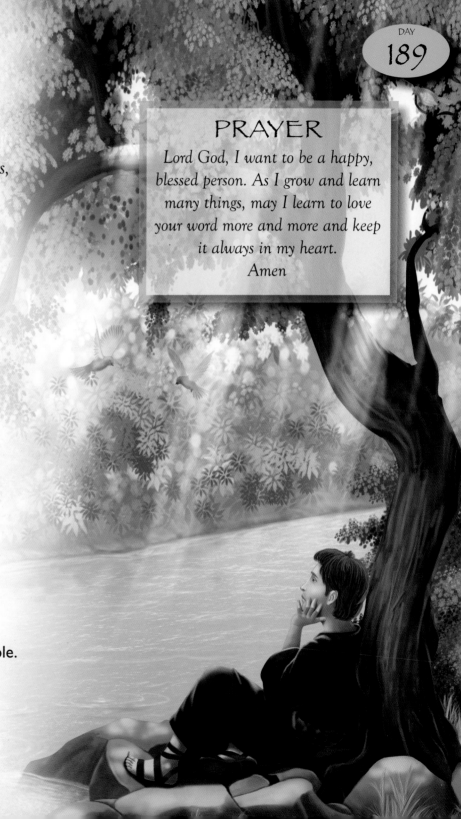

A TREE BY A STREAM

The Book of Psalms is a wonderful collection of prayers, songs, and poetry. Many psalms were written by King David. They are full of different emotions, such as despair, sorrow, joy, and love, and they praise God for his mercy and blessings.

How happy and blessed is the person who
doesn't hang around with wicked people,
or do what they do, or listen to what they say,
but who instead loves God's law
and thinks about his words every day
and every night.

That person is like a tree planted by
a stream of water,
which bears its fruit in the right season
and whose leaves do not wither.
That person will succeed in everything he does.

But not the wicked people!
They are like straw that the wind blows away.
The wicked people will be judged by God
and won't be allowed to stand with God's own people.
God watches over those who try to be good
and obey his laws,
but wicked people are heading
toward destruction!

PRAYER

Lord God, I want to be a happy, blessed person. As I grow and learn many things, may I learn to love your word more and more and keep it always in my heart.

Amen

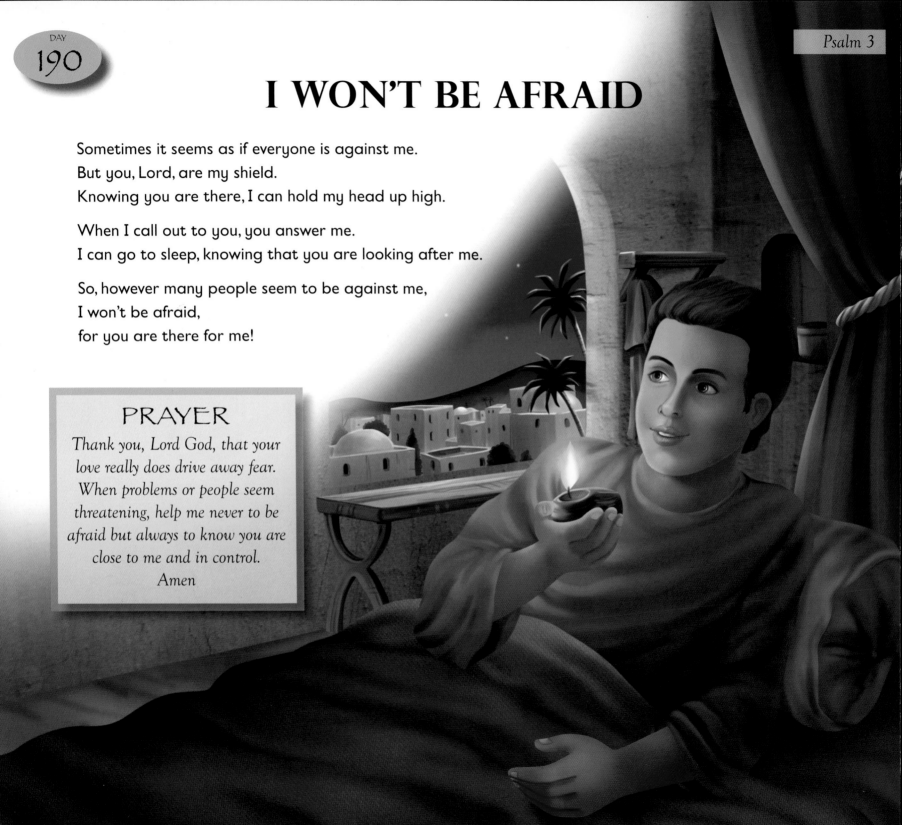

I WON'T BE AFRAID

Sometimes it seems as if everyone is against me.
But you, Lord, are my shield.
Knowing you are there, I can hold my head up high.

When I call out to you, you answer me.
I can go to sleep, knowing that you are looking after me.

So, however many people seem to be against me,
I won't be afraid,
for you are there for me!

PRAYER

*Thank you, Lord God, that your
love really does drive away fear.
When problems or people seem
threatening, help me never to be
afraid but always to know you are
close to me and in control.*
Amen

YOU KEEP ME SAFE

Lord, please listen when I call out to you for help.

Be kind to me and hear my prayer.

All those who mock me should remember that you, Lord, have chosen everyone who is faithful to be your own special people,

and you hear me when I call to you.

Plenty of people ask you to make life easier for them.

But you have made me happier than they could ever be with all their fine food and drinks.

I can go to bed feeling at peace,

and go to sleep knowing that you keep me safe.

PRAYER

Thank you, Lord God, for bringing me into your family and the joy and security this gives me in my heart. Thank you that I can never be safer than I am with you.

Amen

YOUR NAME IS WONDERFUL!

Oh Lord, how wonderful is your name!

Your glory shines down from heaven,
it is seen everywhere on earth.
The praise of young children
silences your enemies and makes you strong.
When I think about how you made the heavens,
how you placed the moon and stars in the sky,
I wonder how you can care about human beings—
we are so small!

Yet you have made us only a little lower
than the angels,
you have made us rulers over
everything you created:
the birds and the beasts, the fish in the sea.
We rule over all of them.

Oh Lord, how wonderful is your name!

PRAYER

*I worship you, Lord God, the great
Creator of the universe. Thank you
that you made the sun, the moon,
the stars, and everything on earth.
I am amazed at your care for me.*

Amen

GOD IS MY FORTRESS

How I love you, Lord!
You are my fortress and my rescuer,
with you I can always be safe,
you are like a shield to me.
The danger of death was all around me,
I was overwhelmed.
When I cried out to you, you heard me
and you reached down from the heavens
and pulled me out of deep waters.
Oh Lord, with your help I can do anything.
You make me strong and keep me safe,
you hold me up, so that I can stand strong and secure.

Lord, I will sing your praises across the land,
I will praise your name wherever I go!

*King David sang Psalm 18
when God saved him
from his enemies.*

PRAYER
*Dear Lord God, please be a fortress
today for people who are in danger.
May people call to you for help.
Thank you that you are always near
to protect and shelter me.*
Amen

DO NOT BE FAR FROM ME

My God, why have you forsaken me?
I cry out every day, but you don't answer,
every night, but I find no rest.
Yet you saved our ancestors.
When they cried out to you they were saved.
They trusted you and you didn't let them down.
But I am nothing but a worm.
Everyone mocks me, saying,
"If he trusts in the Lord, then let the Lord save him!"
Yet it was you that brought me into this world.

Do not be far from me,
for I am surrounded by trouble
and there is no one to help me.
My enemies encircle me like wild beasts,
waiting to pounce, ready to destroy me.
Like a pack of dogs they close in on me,
tearing at my hands and feet.

So don't stay away, my Lord, come quickly to help me.
Rescue me from these wild beasts!
I'll tell everyone what you have done; I'll praise your name.
For you don't neglect the poor or ignore their suffering,
but answer when they call for help.

Everyone will bow down before you,
and future generations will be told
that the Lord saved his people.

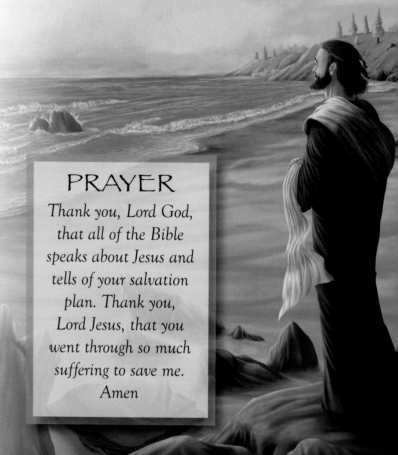

This is another of King David's psalms, which many Christians read or sing on Good Friday because they believe that it is not only about the suffering of King David, but that it is also about the suffering of Jesus.

PRAYER

Thank you, Lord God, that all of the Bible speaks about Jesus and tells of your salvation plan. Thank you, Lord Jesus, that you went through so much suffering to save me.
Amen

THE LORD IS MY SHEPHERD

The Lord is my shepherd,
he will make sure I have everything I need.
He lets me rest in green meadows,
he leads me beside quiet streams to drink,
he refreshes my soul.
He shows me the right way to go,
so that I can bring honor to his name.
Even though I walk through the darkest of valleys,
I will fear nothing, for you are with me;
your rod and your shepherd's crook make me feel safe.
You prepare a feast for me in front of my enemies.
You anoint my head with oil;
I feel so honored that I'm overwhelmed.
Surely your goodness and love will be with me
every day of my life,
and I will live in the house of the Lord
forever.

PRAYER

Thank you, Lord Jesus, that you truly are my Shepherd. Thank you that you will always protect and provide for me and bring me safely into your eternal home. Thank you for your goodness and mercy to me.
Amen

YOUR DAY WILL COME

Don't waste time worrying about people
who do bad things, for they won't last long.
Trust in God and do good,
love him and you will have everything you need.
Follow his ways and your reward will shine
like the brightest sun.
Be calm and patient and your day will come.

God looks after those who love him.
Even though they may stumble, he keeps them from falling,
he holds them up with his hand.
God never lets them down.

God will always make sure those who love him have enough.
Bad people hold on tight to what they have
and it is taken away.
But good people want to share the things they have,
and they will be blessed.
One day, those who do bad things will be punished.
Then God's followers will inherit the land.

God will always take care of his people.
He will look after them when times are bad,
He will rescue them from wicked people
because they turn to him for help.

PRAYER

*Lord God, help me to live the right way. Help
me not to worry about people who do bad
things. Instead help me to concentrate on
following your ways and trusting in your care.*

Amen

WATER IN THE DESERT

PRAYER

Dear Lord God, I do want to always seek you with all of my heart, for all of my life. Please help me. Thank you for the wonderful psalms that show me that people long ago had the same feelings and longings that I have.

Amen

You, God, are my God,
I seek you with all my heart;
I need you just like a dry, parched desert needs water.
I have seen how wonderful and glorious you are.
Your love is better than life itself, and I'll praise you.
I'll praise you as long as I live, and I'll pray to you.
Your love will satisfy me like the richest food.
When I lie in my bed I'll remember you,
and I'll think of you all night long.
You have always been there to help me,
your wings protect me,
and when I cling to you, your hand keeps me safe.

UNDER HIS WINGS

Trust in God and you don't need to be afraid of anything!
He will protect you under his wings,
and cover you with his feathers.
You will have nothing to fear by night or by day.
Whatever happens to those beside you,
nothing bad will happen to you.

If you trust in God for your protection,
no harm will come upon you,
no disaster will befall you.
He will tell his angels to look after you.
Their hands will catch you so that you do not trip.
For the Lord says, "I will save those who love me.
When they call to me, I will answer them;
when they are in trouble, I will be with them.
I will save them!"

PRAYER

Thank you, Lord God, for your
great protection and for your
angels who are guarding me even
though I am not aware of them.
I am so glad to trust in you.
Amen

A LAMP FOR MY FEET

How blessed are they who are good;
who follow the ways of the Lord
and seek him with all their heart.

But how can young people keep their lives pure?
By obeying your commands.
I seek you with all my heart and love your laws.
Please give me understanding
and keep me strong
that I may follow your laws.
Your words taste sweet in my mouth,
they are a lamp for my feet,
a light on the path on which I travel.
You are my refuge and my shield,
I put all my hope and trust in you.
Steady me with your hand,
and help me to honor you.
I am like a sheep that was lost:
Please come and look for me,
for I remember all your commands.

PRAYER

*Thank you, Lord God, for your words, which
show me the right way to live. Thank you that
your way is always the best way. Please light the
way for me and help me to follow that path.*
Amen

HE WILL NEVER SLEEP

I lift up my eyes to the mountains—
where will my help come from?
My help comes from the Lord,
the Maker of heaven and earth.
He won't let me stumble or fall,
he will never sleep while he is
watching over me.
The protector of all Israel never sleeps.

The Lord watches over you,
he is right beside you, shading you;
the sun won't harm you by day,
nor the moon by night.
The Lord will keep you from all harm,
he will watch over you your whole life long;
he will watch over you in your daily life
now and always.

PRAYER

*How wonderful you are, Lord
God. Although you are the Maker
of heaven and earth, you are
interested in my daily life. May I
be aware today that you are right
beside me, watching over me.*
Amen

BY THE RIVERS OF BABYLON

By the rivers of Babylon we sat and wept when we remembered Zion.
There on the willow trees we hung our harps,
for our captors wanted us to entertain them,
our tormentors ordered us to sing songs of joy!
They said, "Sing us one of the songs of Zion!"
How can we sing the songs of the Lord in a foreign land?
If I forget you, Jerusalem, may my right hand forget its cleverness,
and let my tongue stick to the roof of my mouth,
if I don't remember you—
if I don't think about Jerusalem above everything else.

PRAYER

*Dear Lord God, please help me
to sing songs about your kindness
and look forward to your
goodness today and tomorrow.
Help me not to spend time being
sad over bad things in the past.*
Amen

*This psalm is about the
yearning and sorrow of the
Jewish people in exile.*

YOU KNOW EVERYTHING ABOUT ME

Lord, you have looked inside me,
and you know everything about me.
You know when I sit down and when I stand up,
you know exactly what I'm thinking,
and what I'll say even before I have said it!
There is nothing about me that you don't know!

It doesn't matter where I go.
I could go up to heaven, or across the sea,
and you would still be there to guide me.
If I tried to hide from you in the dark,
even the darkness is not dark to you,
but as bright as day.

For you formed me:
You made me inside my mother's womb,
and I'll praise you, for you made me in such a wonderful way!
Lord, make sure I don't go the wrong way,
keep me on the right path!

PRAYER

*Lord God, it's scary to think that you
know even what I am thinking; and yet
it is a comfort too. It is hard for me to
understand how you can be everywhere
and know everything. When I realize
this, help me to trust you completely.*
Amen

Psalm 150

PRAISE HIM WITH MUSIC

Praise the Lord.
Praise God in his temple,
praise him in his mighty heavens.
Praise him for his acts of power;
praise him for his surpassing greatness.
Praise him with trumpets,
praise him with harps and lyres,
praise him with drums and dancing,
praise him with stringed instruments and flutes,
praise him with the clash of cymbals.
Let everything that breathes praise the Lord!

PRAYER

Thank you, Lord God, for the joy of music. Thank you for people who can create marvelous melodies with all kinds of instruments. Help me to praise you with my voice and my whole heart.

Amen

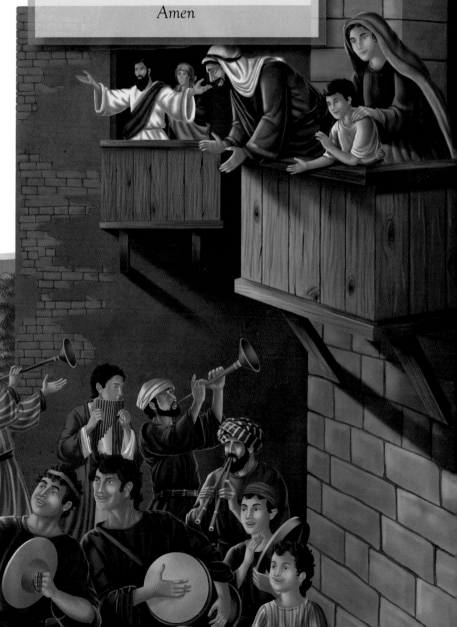

WISE WORDS

The Bible is a wonderful place to look for words of wisdom. The Book of Proverbs is filled with wise sayings, composed by King Solomon and other wise men, or passed down through the ages.

- Wisdom and knowledge are worth more than jewels.
- An honest answer is a sign of true friendship.
- When you give to the poor, it is like lending to God, and God will pay you back.
- The more you talk, the more likely you are to get into trouble.
- Any fool can start an argument—the clever thing is to avoid them.
- Curses cannot hurt you unless you deserve them.
- Sensible people want to be told when they're wrong—it is silly to hate being corrected.
- If you get something by cheating, it might taste delicious at first, but sooner or later it will taste like a mouthful of sand.
- Better to be poor and honest than rich and dishonest.
- Let other people praise you—never do it yourself!
- Being cheerful keeps you healthy.
- We may make our plans, but God has the last word!

You can find some more wise sayings at the end of this book.

PRAYER

Dear Lord God, as I grow up and find knowledge in many places, may I always remember that there is only one place that I can find wisdom, and that is in you. May I always treasure your words and your advice.

Amen

A TIME FOR EVERYTHING

The writer of the Book of Ecclesiastes believed that everything that happens does so at the time God chooses, that we should spend our lives doing the best we can and trying to be happy, and that we should enjoy the things that we work to get, because life is God's gift to us. This is what he wrote:

There is a time and a season for everything:

A time to be born, and a time to die;

a time to plant, and a time to uproot;

a time to kill, and a time to heal;

a time to break down, and a time to build up;

a time to weep, and a time to laugh;

a time to mourn, and a time to dance;

a time to scatter stones, and a time to gather stones together;

a time to embrace, and a time to refrain from embracing;

a time to seek, and a time to lose;

a time to keep, and a time to throw away;

a time to rend, and a time to sew;

a time to keep silent, and a time to speak;

a time to love, and a time to hate;

a time for war, and a time for peace.

PRAYER

Thank you, Lord God, for the life you have given me and the hours of this day. Help me to use my time wisely and well. As I grow, may I rely on your wisdom, not my own.
Amen

A VISIT BY AN ANGEL

Four hundred years had passed since Malachi had warned the people of Israel. Now evil King Herod sat on the throne of Judea, but even he answered to Augustus Caesar, the emperor of the mighty Roman empire. Inside the holy temple in Jerusalem, Zechariah the priest was burning incense when an angel appeared before him! Zechariah was terrified, but the angel said gently, "Don't be afraid. God has heard your prayers. Your wife Elizabeth will bear you a son, and you are to call him John. He will be a great man and will prepare the way for the one who comes after him."

Zechariah was amazed, for he and his wife had longed for a child, but were very old now. "How can I be sure of this?" he asked. "My wife and I are old. How can this be?"

Because of his doubt, the angel told him that he would not be able to speak until what God promised had come to pass. But when Zechariah wrote down the good news for his wife, she was filled with joy.

PRAYER

Thank you, Lord God, that you always hear my prayers, even though I am a child. Help me to listen for your answers. Amen

MARY IS CHOSEN BY GOD

At around the same time, the angel Gabriel visited the house of Mary in the town of Nazareth in Galilee. Gentle Mary was Elizabeth's cousin. She was engaged to Joseph, a carpenter who could trace his family back to King David.

"Don't be afraid, Mary," he told the startled girl. "God has chosen you for a very special honor. You will give birth to a son, and you are to call him Jesus. He will be called the Son of God, and his kingdom will never end!"

Mary was filled with wonder. "How can this be?" she asked softly. "I'm not even married!"

PRAYER

Dear Lord God, as I grow up, please show me the good plan that you have for my life.
Amen

"Everything is possible for God," replied the angel. "The Holy Spirit will come on you, and your child will be God's own Son."

Mary bowed her head humbly, saying, "It will be as God wills it."

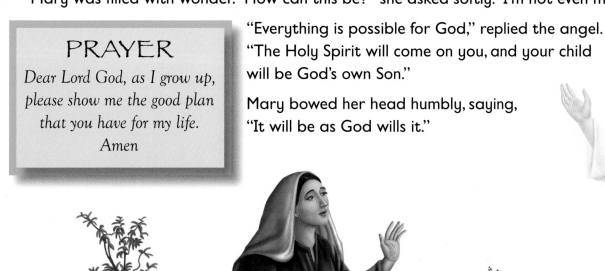

MARY VISITS ELIZABETH

Mary couldn't wait to tell her cousin the good news and traveled to see her. No sooner had she said "Hello," than Elizabeth exclaimed: "Oh Mary, you are truly blessed among women, and so is the child you will bear! How honored I feel when the mother of my Lord visits me! When you greeted me, the baby in my womb leaped for joy. We are so blessed, cousin!"

Mary was so full of thanks and joy that she broke out into a song of praise, thanking God with all her heart. The two women had so much to share that Mary stayed with Elizabeth for several months before returning home.

PRAYER

Dear Lord God, sometimes I just want to sing for joy! Thank you for all the great songs of praise that I can sing on my own and with others.
Amen

JOSEPH LISTENS TO GOD

Not surprisingly, when Joseph found out that Mary was pregnant, he thought she had been unfaithful to him, and he was bitterly disappointed. He decided to break off the marriage, but before he could do anything, God spoke to him in a dream: "Mary has not been unfaithful. The baby she is carrying was conceived from the Holy Spirit. She will give birth to a son, and you will call him Jesus, for he will save his people from their sins."

When Joseph awoke, he felt much happier. Mary had been true to him, and now he would do all he could to keep her and the child safe. So he married her without delay.

PRAYER

Dear Lord God, please help me when things happen in my family that I can't understand. Thank you that I can talk to you about everything.

Amen

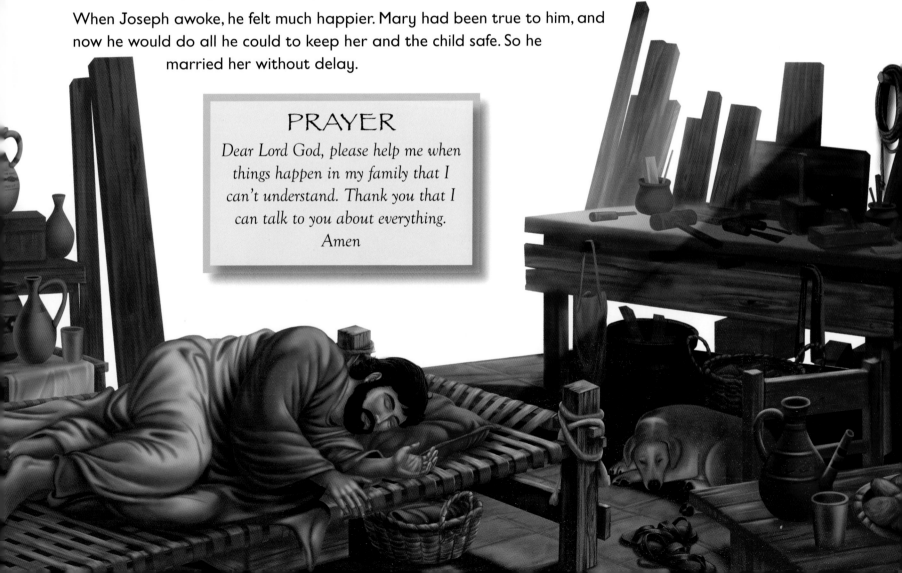

HIS NAME IS JOHN

Soon Elizabeth gave birth to a boy. Her friends and relatives were thrilled and asked what she was going to call him. When she told them he would be named John, they were rather taken aback, for they had expected the child would be named after his father—no one else in the family was called John!

They asked Zechariah and were amazed when he took a tablet and wrote on it in clear, bold letters, "His name is John." At that moment, Zechariah's tongue was freed—and the very first words that he spoke were all in praise of the Lord: "Let us praise the Lord, the God of Israel! He has sent his people a mighty Savior from the house of his servant David. You, my child, will go before the Lord to prepare the way for him, to let his people know that they will be saved, for their sins will be forgiven."

The people looked at one another in wonder. It was clear that this child would grow up to be very special indeed.

PRAYER

Thank you, Lord God, for every new baby that is given to my family and friends. Please be close to very little babies and their parents.

Amen

TRAVELING TO BETHLEHEM

Now, around this time, the emperor of Rome ordered a census of all the people he ruled over. This was when the Roman empire was at the height of its power and covered a vast area, and the emperor wanted to make sure he kept tabs on every single one of his subjects. So it was that all the people throughout the lands ruled by Rome had to go to their hometown to be counted.

For Mary and Joseph, this meant that they had to travel to Bethlehem, the town of Joseph's ancestor, King David. It was a long journey and took several days.

By the time they arrived, they were tired and desperately wanted to find a room for the night, for it was clear that the time had come for Mary's baby to be born. But the town was filled to bursting. Every inn was full!

PRAYER

Dear Lord God, please watch over those I love when they are traveling and keep them safe from harm.
Amen

BORN IN A MANGER

Even though poor Mary sorely needed to find somewhere to stay, there was no room for them anywhere, for the town was full of people who had come to Bethlehem for the census. In the end, an innkeeper showed them to a stable, or room where the animals were kept, and it was in this humble place that Mary's baby was born.

She wrapped him in strips of cloth and laid him gently on clean straw in a manger—the feeding trough from which the animals would have eaten.

Mary and Joseph looked down upon their son with joy, and they named him Jesus, just as the angel had told them to.

PRAYER
Thank you, Lord God, for sending your Son Jesus into our world at the very first Christmas.
Amen

THE SHEPHERDS' STORY

That same night, some shepherds were watching over their sheep in the hills above Bethlehem. Suddenly an angel of the Lord appeared to them, and the dark sky was ablaze with light!

As the shepherds fell to the ground in fear, the angel said, "Don't be afraid. I have brought you good news. Today, in the town of David, a Savior has been born to you; he is the Messiah, the Lord. Go and see for yourselves. You will find him wrapped in cloths, lying in a manger."

Then the sky was filled with angels praising God:

> *"Glory to God in the highest heaven,*
> *and peace on earth and good will to all men."*

PRAYER

Thank you, Lord Jesus, for all the excitement I enjoy at Christmas. It's all because you came into our world to be the Savior.
Amen

Luke 2

THE BABY KING

When the angels had left, the shepherds looked at one another in amazement. They could hardly believe what had just happened! It didn't take long at all for them to make up their minds to go and see the baby with their very own eyes. So the shepherds hurried down to Bethlehem, where they found the baby lying in the manger just as they had been told.

They knelt before him in wonder and told Joseph and Mary what the angels had said to them. When they left, Mary spent much time thinking about what had happened. The shepherds themselves rushed off to tell everyone about this special baby and the wonderful news!

PRAYER
Dear Lord Jesus, help me to take time each day over Christmas to worship you and be thankful for your coming.
Amen

SIMEON AND ANNA

When Jesus was a few weeks old, Joseph and Mary took him to the temple in Jerusalem to present him to God, as was the custom. There they saw an old man named Simeon who was filled with the Holy Spirit and who had been promised by God that he would see the Messiah before his death.

When he saw baby Jesus, Simeon was filled with joy and awe. He asked if he might hold the precious child in his arms, and then he cried out in gratitude, "Lord, you have kept your promise, and you may let your servant go in peace. With my own eyes I have seen the child who will bring salvation to your people!" Then he turned to Mary, "Your child has been chosen by God to bring about both the destruction and salvation of many people in Israel!"

While they stood there, another stranger came up. Anna was an old widow who spent her life worshipping in the temple. She, too, recognized how special Jesus was and gave thanks to God. Jesus meant so much to so many people!

PRAYER

Dear Lord God, thank you for my grandparents and old people around me who love me. Help me to learn from their stories and share time with them.
Amen

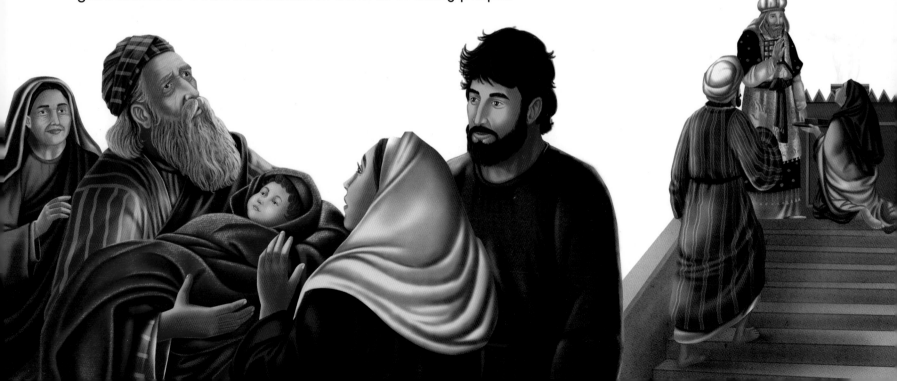

THE BRIGHT STAR

In a distant land far to the east, wise men had been studying the stars. When a really bright star was discovered shining in the skies, they followed it all the way to Judea, for they believed it was a sign that a great king had been born.

They went first to the court of King Herod and asked if he could show them the way to the baby who would be the king of the Jews. Worried, Herod called for his advisors, and they told him that a prophet had foretold that the new king would be born in the city of King David, in Bethlehem.

Then the cunning king directed the wise men to Bethlehem, saying, "Once you have found him, come back and tell me where he is so that I can visit him too."

The wise men followed the star to Bethlehem, where they found baby Jesus in a humble house. They knelt before him and presented him with fine gifts of gold, frankincense, and myrrh before returning home. But they did not stop off at Herod's palace, for God had warned them in a dream not to go there.

PRAYER

Dear Lord God, please guide me each day closer to you, to worship you and to make you my greatest treasure.
Amen

ESCAPE TO EGYPT

Herod was furious when he realized the wise men weren't coming back. He was determined to put an end to this threat to his power and gave an order that all boys under the age of two should be killed.

But no sooner had the wise men left Bethlehem than an angel appeared to Joseph in a dream. "You must take Mary and Jesus and set off at once for Egypt," warned the angel. "You are in danger here, for Herod will be sending soldiers to search for the baby and to kill him."

Joseph awoke with a start. He and Mary swiftly gathered their belongings and, lifting baby Jesus gently from his sleep, set off in haste that very night on the long journey to Egypt, where they lived until wicked King Herod died. Then they came back to Nazareth once more, and as the years passed, Jesus grew to be filled with grace and wisdom.

PRAYER

Thank you, Lord God, for protecting the child Jesus from evil. Thank you that you protect me too.
Amen

"MY FATHER'S HOUSE"

When Jesus was about twelve years old, his mother and father took him to Jerusalem to celebrate Passover—the festival that reminded the Jews of how God had rescued them from slavery in Egypt so many years before. For one whole week the city was filled to bursting.

At the end of this time, Mary and Joseph set off for home with a host of other people, but on the way they realized Jesus was missing. Frantic with worry, they rushed back to the crowded city to search for him.

At last, on the third day, they found him in the temple courts, talking with the teachers of the law, who were amazed by how much he knew.

"Jesus!" cried his parents. "We've been so worried about you!"

"But why were you looking for me?" answered the young boy. "Surely you knew that I would be in my Father's house?" For while Jesus loved Mary and Joseph dearly, he understood that God was his Father in a very special way.

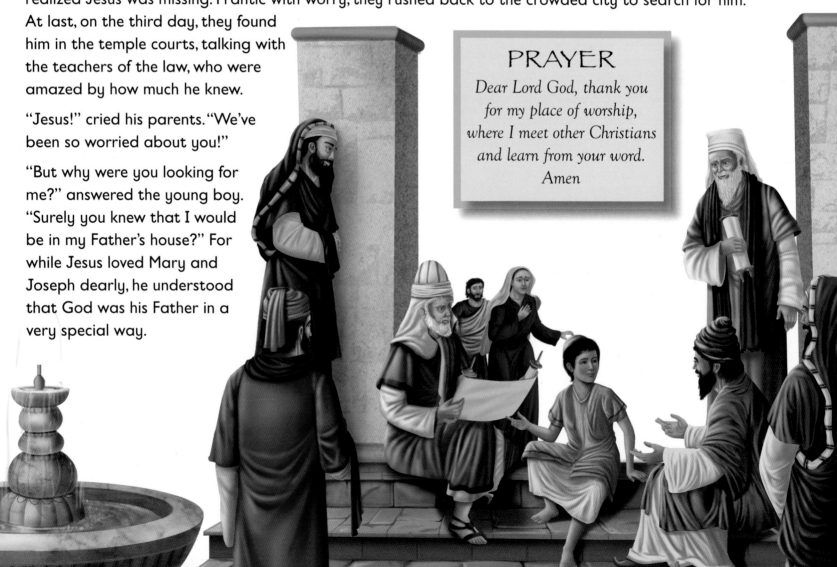

PRAYER

Dear Lord God, thank you for my place of worship, where I meet other Christians and learn from your word.

Amen

A VOICE IN THE WILDERNESS

Jesus' cousin, John, was living in the desert when God called him. He wore clothes made of camels' hair and lived on locusts and wild honey. God wanted John to prepare the world for the coming of his Son, so John traveled throughout the land preaching to people.

"Be sorry for your sins and God will forgive you," he would say. He told those who came to hear him that it wasn't enough to say that they were descended from Abraham to be saved. They needed to truly repent and to change their ways.

People came from all around to listen. Many were truly sorry, and John baptized them in the River Jordan as a sign that their sins had been washed away and that they could start afresh.

Some wondered if John himself could be the promised King, but he said, "I baptize you with water, but the one who comes after me will baptize you with the Holy Spirit and with fire! I'm not even worthy to tie up his sandals!"

PRAYER

Thank you, Lord God, for people who stand up to preach your word. Make them strong to tell your message clearly.

Amen

JESUS IS BAPTIZED

At that time, Jesus came from Nazareth to the River Jordan where John was preaching. John knew at once that this was the promised King, the Lamb of God. So when Jesus asked him to baptize him, John was shocked.

"You shouldn't be asking me to baptize you!" he protested. "I should be asking you to baptize me!" But Jesus insisted.

Just as Jesus was coming up from the water, the heavens opened, the Spirit descended on him like a dove, and a voice came from heaven, "You are my Son, whom I love; with you I am well pleased."

PRAYER

Help me to know, Lord God, that you are one God in three persons: Father, Son, and Holy Spirit.
Amen

TESTED IN THE DESERT

Jesus spent forty days and nights in the dry, hot desert as a test. He ate nothing and was desperately hungry. The devil came to him and said, "If you are the Son of God, surely you can do anything. Why don't you tell these stones to become bread?"

Jesus answered calmly, "It is written: 'Man shall not live on bread alone, but on every word that comes from the mouth of God.'" Jesus knew that food wasn't the most important thing in life.

The devil took Jesus to the top of the temple and told him to throw himself off, for surely angels would rescue him. But Jesus said, "It is also written: 'Do not put the Lord your God to the test.'"

From a high mountain the devil offered him all the kingdoms of the world, if Jesus would simply bow down and worship him. But Jesus replied, "Away from me, Satan! For it is written: 'Worship the Lord your God, and serve him alone.'"

When the devil realized that he could not tempt Jesus, he gave up and left him, and God sent his angels to Jesus to help him to recover.

PRAYER

Thank you, Lord Jesus, that you know what it feels like to be human and tested just like me.
Amen

FISHING FOR MEN

Now Jesus returned to Galilee and began to preach. Word soon spread, and people traveled to hear him. One day, on the shore of Lake Galilee, the crowd was so large that Jesus asked a fisherman if he would take him out in his boat a little way so everyone could see him.

Afterward, Jesus told Simon, the fisherman, to take the boat out further and let down his nets. "Master," Simon answered, "we were out all night and caught nothing. But if you say so, then we will try again."

He couldn't believe his eyes when he pulled up his nets full of fish! He called to his brother, Andrew, and to his friends James and John to help, and soon the two boats were so full of fish that they were ready to sink!

Simon fell to his knees, but Jesus smiled. "Don't be afraid, Simon. From now on you shall be called Peter* for that is what you will be." Then he turned to all the men. "I want you to leave your nets," he said, "and come with me and fish for men instead so that we can spread the good news!" The men pulled the boats up on the beach, left everything, and followed Jesus!

The name Peter comes from the Greek word for rock.

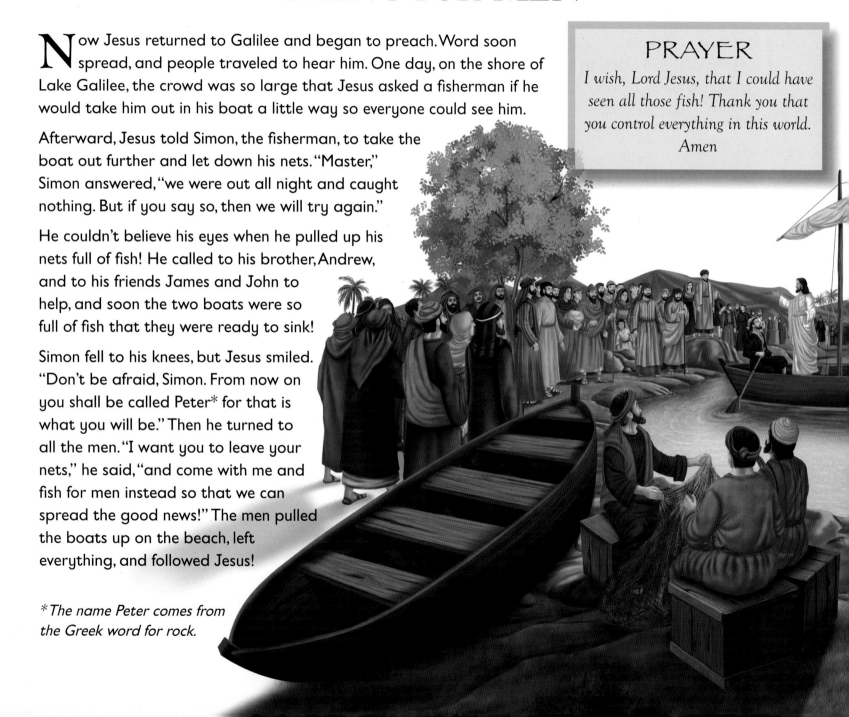

> ## PRAYER
> *I wish, Lord Jesus, that I could have seen all those fish! Thank you that you control everything in this world.*
> *Amen*

WATER INTO WINE

PRAYER
Thank you, Lord Jesus, that you want to be part of special days in my family, like birthdays and parties and weddings.
Amen

Jesus was invited to a marvelous wedding party along with his friends and his mother. Everything was going well until the wine ran out! Mary came to tell Jesus, who asked her, "Why are you telling me this? It is not yet time for me to show myself." But Mary still hoped he would help and spoke quietly to the servants, telling them to do whatever Jesus told them to.

There were several huge water jars nearby. Jesus told the servants to fill them with water, pour the water into jugs, and take it to the head waiter to taste. When the head waiter tasted it, he exclaimed to the bridegroom, "Most people serve the best wine at the start of a meal, but you have saved the best till last!" For the jugs were now filled with delicious wine!

This was the first of many miracles that Jesus would perform.

DEMONS IN THE SYNAGOGUE

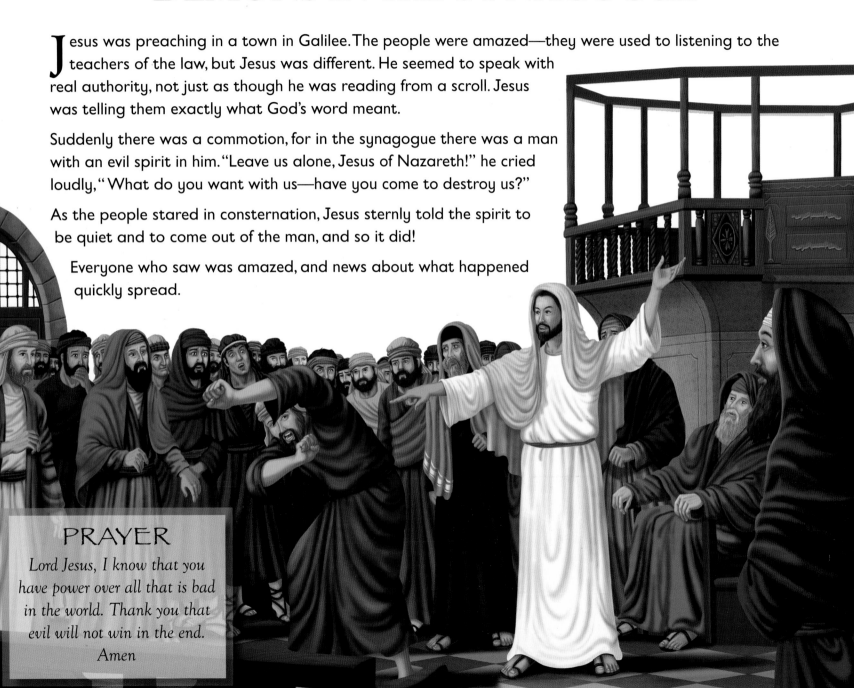

Jesus was preaching in a town in Galilee. The people were amazed—they were used to listening to the teachers of the law, but Jesus was different. He seemed to speak with real authority, not just as though he was reading from a scroll. Jesus was telling them exactly what God's word meant.

Suddenly there was a commotion, for in the synagogue there was a man with an evil spirit in him. "Leave us alone, Jesus of Nazareth!" he cried loudly, "What do you want with us—have you come to destroy us?"

As the people stared in consternation, Jesus sternly told the spirit to be quiet and to come out of the man, and so it did!

Everyone who saw was amazed, and news about what happened quickly spread.

PRAYER

*Lord Jesus, I know that you
have power over all that is bad
in the world. Thank you that
evil will not win in the end.
Amen*

HEALING

Later, Jesus went to the home of Simon Peter and Andrew. Simon Peter's mother-in-law was ill in bed with a fever, but Jesus gently took her hand and helped her sit up. Instantly, she felt better. "I should be looking after you," she smiled at Jesus, and she jumped straight out of bed and began to get dinner ready for everyone!

News of her wonderful recovery spread like wildfire, and by evening a large crowd gathered outside, people who were sick or lame or blind or crippled, others who were troubled by evil spirits like the man in the synagogue. Many had brought their friends or loved ones here. They had all come to see if this amazing man could heal them too. And Jesus went out to them, and laying his hands on each one, he healed them.

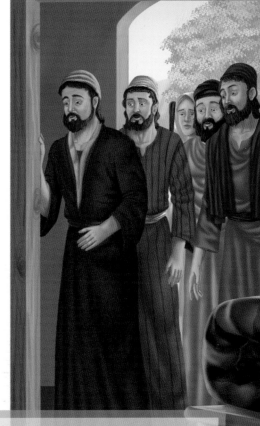

PRAYER

Dear Lord Jesus, when I am feeling unwell, please be near me. Thank you that you still heal today.
Amen

THROWN OUT!

One day Jesus was in his home town of Nazareth, reading from Isaiah's scroll foretelling the coming of the Messiah. At first the people were impressed, but when he said, "Today this Scripture has been fulfilled in your hearing," they were taken aback. Jesus—the son of Mary and Joseph the carpenter—was telling them that he was God's special servant! How could he dare to say such a thing!

Jesus knew that the people would doubt him, that they would expect him to perform some miracle to prove himself, like a showman. He also knew that prophets were never appreciated by the people in their hometowns.

The people became angry with Jesus and forced him out of the synagogue. Some were so furious that they wanted to push him off a steep cliff, but when they tried, he simply walked through the crowd and left them standing there in confusion!

PRAYER

Lord Jesus, I feel sad when people today still don't recognize who you are and don't want to listen to you. Please change their hearts.

Amen

JESUS AND THE TAX COLLECTOR

Matthew had a well-paid job as a tax collector, but when Jesus told him to follow him, he gave up his job on the spot. He wanted all his friends to meet Jesus too. But when the Jewish religious leaders learned that Jesus was meeting with tax collectors and sinners, they were disgusted. "Why is he mixing with the likes of them?" they asked one another. "Everyone knows that tax collectors are greedy and dishonest!"

But Jesus told them, "If you go to a doctor's office, you don't expect to see healthy people—it is people who are sick who need to see the doctor. I am God's doctor. I have come here to save those people who are sinners and who want to start afresh. Those who have done nothing wrong don't need me."

PRAYER

Dear Lord Jesus, help me to be like you and to see that all people have needs. Help me never to despise or prejudge anyone.
Amen

"YOU CAN MAKE ME CLEAN!"

One time, a man with leprosy, an awful skin disease, came up to Jesus and fell to his knees on the ground. "Sir, if you want to, you can make me clean," he begged humbly.

Filled with compassion, Jesus reached out to touch the man. "I do want to," he said. "Be clean!" And immediately the man's skin was perfectly smooth and healthy!

The grateful man simply couldn't keep the wonderful event to himself, and before long so many people wanted to come and see Jesus that he could no longer go anywhere without being surrounded by crowds.

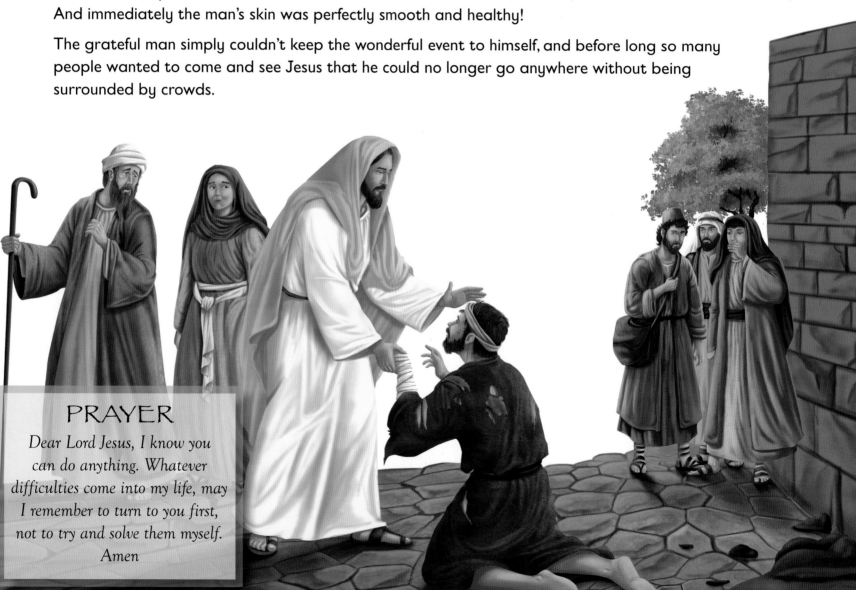

PRAYER

Dear Lord Jesus, I know you can do anything. Whatever difficulties come into my life, may I remember to turn to you first, not to try and solve them myself.
Amen

WHERE THERE'S A WILL...

One time, some men brought their paralyzed friend to be healed, but the house where Jesus was staying was so crowded they couldn't get in! Refusing to give up, they made a hole in the roof and lowered the man down through it on a mat!

When Jesus saw how strongly they believed in him, he said to the man, "Your sins are forgiven, my friend."

This offended the teachers of the law, for only God could forgive sin. But Jesus said, "Is it easier to say to this man, 'Your sins are forgiven,' or to say, 'Get up and walk'? The Son of Man has authority on earth to forgive sins." Then he said to the man, "Get up, pick up your mat, and go home." The man stood up, picked up the mat, and walked out, and everyone was filled with wonder.

PRAYER

Lord Jesus, help me to be so eager to help others that I will not easily give up, but keep looking until I find a way.

Amen

THE UNHOLY TEMPLE

Jesus and his followers went to the temple in Jerusalem to pray. But when Jesus entered, he was appalled, for it was full of money lenders and people selling animals. It looked more like a marketplace than a holy temple! Jesus was furious. He drove the animals out of the temple and knocked over the tables of the money lenders. "Get out!" he shouted. "How dare you turn my Father's house into a marketplace? Begone!"

PRAYER

Thank you, Lord Jesus, that there are special places in my home, my garden, and my church where I can find peace and quiet and worship you.
Amen

Once the temple was quiet and peaceful once more, Jesus began to teach his followers about God's kindness and mercy. Many of the priests and leaders were jealous of Jesus and wished to stop him, but they couldn't do anything because the people paid attention to what Jesus said and listened to him.

THE VISITOR AT NIGHT

Nicodemus was one of the Jewish leaders. He was impressed by Jesus but didn't want anyone to know, so he went to speak to Jesus late at night so he would not be seen. He said he knew Jesus had been sent by God because of the wonderful miracles he had performed.

Jesus was not impressed with flattery. "No one can see the kingdom of God unless they are born again," was all he said. Nicodemus was confused—he couldn't understand how an old person could be born again.

Then Jesus replied, "Unless you are born of water and the Spirit, you cannot enter the kingdom of God." And when Nicodemus still did not understand, Jesus continued, "The Son of Man must be raised up so that whoever believes in him may have eternal life. For God so loved the world that he gave his only Son, so that those who believe in him should not perish but have eternal life. For God sent his Son into the world, not to condemn it, but so the world might be saved through him."

Jesus was talking about a spiritual birth, not a physical birth—one that would come about by believing in Jesus himself.

PRAYER

Dear Lord Jesus, please help me to understand how to be born again into God's family. Thank you for your kingdom, which is like one big family, made up of all who believe in you.
Amen

THE WOMAN AT THE WELL

Passing through Samaria, Jesus stopped to rest at a well. When a local woman came to get water, Jesus asked her for a drink. She was taken aback because normally Jews wouldn't talk to Samaritans. She was even more surprised when he said, "If you knew what God can give you and who it is that asks for a drink, you would have asked, and he would have given you living water."

The puzzled woman asked where he could get such water, and Jesus replied, "Those who drink this water will get thirsty again, but those who drink the water that I will give them will never be thirsty again."

At this, the Samaritan woman asked eagerly, "Please give me this wonderful water!" But when Jesus told her to fetch her husband, she blushed and said she didn't have one.

Jesus said, "No, you have had five husbands and aren't married to the man you are living with now."

The astonished woman ran to tell her friends about the amazing man who knew so much about her. "Do you think he could be God's promised king?" she asked. Many went to see him for themselves and believed because of that day.

PRAYER

Thank you, Lord Jesus, that you know everything about me and you still love me and want to satisfy the deep thirst inside me that sometimes I feel very much.

Amen

THE OFFICER'S SERVANT

In Capernaum there lived a Roman officer. Romans did not normally get on well with the Jews, but this officer was a good man who treated the Jews well. He was also kind to the people in his household, but one of his servants was sick and close to death. When the officer heard that Jesus had come to Capernaum, he came to ask for his help.

Jesus asked him, "Shall I come and heal him?"

Then the officer replied, "Lord, I do not deserve to have you come to my own house, but I know that you don't need to in any case. If you just say the word, I know that my servant will be healed, just in the same way that when I order my soldiers to do something, then they do it!" The officer believed in Jesus so completely that he did not even need him to visit the sick man himself!

Jesus said to the crowd following him, "I tell you all, I have never found faith like this, even in Israel!"

And when the officer returned to his house, sure enough he found his servant up on his feet and feeling perfectly well again!

PRAYER
Help me, Lord God, to always remember that you have all power and whatever you say will always come true.
Amen

TEARS OF JOY

One day when Jesus and his disciples were entering a town, they arrived in time to see a funeral procession coming out through the city gates. The dead man was the only son of a widow, and she was heartbroken. When Jesus saw her, his heart was filled with pity, and he came up to her and said gently, "Don't cry." Then he walked over and touched the coffin, and the men carrying it stopped.

Jesus said, "Young man! Get up, I tell you!"

At his words, to the astonishment and awe of the mourners, the dead man sat up and began to talk, and Jesus led him to his mother, who was filled with joy and thankfulness.

PRAYER

Dear Lord Jesus, please speak words of comfort today to all people who are sad, especially when those who love one another are separated.

Amen

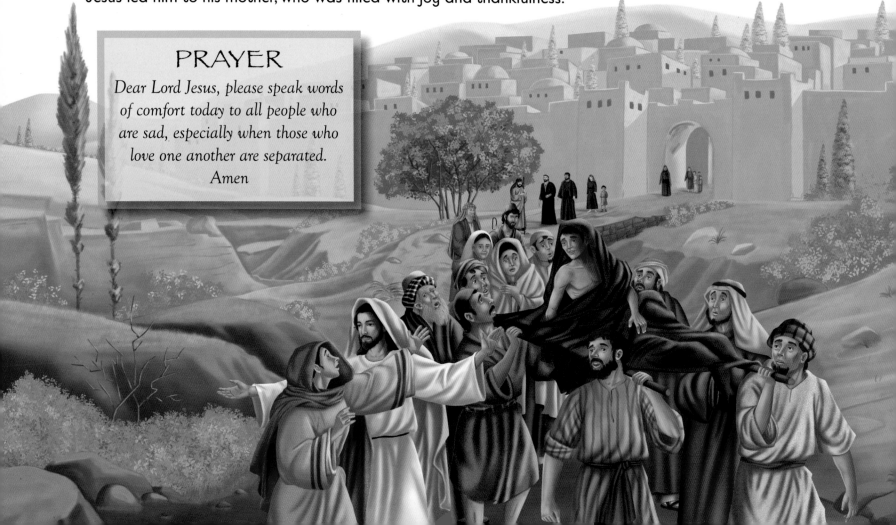

JUST A TOUCH

Jairus was desperate! His little girl was dreadfully ill, and he was worried that Jesus wouldn't be able to make his way through the crowds to heal her in time. Then Jesus stopped still and asked who had touched him. "Master, everyone is touching you in this crowd!" said a disciple, but Jesus knew that he had been touched in a special way.

As he looked around, a woman stepped forward and knelt at his feet. "Lord, it was me," she said nervously. For years she had been ill, and nobody had been able to help her. But she had known that if she could just get close to Jesus, she would be healed. Sure enough, the moment she had managed to touch the edge of his cloak, she was well!

Jesus wasn't angry. "Woman," he said to her kindly, "your faith has healed you. Go home now."

PRAYER
Lord Jesus, help me to always keep close to you and to know that you are the great Healer who can sort out any kind of problem in my life.
Amen

JUST SLEEPING

Just then, someone came running up to say that Jairus' daughter was dead! Jairus was heartbroken, but Jesus kept on walking. "Trust me, Jairus," he said. "Don't be afraid."

He arrived at the house to the sound of weeping. "Why are you carrying on so?" he asked. "The girl is not dead, she is just sleeping." The people there laughed at him, for they knew that the child was dead. But Jesus ignored them and went to her room, where he took one of her hands in his own, and whispered, "Wake up, my child!"

In that instant, the child opened her eyes. She smiled at Jesus and hugged her overjoyed parents!

PRAYER
Thank you, Lord Jesus, that you know all about sick children, and you care about them and their parents. Please be near to them today.
Amen

LORD OF THE SABBATH

Jesus and his disciples were walking through a wheat field on a Sabbath. Some Pharisees spotted his disciples picking heads of grain to eat. They felt this was wrong, for it was like working, and God had commanded them to keep the Sabbath holy. The Pharisees loved their rules—they didn't even think a doctor should work on the Sabbath unless his patient was about to die!

Jesus knew that these laws missed the true spirit of what the Sabbath was about.

He reminded the Pharisees, "When David and his men were hungry, he went into the temple and took the bread that was there for the priests to eat."

Jesus wanted the Pharisees to think about things in a different way. The bread that David and his men ate was holy, not to be eaten as normal food. But David and his men needed food, and so it was okay for them to eat the holy bread. They were God's people and the needs of God's people are more important than religious rituals, however important those rituals might be.

Then Jesus finished by saying, "The Son of Man is Lord of the Sabbath." As Jesus is Lord of the Sabbath, it is his right to do as he wishes on the Sabbath.

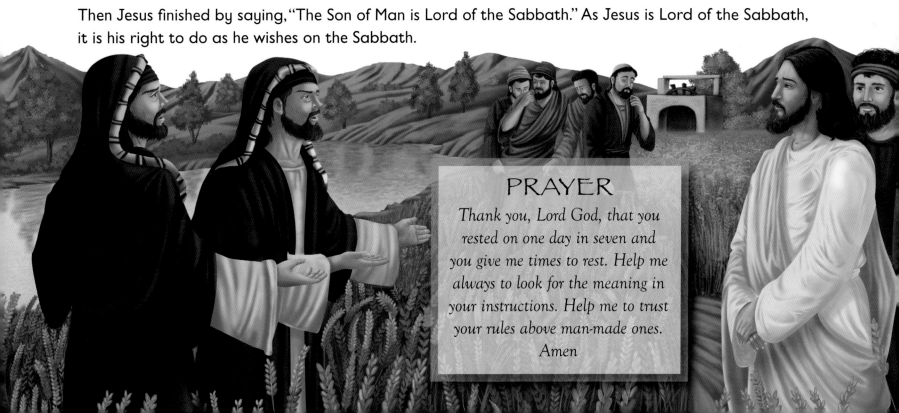

PRAYER

Thank you, Lord God, that you rested on one day in seven and you give me times to rest. Help me always to look for the meaning in your instructions. Help me to trust your rules above man-made ones.

Amen

HEALING ON THE SABBATH

On another Sabbath, when Jesus was teaching the people in a synagogue, he noticed a man with a crippled hand. Jesus knew that the Pharisees and the religious teachers were watching him and waiting to catch him doing something wrong—like working on the Sabbath!

Jesus told the man to stand up so that everyone could see him, and then he turned to the crowd, asking, "What do you think our Law really wants us to do on the Sabbath? Does it want us to help people or harm them?" Then he told the man to hold out his hand, and it was healed!

The Pharisees and the teachers were furious, but Jesus was trying to explain that the laws God had given them were there to teach them right from wrong, not to be used just to punish and judge. They were supposed to love one another and help one another.

PRAYER

Dear Lord God, thank you that Jesus showed love and helped people whatever day of the week it was. Help me to show love to people whenever there is a need.

Amen

CHOOSING THE TWELVE

A round this time, Jesus chose twelve men to be his special disciples* to carry on his work after his death. They were a mixed bunch: Simon Peter and his brother Andrew, and brothers James and John, were all fishermen; Matthew (or Levi) was a tax collector, while Simon (not Simon Peter) was a patriot who wanted to fight the Romans; and the other six were Bartholomew, Thomas, James son of Alphaeus, Philip, Judas (or Thaddeus) son of James, and Judas Iscariot.

Jesus knew they had a hard task ahead of them. He wanted them to teach the people that God's kingdom is near, and to heal people too. He sent them out to travel from village to village, taking nothing with them except for a staff, because God would provide everything they needed. They were to rely on people's hospitality, and if they were not made welcome, then they were to leave. But those who welcomed them were really welcoming Jesus himself.

These men became known as apostles, or messengers, for Jesus chose them to pass on his message of good news

PRAYER
Dear Lord God, I pray for all preachers and Bible teachers and those who travel to many places to tell of Jesus. Please make them strong and bold today.
Amen

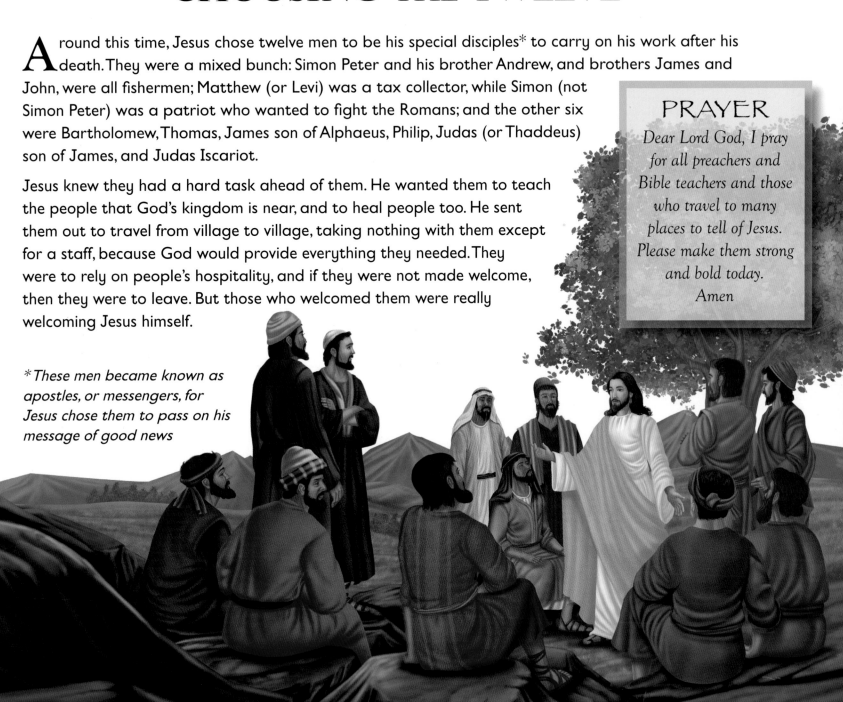

THE HEALING AT THE POOL

In Jerusalem there was a pool called Bethesda, where the sick gathered. They believed that from time to time an angel would move the water and that the first person who stepped into it would be healed. One man was there who had been sick for thirty-eight years! He told Jesus that he had no one to help him into the pool. But Jesus simply replied, "Get up, pick up your mat, and walk."

Then the man got up from the ground, picked up the mat that he had been lying on for so many years and walked away, perfectly healthy!

Once again, the religious leaders were angry with Jesus for healing on a Sabbath. They were even more offended when he told them, "My Father is always working, and I too must work." Who did he think he was? This was outrageous! But Jesus answered, "I do nothing on my own authority— I'm only doing what God wants me to do and has authorized me to do."

PRAYER

I am so glad, Jesus, that you helped a man who had no friends. Please show me how I can be helpful and useful today.

Amen

THE SERMON ON THE MOUNT

Jesus wasn't always welcome in the synagogues, so he would often teach his disciples and the large crowds that gathered to hear him outside in the open air. One of the most important talks he gave was on a mountain near Capernaum. It has become known as the Sermon on the Mount. Jesus taught the people about what was truly important in life and gave comfort and advice:

"How happy are the poor and those who are sad or who have been badly treated, those who are humble, gentle and kind, and those who try to do the right thing—for all these people will be rewarded in heaven! They will be comforted and know great joy. Those who have been merciful will receive mercy, and God will look kindly on those who have tried to keep the peace, for they are truly his children. So be glad when people are mean to you and say nasty things about you because of me—for a great reward is waiting for you in heaven!"

PRAYER

Thank you, Lord Jesus, for your wonderful words that I can read and learn today. Help me to see that your way is the best way of living.
Amen

LET YOUR LIGHT SHINE BRIGHTLY

Jesus went on, "It is important to obey all of God's laws, but you need to understand the meaning behind them. It isn't enough just not to kill someone—you must learn to truly forgive to become close to God. So instead of thinking, 'An eye for an eye, and a tooth for a tooth,' if someone slaps you on the cheek, offer him the other one too! Anger will eat you up. It's easy to love those who love you, but I say, love your enemies! God gives his sunlight and rain to both good and bad people!

"And let your life be an example to others, so that your light shines brightly, and all who see it praise God too. But don't do good things just so people will look at you and think how good you are. You don't need their praise. Do your good deeds in private, and your Father, who sees everything, will reward you.

"Treat others in the same way that you would like them to treat you. Don't judge them. Think about your own faults first!"

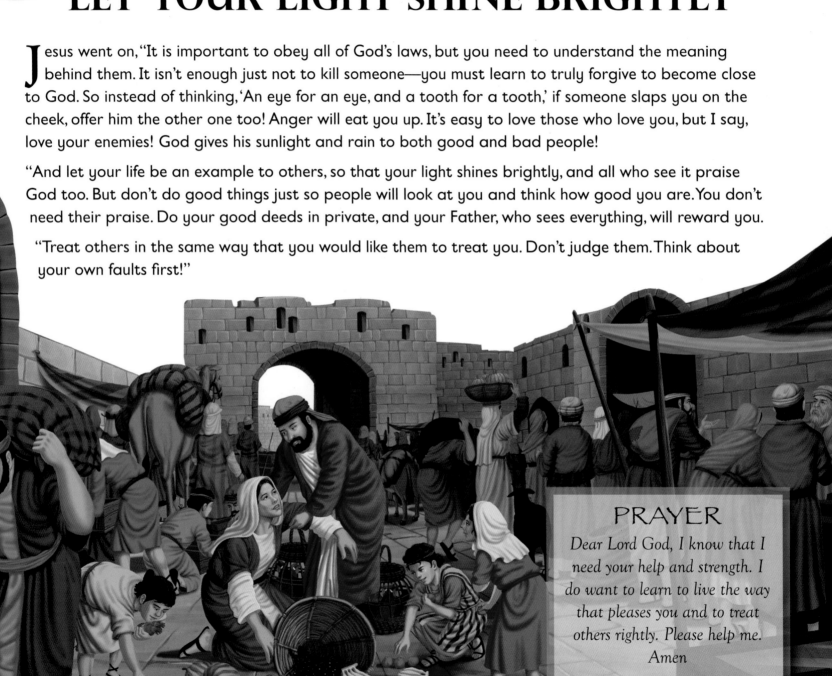

PRAYER

Dear Lord God, I know that I need your help and strength. I do want to learn to live the way that pleases you and to treat others rightly. Please help me.

Amen

TREASURES IN HEAVEN

Jesus also told the people that they shouldn't spend their time trying to make themselves comfortable now. Instead, they needed to focus on the big picture. "Don't store up wealth on earth," he told them. "It won't last! Store up treasures in heaven, for where your treasures are, your heart will be too. And don't worry about what clothes you're wearing or where your next meal will come from. There is more to life than food and clothes. Look at the birds in the sky. They don't have to plant and harvest and store their food— God feeds them.

"And what about the beautiful wildflowers that grow everywhere? They don't have to work hard either, for God himself clothes them, and even King Solomon in all his glory never looked as splendid as any one of these colorful flowers!

"If God cares for the birds and the flowers, how much more does he love you?"

PRAYER

Dear Lord Jesus, when I see the birds and the flowers, may they always be reminders to me that I can trust you for everything. Help me never to think that money or things can bring happiness.

Amen

THE RIGHT WAY TO PRAY

Jesus also taught people the right way to pray. They shouldn't try to impress others by praying in public, but should go to a quiet place and pray to God alone. Nor should they keep repeating meaningless words. God knows what is in our hearts, and this is the way Jesus told people to pray to him:

Our Father in heaven,
hallowed be your name.
Your kingdom come.
Your will be done,
on earth as it is in heaven.
Give us today our daily bread,
and forgive us our sins,
as we forgive those who sin against us.
Lead us not into temptation,
but deliver us from evil.
For yours is the kingdom,
the power, and the glory, forever.
  Amen.

"Keep on asking," said Jesus, "and you will receive. Keep on seeking, and you will find. Keep on knocking, and the door will be opened to you."

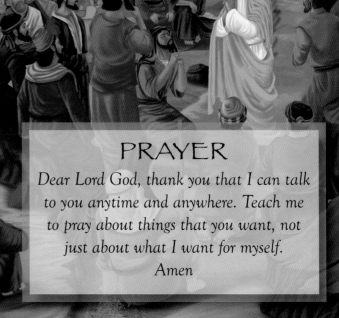

PRAYER

Dear Lord God, thank you that I can talk to you anytime and anywhere. Teach me to pray about things that you want, not just about what I want for myself.

Amen

A FIRM FOUNDATION

Before Jesus ended his sermon, he said one last thing: "If you listen to my teaching and follow it, then you are wise, like the person who builds his house on solid rock. Even if the rain pours down, the rivers flood, and the winds rage, the house won't collapse, for it is built on solid rock. But he who listens and doesn't obey is foolish, like a person who builds a house on sand, without any foundations. The house is quickly built, but when the rains and floods and winds come, the house won't be able to stand against them. It will collapse and be utterly destroyed."

As the crowds slowly dispersed, their heads were filled with all these new ideas. Jesus was nothing like their usual teachers, but what he said made sense. They had a lot to think about!

PRAYER

Dear Lord God, I do so much want to build my life on the first foundation of obeying you. Please help me day by day to build well.
Amen

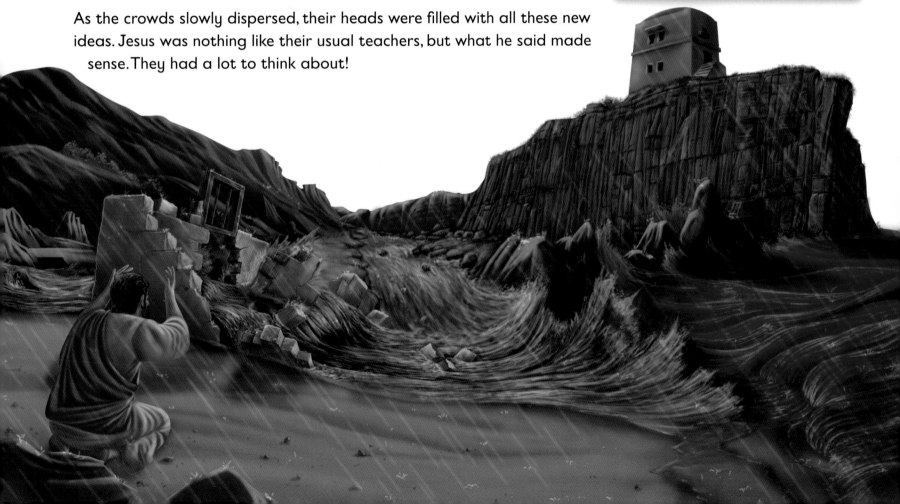

THE DEADLY DANCE

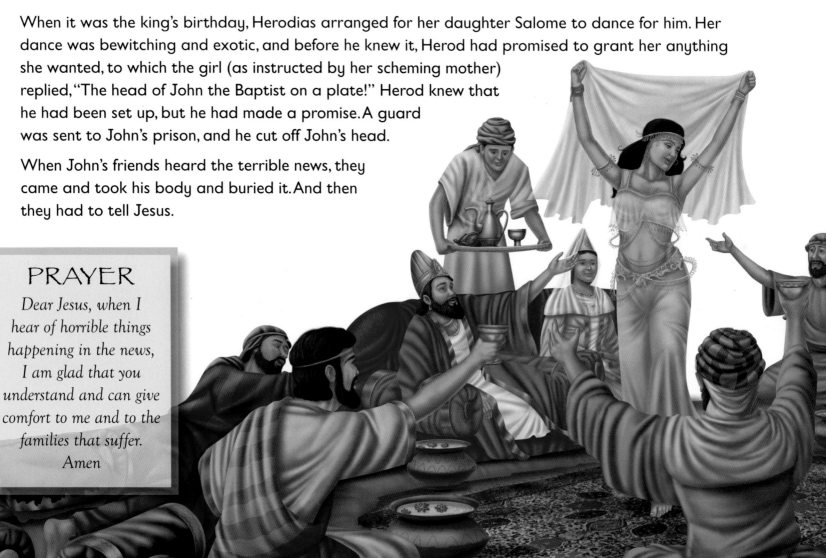

Some time before this, King Herod had given orders to have John the Baptist thrown in prison. He and the queen had been furious with John for telling everyone that Herod had been wrong to divorce his own wife in order to marry his half-brother's wife, Herodias. In fact, Queen Herodias wanted her husband to execute John!

When it was the king's birthday, Herodias arranged for her daughter Salome to dance for him. Her dance was bewitching and exotic, and before he knew it, Herod had promised to grant her anything she wanted, to which the girl (as instructed by her scheming mother) replied, "The head of John the Baptist on a plate!" Herod knew that he had been set up, but he had made a promise. A guard was sent to John's prison, and he cut off John's head.

When John's friends heard the terrible news, they came and took his body and buried it. And then they had to tell Jesus.

PRAYER

Dear Jesus, when I hear of horrible things happening in the news, I am glad that you understand and can give comfort to me and to the families that suffer.
Amen

FEEDING FIVE THOUSAND

When Jesus heard about John, he tried to go somewhere quiet. But the people followed, and he could not bring himself to send them away. When evening came, there was still a huge crowd. Jesus told his disciples to give them something to eat. "But Master," the disciples said, "there are thousands of people, and we only have five loaves of bread and two fish!"

Jesus commanded them to tell the people to sit down. Then, taking the five loaves and the two fish and looking up to heaven, he gave thanks to his Father and broke the loaves into pieces. He gave them to the disciples, who took them to the people and then came back to Jesus for more bread and fish. He filled up their baskets again . . . and again . . . and again! To their astonishment there were still bread and fish left in the baskets when they came to feed the very last people! More than five thousand people had been fed that day—with five loaves of bread and two fish!

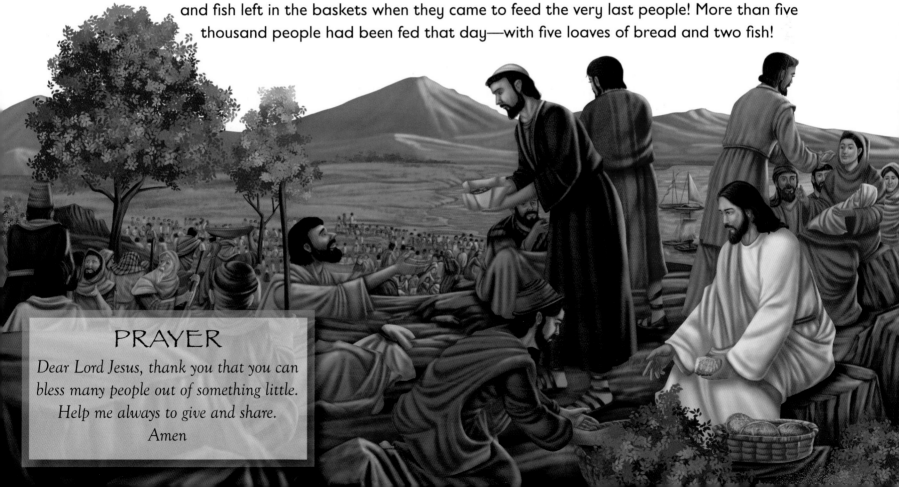

PRAYER
Dear Lord Jesus, thank you that you can bless many people out of something little. Help me always to give and share.
Amen

Matthew 8; Mark 4; Luke 8

JESUS CALMS THE STORM

Jesus and his disciples climbed into a boat to travel across to the other side of the lake. Jesus was so tired that he lay down and fell asleep. Suddenly, the skies darkened, rain came pelting down, and a fierce storm struck the lake. Huge waves tossed the boat, and the disciples were terrified that they would capsize.

Jesus still lay sleeping. The frightened disciples went over and woke him up, begging him to save them. Jesus opened his eyes and looked up at them. "Why are you afraid? You have so little faith!" he said sadly. Then he stood up calmly, his arms spread wide, and facing into the wind and rain, commanded, "Be still!" At once the wind and waves died down, and all was calm.

The disciples were amazed. "Who is this man?" they asked themselves. "Even the winds and waves obey him!"

PRAYER

*Lord Jesus, whenever I feel afraid,
remind me that you are near
and that you have all power over
everything in the world.
Amen*

DEMONS AND PIGS

Jesus stepped ashore and was met by a man possessed by evil spirits. For a long time this man had lived in the wild. People were frightened of him and had bound him with chains, but he was so strong that he had torn them apart! When he saw Jesus, he fell to his knees, screaming, "What do you want with me, Son of the Most High God? Please don't torture me!" for he was possessed by many demons that begged Jesus not to banish them.

A herd of pigs was feeding on the nearby hillside. Jesus let the evil spirits go into the pigs. The entire herd rushed down the hillside into the lake, and every last pig was drowned!

The people all around were so shocked when they saw the change in the wild man that they asked Jesus to leave, but the man who had been demon-possessed told his wonderful story far and wide, and everyone who heard was amazed.

PRAYER

Thank you, Lord Jesus, that you really are the Son of God and you are stronger than everything that is evil in this world.
Amen

PARABLE OF THE SOWER

Many of the people who came to listen to Jesus were farmers. Jesus tried to pass on his message in a way that they would understand. His stories, often called parables, let people think things through for themselves. To some they would just be stories, but others would understand the real message.

"A farmer went out to sow his seed. As he was scattering it, some fell along the path and was trampled on or eaten by birds. Some fell on rocky ground where there was no soil, and when they began to grow, the plants withered because their roots could not reach water. Other seeds fell among weeds that choked them. Still others fell on good soil and grew into tall, strong plants and produced a crop far greater than what was sown."

Jesus was telling them that he was like the farmer, and the seeds were like the message he brought from God. The seeds that fell on the path and were eaten by birds are like those people who hear the good news but pay no attention. Those on the rocky ground are like people who receive the word with joy when they hear it, but they have no roots. They believe for a while, but when life gets difficult they give up easily. The seeds among weeds are like those who hear but let themselves become choked by life's worries and pleasures. But the seeds that fell on good soil are like those people who hear God's message and hold it tight in their heart. Their faith grows and grows.

PRAYER

*Thank you, Lord Jesus,
for your wonderful stories.
I do want the good seed
of your words to grow
strong in my heart and
give you a great harvest.
Amen*

A LAMP ON A STAND

Jesus tried to explain how important it was for his followers to hear his message, take it to heart, and then pass it on. He said to them, "No one lights a lamp and then covers it with a bowl or hides it under a bed. Instead, they put the lamp on a stand so that anyone who comes in will see the light. Everything that is hidden will become clear, and everything that is secret will be brought out into the open."

He wanted them to think very carefully about what he was telling them so that they themselves could be lamps, shining forth in the world, bringing light into the lives of those around them. A light is made to be seen, it is made to be used—we must use what God has given us!

They weren't to keep his wonderful news a secret for themselves. They should share it, and in doing so would be filled with light. Jesus is the light of the world, and he came into it, not to stay hidden, but to light up the world with the truth about God. And when we let Jesus into our hearts, we shine too!

PRAYER

Thank you, Lord Jesus, that you are the truth and the truth always brings light. Help me to live in your light and share the truth with others.

Amen

PARABLE OF THE WEEDS

Jesus told another parable: "Once a farmer sowed good seed in his field, but that night, his enemy sowed weeds among the wheat. When the wheat began to grow, weeds grew too. His servants asked if they should pull them up, but the owner said, 'If you pull the weeds up, you may pull some of the wheat up too. We must let both grow until harvest. Then we will collect and burn the weeds, gather the wheat, and bring it into my barn.'"

Jesus later explained, "The farmer who sowed the good seed is the Son of Man. The field is the world, and the good seed is the people of the kingdom. The weeds were sown by the devil, and they are his people. The harvest will come at the end of time. Then the Son of Man will send out his angels, and they will weed out of his kingdom everything that causes sin and all who do evil. They will be thrown into the blazing furnace, but the righteous will shine like the sun in the kingdom of their Father."

PRAYER

Thank you, Lord God, that you know everything and one day, when you come as Judge, everything will be absolutely fair.
Amen

WALKING ON WATER

It was late at night, and waves tossed the boat violently. Jesus had gone ashore to pray, and the disciples were afraid. At the first light of dawn, they saw a figure walking toward them on the water! They thought it was a ghost and were scared until they heard the calm voice of Jesus, "It is I. Don't be afraid."

Simon Peter was the first to speak. "Lord," he said, "if it is you, command me to walk across the water to you," and Jesus did so.

He put one foot gingerly in the water. Then he lowered the other and bravely stood up, letting go of the boat. He didn't sink! But when he looked around at the waves, his courage failed him. As he began to sink, he cried, "Lord, save me!"

Jesus reached out and took his hand. "Oh, Peter," he said sadly, "where is your faith? Why did you doubt?" Then together they walked back to the boat. The wind died down and the water became calm. The disciples bowed low. "Truly you are the Son of God," they said humbly.

PRAYER

Dear Lord Jesus, you truly are the Son of God, and there is nothing you cannot do. Help me not to doubt you.
Amen

THE BREAD OF LIFE

People were always wanting another miracle. Jesus told them that God wanted them to believe in his Son, but they asked him, "What miracle will you perform for us so that we might believe in you? Moses gave our ancestors bread from heaven when they were in the desert. What will you do?"

Jesus reminded them that it was not Moses who provided the bread, but God: "It is my Father who gives you the true bread from heaven, for the bread of God is the bread that comes down from heaven and gives life to the world."

Then the people said to Jesus, "Well, give us this bread, then."

So Jesus explained, "I am the bread of life. Whoever comes to me will never go hungry, and whoever believes in me will never be thirsty. For what my Father wants is that whoever sees his Son and believes in him shall have eternal life!"

The people didn't like the sound of this. "He's the son of Mary and Joseph the carpenter! How can he say these things?!"

Jesus continued, "I am telling you the truth: He who believes has eternal life. Your ancestors ate manna in the desert but died. I am the living bread that came down from heaven. This bread is my body, and whoever eats it will live forever. I will give my body so that the people in the world can live."

PRAYER

Lord Jesus, you came from heaven to give us everything we need for this life and for eternal life. Help me to remember that I need more than the things I see around me: I need the bread of life.

Amen

CRUMBS FROM THE TABLE

One day, a Canaanite woman threw herself at Jesus' feet, crying out in anguish and hope, "Lord, have mercy on me! My daughter is possessed by a demon!" Jesus remained silent, but his disciples urged him to send her away.

Jesus told the woman gently, "I was sent only to the lost sheep of Israel," and when she begged him again, he replied, "It is not right to take the children's bread and toss it to the dogs."

"Lord," she replied, "Even the dogs eat the crumbs that fall from their master's table."

Jesus was touched by her faith and said, "Woman, you have great faith! Your request is granted." And when the woman went home she found her beloved child sleeping peacefully, safe and well once more.

PRAYER

Thank you, Jesus, that your love and healing are for all people, all over the world, and that includes me.
Amen

THE TRANSFIGURATION

Jesus climbed up a mountain to pray, taking with him Peter, James, and John. All of a sudden, as Jesus prayed, the disciples looked up to see him changed. Light shone from his face and clothes, and as they watched in wonder, Moses, who had led his people out of Egypt, and Elijah, greatest of all the prophets, were suddenly there before their very eyes, talking with Jesus! Then a bright cloud covered them, and a voice said, "This is my Son, whom I love. Listen to what he has to say, for I am very pleased with him!"

The disciples fell to the ground, too frightened to raise their eyes. But Jesus came over and touched them. "Don't be afraid," he said softly, and when they looked up, they saw no one there except Jesus.

PRAYER

Thank you, Lord Jesus, that you are greater than anyone else who has ever lived. You are God's Son. Help me to listen to what you say above everyone else.

Amen

THE FRANTIC FATHER

The very next day, when they came down from the mountain, a large crowd came to meet them, and out of the crowd a man called out in anguish, "Teacher, please look at my son! He is possessed by a demon and he has dreadful fits. Sometimes he can't speak, or he is thrown to the ground and foams at the mouth! I beg you to help him. I asked your disciples to, but they couldn't drive it out."

Jesus was disappointed. "Why don't you people believe? How long must I put up with you? Bring the boy to me."

When the boy came close to Jesus, the spirit threw the child to the ground, where he rolled around, foaming at the mouth.

"If you can do anything, please help us!" begged the father.

"'If you can?'" repeated Jesus. "Anything is possible for one who believes."

The father exclaimed, "I do believe! Help me believe more!"

Then Jesus commanded the spirit to come out, and the boy was healed.

Later, the disciples asked Jesus why they hadn't been able to drive out the demon themselves, and he told them that they had needed to pray. They hadn't had enough faith. And he told them, "The truth is, if you really have faith, even if your faith is as small as a mustard seed, you can say to this mountain, 'Move from here to there,' and it will move. Nothing will be impossible for you."

PRAYER
Thank you, Lord God, for the strong love of my family. For my parents and grandparents and others who I know really want the best for me.
Amen

JESUS AND THE CHILDREN

Jesus loved little children, for they were good and innocent. He was always surrounded by children, and sometimes his disciples tried to shoo them away. "Don't stop little children from coming to me," he told them sternly. "The kingdom of heaven belongs to them and all those like them."

Once, when the disciples began arguing about which of them was the most important, Jesus beckoned to a little child and put his arm around him. He turned to his disciples, saying, "Whoever welcomes this child in my name welcomes me, and whoever welcomes me welcomes the one who sent me. For it is the one who is least among you who is the greatest. To enter heaven, you must be like a little child!"

PRAYER

Thank you, Jesus, that you have a special love for children. Thank you that the door of heaven is wide open to children and also to adults who have simple trust like a child.

Amen

"I WILL GIVE YOU REST"

Jesus wanted everyone to know that he was there to help. Many people have burdens to carry in life. Maybe someone in their family is out of work and they have trouble making ends meet. Someone they love might be ill, or they themselves might be unwell or have some disability. They might struggle to keep up at school or to do well at work. Maybe they simply feel overwhelmed by all the details of life, all the rules and chores and running around, and can't see the big picture anymore. Some things we just can't seem to handle by ourselves. But we don't have to!

Jesus wanted people to turn to him for help. He said, "Come to me, everyone who is weary and carrying a heavy burden, and I will give you rest. Take my yoke upon you and learn from me, for I am gentle and humble at heart, and you will find rest for your souls. For my yoke is easy, and my burden is light."

A yoke is something that we put on an ox when we want it to pull something. Jesus wasn't saying that God will take away all our burdens if we ask him to. Sometimes it is the troubles that we go through that strengthen us and bring us closer to God. But Jesus was saying that we don't have to struggle on our own. He can help us carry our burdens—he can comfort us and make us feel at peace.

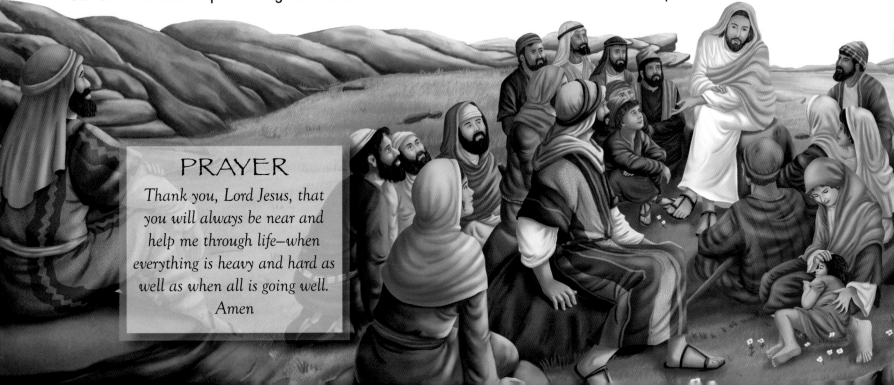

PRAYER

Thank you, Lord Jesus, that you will always be near and help me through life—when everything is heavy and hard as well as when all is going well.

Amen

THE SECOND CHANCE

Once, when Jesus was teaching, the Pharisees brought in a woman who had been caught with a man who was not her husband. "According to the laws laid down by Moses, she should be stoned to death," they said. "What do you say?" For they wanted to see what Jesus would do.

Jesus bent over and wrote on the ground. After a long silence he looked them in the eye. "Whoever has committed no sin may throw the first stone." Then he bent over again.

No one said a word. People lowered their eyes uncomfortably until one of the men turned and walked away. Then another person edged away, and another, and soon only Jesus and the woman remained.

Jesus stood up and said to the woman, "Where has everyone gone? Is there no one left to condemn you?" She fearfully shook her head. "Well," said Jesus, "I don't condemn you either. Go home, but don't sin again," and the woman went home, filled with gladness and gratitude at being given a second chance.

PRAYER

Dear Lord Jesus, help me not to judge other people when they go wrong. Help me to be like you—you came to save, not to condemn.
Amen

FORGIVENESS

Jesus tried to make his followers understand how important forgiveness was. Peter asked, "Lord, how many times should I forgive someone who has wronged me? Up to seven times?"

Jesus looked him straight in the eyes. "Don't just forgive him seven times. Forgive him seventy-seven times!" he answered, and he continued, "The kingdom of heaven is like the master whose servant owed him a great deal of money. The man could not pay and he begged for more time. The kind master canceled the debt and sent him home.

"This same servant was owed a small amount of money by another servant, and when he couldn't pay him back, he had the second servant thrown into prison!

"When the master learned of this, he called the first servant in. 'You've been cruel and unkind,' he said. 'I canceled your debt because you begged me. Shouldn't you have shown mercy just as I showed you?' He was so furious that he handed him over to the jailers until he could pay back all he owed."

Jesus looked at his followers. "This is how my Father will treat you unless you forgive your brother or sister from your heart."

PRAYER

Lord Jesus, thank you for the happiness and relief I feel when I am forgiven. Help me to be ready to forgive others who hurt me.
Amen

THE GOOD SHEPHERD

People asked Jesus who he really was, and he explained that he was like a shepherd. "The good shepherd would do anything for his sheep—even lay down his life to save them. A hired hand would run away if he saw a wolf coming, but the shepherd would never leave them. The sheep will listen to him and follow where he leads, but will never follow a stranger.

"I am the gate for the sheep. I will let my own sheep through. I know my sheep and they know me. I will lay down my life for them of my own free will, and for this my Father loves me."

When people grumbled that Jesus spoke with people who had done bad things, he said, "Imagine you had a hundred sheep and lost one of them. How would you feel? Wouldn't you leave the other ninety-nine safe and rush off to look for the lost one? And when you found it, don't you think you would be so thrilled that you would rush home and celebrate? In the same way, there will be more rejoicing in heaven over one sinner who repents than over ninety-nine people who don't need to repent."

PRAYER

Thank you so much, Lord Jesus, that you are such a wonderful shepherd and that you really did give your life for us, the sheep. Thank you that you care for every single lost sheep.

Amen

THE LOST SON

Jesus told another story to explain how happy God was when sinners returned to him: "There was once a man with two sons. The younger one asked for his share of the property so he could go out into the world, and he soon spent it all on enjoying himself. He ended up working for a farmer and was so hungry that sometimes he wished he could eat the food he was giving to the pigs! But at last he came to his senses and set off for home to tell his father how sorry he was. 'I'm not worthy of being his son,' he thought, 'but maybe he will let me work on the farm.'

"When his father saw him coming, he rushed out and threw his arms around him. The young man tried to tell him that he was not fit to be called his son, but the father told his servants to bring his finest robe for his son to wear and to kill the prize calf for a feast.

"The older son was outraged! He had worked hard for his father all this time, and nobody had ever held a feast for him! Yet here came his brother, having squandered all his money, and his father couldn't wait to kill the fattened calf and welcome him home!

"'My son,' the father said, 'you are always with me, and all I have is yours. But celebrate with me now, for your brother was dead to me and is alive again; he was lost and is found!'"

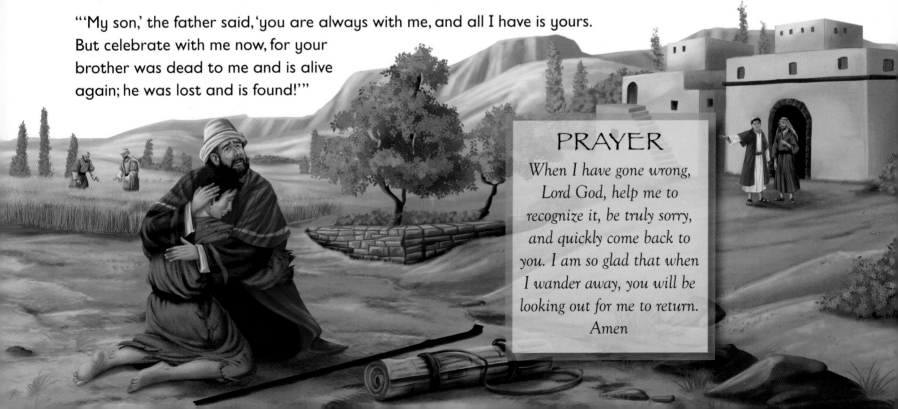

PRAYER

When I have gone wrong, Lord God, help me to recognize it, be truly sorry, and quickly come back to you. I am so glad that when I wander away, you will be looking out for me to return.
Amen

THE GREATEST COMMANDMENT

One day one of the teachers of the law came up to Jesus. He asked him which of the commandments was the most important.

Jesus answered, "'You must love the Lord your God with all your heart, all your soul, all your strength, and all your mind.' This is the most important commandment of all. And the second-most important commandment is this: 'Love your neighbor as yourself.' There is no commandment greater than these."

Jesus knew that when we love God more than we love ourselves, we can love other people as much as we love ourselves. If we can keep these two commandments, then we won't have trouble keeping the others! Love is the most important thing of all.

PRAYER

Thank you, Lord God, for the power of love. Thank you for your great love to me. Help me in return to love you with all my heart and to love those around me.
Amen

THE GOOD SAMARITAN

Once someone asked Jesus what the Law meant when it said we must love our neighbors as much as ourselves. "Who is my neighbor?" he asked, and Jesus told him a story:

"A man was going from Jerusalem to Jericho when he was attacked by robbers who beat him and took everything from him before leaving him by the roadside, half dead. Soon a priest passed by. When he saw the man, he crossed to the other side of the road and continued on his way. Then a Levite came along. He also hurried on his way without stopping.

"The next person to come along was a Samaritan, who are not friends of the Jews. Yet when this traveler saw the man lying bleeding by the roadside, his heart was filled with pity. He knelt beside him and carefully washed and bandaged his wounds before taking him on his donkey to an inn, where he gave the innkeeper money to look after the man until he was well."

Jesus looked at the man who had posed the question, and he asked who he thought had been a good neighbor to the injured man.

The man sheepishly replied, "The one who was kind to him."

Then Jesus told him, "Go, then, and be like him."

PRAYER

Lord Jesus, please help me to be like you. Help me to stop what I am doing and be willing to help others.
Amen

MARTHA AND MARY

Jesus was fond of two sisters—Mary and Martha. One day, Jesus stopped to visit. Martha rushed off to make sure everything was clean and tidy and to prepare food, but Mary sat by his feet, listening to everything he said, not wanting to miss a single word.

Martha was angry. "Lord," she said to Jesus, "won't you tell Mary to help me? There is so much to get ready, and she is sitting there doing nothing while I do all the work!"

"Martha," said Jesus in a soothing voice, "you are worrying about small things, but they are not what is really important. Your sister understands what is truly important, and it won't be taken away from her." He was trying to explain that the most important thing in life is to love Jesus and listen to his words!

PRAYER

Lord Jesus, I am sorry that I sometimes get too busy with other good things, and I forget the most important thing of all, which is to listen to you.

Amen

LAZARUS LIVES!

Jesus received a message from Martha and Mary, telling him that their brother, Lazarus, was very ill, but by the time Jesus arrived at their house, Lazarus was dead. Martha wept, saying, "Oh Lord, if you had been here, my brother would not have died. But I know that God will give you whatever you ask."

Then Jesus said gently, "He will rise again. Everyone who believes in me will live again, even though he has died." But when Mary came up weeping, and he saw the other relatives crying, then Jesus wept, too, and asked to be taken to the cave where Lazarus had been laid. He told the men to open it.

Now, Lazarus had been dead for four days, but Jesus prayed and gave thanks to God. Then he said loudly, "Lazarus, come out!"

Everyone watched in silent wonder as a figure emerged from the dark cave, his hands and feet wrapped with strips of linen, and a cloth around his face. It was Lazarus, and he was alive!

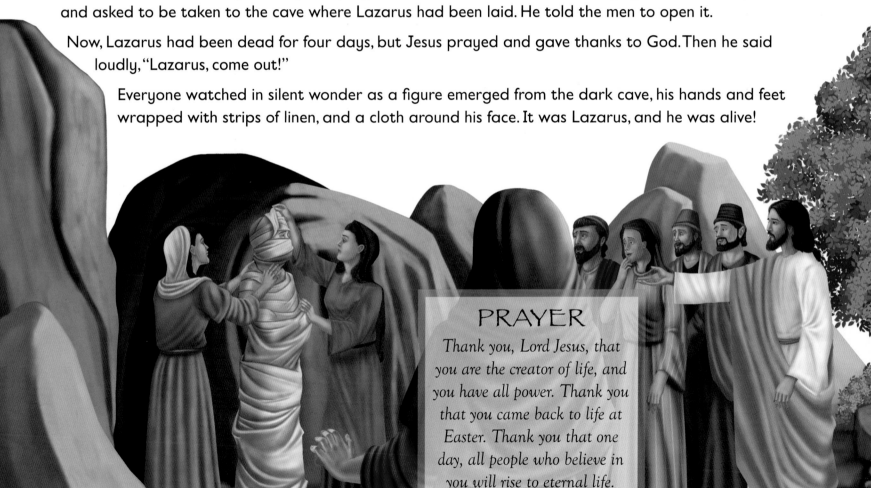

PRAYER

Thank you, Lord Jesus, that you are the creator of life, and you have all power. Thank you that you came back to life at Easter. Thank you that one day, all people who believe in you will rise to eternal life.

Amen

THE RICH FOOL

Jesus wanted to warn his followers to be on their guard against all kinds of greed. Life shouldn't be about owning lots of things or making lots of money. He explained this to them in a parable: "Once there was a rich man with a lot of land. One year he had a truly wonderful harvest. He had so many crops that he didn't have enough room to store them all! So he had an idea. He had plenty already and could have chosen to share the extra crops, but he didn't want to do that. Instead, he decided to knock down all his barns and build bigger and better ones so that he could store all his grain. That way he would have enough put aside for years, and he could spend his time enjoying himself with lots of good food and drink and generally taking life easy.

"But God said to him, 'You fool, this very night your life will be over, and who will have all this then?'"

The rich man couldn't take all his wealth with him after his death. His greed and selfishness would do him no good in the end.

Jesus was saying that we shouldn't spend our lives laying up treasure for ourselves. If God blesses us, we should use what he gives us to help others, and then we will be rich toward God.

PRAYER

Dear Lord Jesus, help me to guard my life against selfishness. Help me not to make riches my goal in life but rather to set my heart on you and heaven.
Amen

WATCHFULNESS

Jesus told his followers that they needed to be ready at all times for the day when he would come again. He told them about the watchful servants who were waiting for their master to return from a wedding feast. They didn't know when he would be back, for in those times wedding feasts could last for days! Nevertheless, the faithful servants stayed dressed and ready for action, and they kept the lamps cheerfully burning so that the instant he knocked on the door, they could open it for him.

Jesus went on to say that the servants would be richly rewarded for their readiness, for the master would put on an apron, sit them down at the table, and wait on them himself! This is how Jesus will reward us if he returns to find us ready for him.

But woe to those who are unprepared, who are sleepwalking their way through life. They will be like the bad servant who loses patience while waiting for his master's return, and starts being mean to the other servants, and helps himself to food and too much drink. When the master comes back unexpectedly, he will be very angry, and the servant will surely be punished!

So let us be ready, for if we are not prepared when Jesus comes, there will be no time to get ready then. Let him instead find us watching, waiting, and serving God as best we can.

PRAYER

Thank you, Lord Jesus, that one day you will come back to earth. Help me every day to live in a way that shows I am ready for your coming.

Amen

THE MUSTARD SEED AND THE YEAST

Jesus told another parable: "The kingdom of heaven is like a mustard seed, which a man took and planted. Even though it is the smallest of all seeds, when it grows, it outgrows all the other herbs and becomes a tree, big enough that the birds come and perch in its branches."

Then he continued, "The kingdom of heaven is like yeast that a woman took and mixed into about sixty pounds of flour until it worked all through the dough." You only need a very small amount of yeast to add to some flour and water and a bit of salt and sugar to make a lovely big loaf of bread. Just a small piece of yeast will have a huge effect.

Jesus was saying that we are never too small to be important in God's eyes, and that however little we are, we can help to grow the kingdom of God. From small beginnings can come wonderful things!

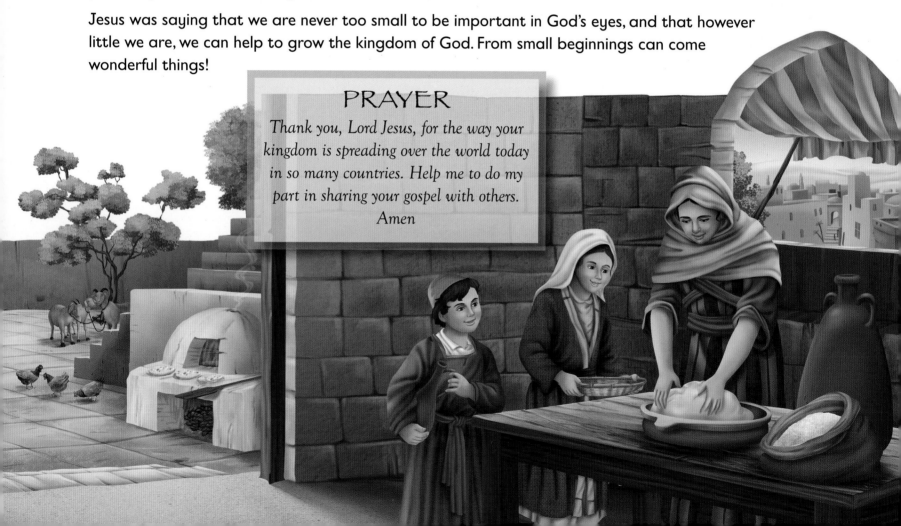

PRAYER

Thank you, Lord Jesus, for the way your kingdom is spreading over the world today in so many countries. Help me to do my part in sharing your gospel with others.

Amen

THE USELESS FIG TREE

Jesus told a story about a man who had a fig tree in his vineyard. He went to look at it, hoping to find some fruit, and was disappointed to see that there was none on it. He found the gardener and told him that he had been looking for fruit on this tree for three years now, and it was about time that it was cut down! It was using up precious soil for nothing.

But the gardener pleaded with his master to leave the tree for one more year to see if it would bear fruit. He offered to dig up the soil around the tree and add fertilizer to it. After a year, if it still produced no fruit, he would cut it down. His master agreed.

The parable was referring to the nation of Israel, but the message is for all of us even today: God is the owner of the vineyard, and Jesus is his gardener. Jesus has come to plead for more time for us to bear fruit—and, more than that, he is prepared to help us by tending the soil around us! Let's make the most of his tender care and bear fruit for him.

PRAYER

Thank you, Lord Jesus, for your great patience. Please help me to follow your example and learn to wait patiently for things to come at the right time.
Amen

THE GREAT BANQUET

Jesus told a story about a man who was preparing a great feast. It was to be a very special occasion, for it was in honor of his son's wedding. He had invited many guests, and when the food was ready he sent his servant to tell them it was time to come. But every last one of them had an excuse and would not come—and some were rude and nasty to the servant!

When the man heard this, he was furious. He told his servant to go back outside, and this time he was to invite all the poor people, anyone who was blind or crippled or lame, and bring them in to enjoy the banquet. And when this had been done, the servant told his master that all the places at the table weren't yet full. The man told him to search further afield and find yet more people and make them come in so that his house would be full. As for his original guests, he promised that not a single one of them would get even a taste of his feast!

God had invited his people to be saved through his Son, Jesus Christ, but many of them, especially the Pharisees and the teachers of the law, had refused to accept Jesus as their Savior. They had made all kinds of excuses to explain why he wasn't the Son of God and had taken refuge in all their laws and traditions. So God extended his invitation all across the world to everybody, not just the Jews.

God has invited us all to his wonderful feast—let's not miss out!

PRAYER

I am so glad, Lord Jesus, that you welcome all kinds of people into your family. Make me glad to share with them all the good things you provide for us all.

Amen

LOST AND FOUND

The Pharisees and the teachers of the law muttered among themselves when they saw Jesus mixing with tax collectors and sinners. Jesus explained how there will be far more rejoicing in heaven over the one sinner who repents than over the ninety-nine good people who don't need to repent.

He had told them about the shepherd who would search high and low for one missing sheep even though his other ninety-nine sheep were safe and sound, and how thrilled the shepherd would be when he found the lost sheep.

Now he told them to picture a woman who had ten silver coins and who had lost one of those coins. "Wouldn't she light a lamp?" Jesus asked them. "Don't you think she would take a brush, sweep every corner of the room, and search every nook and cranny until she found it? And when she did, how happy and relieved would she be? Surely she would get all her friends and neighbors together and tell them about the lost coin and how she had found it, and ask them to be happy for her."

Jesus finished by saying, "In the same way, the angels will rejoice over every single sinner who repents."

Jesus cares about each and every one of us. He is never satisfied with all the people who do believe in him and try to live in the way he teaches. No, we are all so important to him that he will try to save every last one of us.

PRAYER

Lord Jesus, I am trying to imagine all the joy of heaven when someone turns to you. I always want to make you happy, so please help me to always be turning away from sin.
Amen

HIDDEN TREASURE

Jesus was speaking to his disciples. Everyone else had gone, but he had a special message for his friends: "The kingdom of heaven is like treasure hidden in a field. When a man found it, he hid it again, and he was so happy and full of joy that he sold all he had and bought that field!"

He continued, "The kingdom of heaven is like a merchant on the lookout for beautiful pearls. When he found one of great price, he went away and sold everything he had so that he could buy it."

Jesus was talking about the most important thing of all—God's love. This love is the greatest treasure that we can possibly find. It is more precious than silver or gold or jewels—and absolutely worth giving everything else up for!

PRAYER

Lord Jesus, help me to be as thrilled about your kingdom as when someone discovers buried treasure. Help me to value your love above everything else.

Amen

THE RICH MAN AND THE BEGGAR

Jesus told another story: "There was once a rich man who lived in a grand house and whose table was laid every day as if for a feast. At his gate lay a poor, hungry beggar called Lazarus, who used to long for the crumbs that fell from his table! But the rich man was selfish and never stopped to think about poor Lazarus. At last Lazarus died, and the angels carried him to Abraham's side, where he felt no more pain or hunger.

"Some time after, the rich man also died, but no angels came for him. He was sent to the place for wicked people. In torment he begged, 'Father Abraham, have pity and send Lazarus to dip his finger in water and cool my tongue, for I'm so thirsty!'

"But Abraham replied, 'Son, remember that you received your good things in your time on earth while Lazarus suffered greatly, but now he is comforted here and you are in agony.'

"The rich man pleaded that his brothers might be warned, but Abraham told him they already had the writings of Moses and the prophets to warn them. It would be their own fault if they didn't change their ways in time to avoid the same fate as him!"

PRAYER

Thank you, Lord Jesus, for your stories, which teach me the truth. Help me always to know that eternity is real and that through your death I can have a place in heaven forever.
Amen

THE GRATEFUL LEPER

One time, when Jesus was going into a village, he was met by a sad sight—ten men, all suffering from leprosy. They stayed well back, but they cried out in loud voices, "Jesus, please take pity on us!"

Jesus told them to go straight to the priests, and as they went they saw that their sores had gone— their skin was smooth once again! They shouted and danced in joy and made their way to the priests as quickly as they could.

But one of the men, as soon as he realized that he was healed, rushed straight back to Jesus, praising God at the top of his voice. He threw himself to the ground before Jesus and thanked him with all his heart.

Jesus looked down at the grateful man. "Didn't I clean ten men? Where are the other nine? Are you the only one to come back to thank God?" Then he said kindly, "Go on your way now. Your faith has made you well."

Let us always remember to thank God for all the wonderful things he gives us and for his everlasting love.

PRAYER

Lord Jesus, I am so grateful for your saving love to me: thank you. Help me also to always say "thank you" to those around me who do so much for me.
Amen

THE HUMBLE WILL BECOME IMPORTANT

On another occasion, Jesus looked around at his followers. Some among them thought very well of themselves, and so Jesus told this story: "Two men went into the temple to pray. One was a Pharisee, who always paid great attention to the letter of the law, while the other was a despised tax collector. In the temple, the Pharisee stood by himself and prayed: 'God, I thank you that I'm not like other people—robbers, criminals, adulterers—or even like this tax collector. I fast twice a week and give a tenth of all I get!' He thought he was very good and far better than everyone else!

"But the tax collector stood humbly at a distance. He would not even look up to heaven, but beat his breast and said, 'God, have mercy on me, for I'm nothing but a miserable sinner.'"

Jesus looked around at those who were listening. "It wasn't the self-important Pharisee who earned God's love and forgiveness that day—it was the humble tax collector. For all those who show off and think themselves important will be humbled, and those who humble themselves will become important."

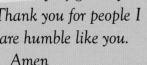

PRAYER

As I grow up, Lord Jesus, keep me humble and save me from ever feeling I can make myself good by the things I do. Thank you for people I know who are humble like you.
Amen

THE RICH RULER

Once, a rich ruler came to ask Jesus what he must do to inherit eternal life. Jesus told him that he must keep all the commandments that Moses had been given, and the ruler replied, "All these I have kept since I was a boy."

Jesus looked at him. "You still lack one thing. Sell everything you have and give to the poor, and you will have treasure in heaven. Then come and follow me."

When he heard this, the ruler was sad, for he was very wealthy.

"How hard it is for the rich to enter the kingdom of God!" Jesus said. "In fact, it is easier for a camel to go through the eye of a needle than for someone who is rich to enter God's kingdom."

But he told his disciples who had left all they had to follow him, "You can be sure that everyone who has left behind their home or their loved ones for my sake will be given so much more in return, as well as eternal life."

PRAYER

I pray today, Lord Jesus, for missionaries across the world who have left everything behind to spread your message. Please be near to them and give them much in return.

Amen

BAGS OF GOLD

Once there was a man heading off on a journey. He entrusted his wealth to his servants before he left according to their abilities, giving one of them five bags of gold, another two bags, and one bag to the third.

When he returned and called the servants before him, the first one announced, "Sir, I put your money to work, and with the five bags of gold you gave me I have made five more." His master was very pleased and told him that since he had been able to trust him with a few things, he would gladly put him in charge of many things.

The second servant told him he had gained two more bags on top of the ones given to him, and again, the master was pleased that he could be trusted and put him in charge of many things.

Last of all, the third servant spoke up. "Master," he said, "I know that you are a hard man, and I was scared, so I hid the gold in a hole in the ground so it would be safe. Here it is now," and he handed over the bag of gold.

The master was angry. "You have been wicked and lazy," he exclaimed. "You could at least have put my money in the bank so it could earn some interest!" He gave the bag of gold to the one who had ten bags and then had the worthless servant thrown out of the house!

God expects us to use whatever gifts he has given to us. If we do, he will give us even more, but if we don't, he may take them away and give them to someone who will use them.

PRAYER

*Lord Jesus, thank you for the
things I can do well and enjoy.
Help me to use the abilities
you have given me to please
you and to serve others.*

Amen

THE LAST WILL BE FIRST

Jesus told a parable: "The kingdom of heaven is like the vineyard owner who went out one morning to hire workers. He agreed to pay them a certain sum of money for the day and set them to work. Later on, he went back to the marketplace and hired more men and told them he'd pay them whatever was right. He did the same thing at lunchtime, again in the afternoon, and once more at about five. When evening came, he told his foreman to pay the workers, beginning with the last ones hired.

"The workers who were hired late received the same amount that had been promised to the first workers. So when those came who were hired first, they expected to receive more, and when they didn't, they began to grumble. 'These worked only one hour,' complained one, 'and you have given them the same as those of us who worked all day long in the blazing heat!'

"The owner answered, 'I'm not being unfair. Didn't you agree to work for this amount? I want to give the one hired last the same as you. Don't I have the right to do what I want with my own money? Or are you annoyed because I'm generous?'

"So the last will be first, and the first will be last."

PRAYER

Lord Jesus, help me not to be jealous when you are good to other people. Help me not to be a grumbler, but to be glad for all you have given me.
Amen

WISE AND FOOLISH GIRLS

Jesus tried to make his followers understand that they must be ready at all times for his return, for they would never know when it might happen. He told them a story: "Once ten girls were waiting to join a wedding feast. Five were foolish, and while they brought lamps, they had no spare oil. The other five were sensible and brought extra oil. It was late and the girls fell asleep, for the bridegroom was long in coming.

"Suddenly, at midnight, a cry rang out, for the bridegroom was coming. Excitedly, the girls went to light their lamps, but those of the foolish girls began to flicker, for their oil had run out. They begged for more oil, but the wise girls replied, 'No, for there is not enough for all of us. You will have to go and buy some more!' And they went off to join the bridegroom and went in with him to the feast.

"By the time the foolish girls returned with lighted lamps, the door was shut, and though they knocked loudly, they were told, 'You are too late. I don't know who you are!'"

Jesus told his disciples, "Always be ready, because you don't know the day or the hour of my return!"

PRAYER

Lord Jesus, thank you that you teach me true wisdom and you show me how to live well. Please remind me to always be ready for your return.
Amen

BLIND BARTIMAEUS

Jesus was passing through Jericho on his way to Jerusalem. Blind Bartimaeus was begging by the roadside when he heard a great commotion around him. When he learned that it was Jesus of Nazareth, of whom he had heard so many wonderful things, he struggled to his feet and called out, "Jesus, Son of David, have mercy on me!"

People shushed him, but he kept calling. Jesus heard him and stopped by the roadside. "What do you want me to do for you?" he asked gently.

Bartimaeus fell to his knees. "Lord, I want to see!" he begged.

"Receive your sight," said Jesus. "Your faith has healed you." Immediately Bartimaeus' eyes were cleared and he could see everything around him! Instantly, he jumped up and followed Jesus, praising God. When all the people saw him, they praised God too!

PRAYER

*Lord Jesus, so often I am blind to who you are. Please open the eyes of my heart so that I may see you, follow you, and praise God.
Amen*

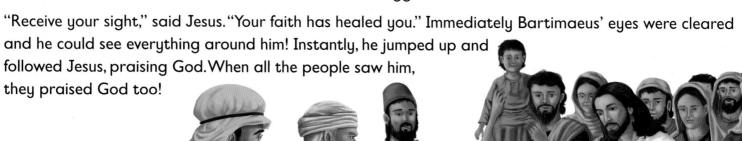

ZACCHAEUS IN THE TREE

The streets of Jericho were lined with people eager to catch a glimpse of Jesus. Among them was a tax collector called Zacchaeus. Everyone hated tax collectors and believed that they stole some of the taxes to line their own pockets, so no one would make way for him, and he was too short to see over the crowd. He was feeling frustrated. Then he had a great idea: he would climb a tree! From its branches, he could see the procession as it made its way toward him. Perfect!

He almost fell off the branch when Jesus stopped right below and said, "Zacchaeus, come down now. I must stay at your house today." He scrambled down and bowed before Jesus as the crowd muttered angrily about Jesus visiting a sinner!

But Zacchaeus was already a changed man. He said to Jesus, "Lord! I'm going to give half of everything I have to the poor, and if I have cheated anybody out of anything, I'll pay back four times the amount!"

Then Jesus turned to the crowd and said, "It is lost people like Zacchaeus that I came to save. Today he has found salvation!"

PRAYER

Thank you, Lord Jesus, that you know all about me. You know my name and you know where I live and you want to come into my life. Thank you that when you are part of my life, everything is so different.

Amen

THE EXPENSIVE PERFUME

One evening, shortly before Passover, Jesus was dining with his disciples and friends in Bethany. Mary came to him, carrying an expensive jar of perfume. Kneeling before him, she carefully poured the perfume on his feet, using her own hair to wipe them. The house was filled with the wonderful fragrance.

Some started to scold her, for the perfume could have been sold to raise money for the poor. Jesus hushed them. "She has done a beautiful thing," he said. "You will always have the poor, and you can help them anytime you want. But you won't always have me. People will remember Mary's kindness to me."

For Jesus would not be with them in this way for much longer. The final stage of his time on earth was about to begin.

PRAYER

Lord Jesus, help me to copy Mary's example and give my very best to you. Help me to honor you with what I have and by kneeling in worship to you.
Amen

JESUS ENTERS JERUSALEM

Jerusalem was packed. It was the week of the Passover festival, and everyone had gathered to celebrate. It was also time for Jesus to start the last stage of his earthly life.

Jesus entered Jerusalem riding a humble donkey. Some of his followers threw their cloaks or large palm leaves on the dusty ground before him, and he was met by an enormous crowd, for many had heard of the miracles he had performed. Some of the religious leaders feared and hated Jesus, but many of the people truly saw him as their King, and they tried to give him a king's welcome.

His followers cried out, "Hosanna to the Son of David! Blessed is the king who comes in the name of the Lord!"

But Jesus was sad, for he knew that in a very short time these people cheering him would turn against him.

PRAYER

Thank you, Lord Jesus, that you are the promised Son of David, and you truly are the King of kings. Thank you that one day, everyone will honor your name. Help me to praise you today.

Amen

TROUBLE IN THE TEMPLE

The first thing Jesus did in Jerusalem was to visit his Father's temple. He was appalled to find that all the greedy, cheating people that he had thrown out before were back again, trying to make money out of the poor people who came to make sacrifices to God. He looked around in anger, shouting, "No! God said that this temple was to be a place where people from all nations could come to pray to him. But you have made it a den of robbers!" And with these words he tore through the temple, throwing everyone out who shouldn't be there.

When he had finished and the temple was once again calm and tranquil, the poor people, the beggars, and the sick began to find their way back in and came to Jesus to be healed and to feel better. Children danced for joy around him, and everyone was happy—apart from the Pharisees, who plotted to get rid of him.

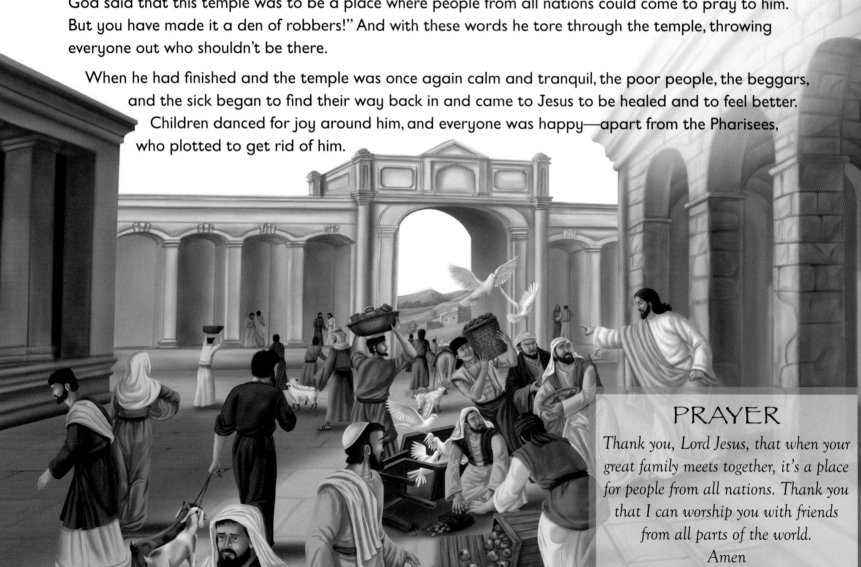

PRAYER

Thank you, Lord Jesus, that when your great family meets together, it's a place for people from all nations. Thank you that I can worship you with friends from all parts of the world.

Amen

BY WHOSE AUTHORITY?

Each day Jesus would go to the temple to teach his followers and to offer comfort and healing to those in need of it. The priests, the teachers of the law, and the elders were not happy about this.

"Who gave you authority to do these things?" they asked him, and Jesus replied, "I'll ask you one question. If you can answer me, then I will tell you by what authority I'm doing these things. Tell me, was John's baptism from heaven, or of human origin?"

The priests and elders didn't know how to answer. If they said it was from heaven, then he would ask why they didn't believe him. But if they said it was of human origin, then the people would be angry, for they truly believed that John was a prophet. In the end, they mumbled, "We don't know."

Jesus said, "Then I won't tell you by what authority I'm doing these things."

PRAYER

Thank you, Lord Jesus, that all authority is given to you in heaven and on earth. Help me to understand what this means and to know that I can trust you for everything.

Amen

THE WICKED TENANTS

Jesus told a parable: "Once a man planted a vineyard, rented it to some farmers, and then went away. At harvest time he sent a servant to collect his share of the fruit. But the tenants beat the servant and sent him away with nothing. He sent another servant, but again they beat him and sent him away empty-handed. He sent a third, and that one was killed!

"In the end, he decided to send his beloved son. 'Surely they will respect him,' he thought to himself.

"But when the tenants saw him coming, they plotted among themselves. 'This is the heir,' they said. 'If we get rid of him, we will become the new owners!' And they threw him out of the vineyard and killed him."

Jesus looked at the priests and Pharisees who were listening. "What do you think the owner of the vineyard will do to the tenants when he finds out?"

"Kill them and give the vineyard to others who will give him his rightful share," they replied. But when they realized Jesus had been talking about them, they felt tricked and angry!

PRAYER

Lord Jesus, I am so glad you came from heaven to save us. I am sorry that bad people hated you and plotted to kill you. Help me never to stand with those who despise you, even if I am the only one.
Amen

GIVE TO CAESAR . . .

The chief priests and Pharisees sent spies to try to find evidence against Jesus. Once, they asked him, "Teacher, please tell us, is it right for us to pay taxes to Caesar or not?" They thought they had trapped him, for if he answered that they shouldn't pay taxes, then they could hand him over to the Romans for rebellion. But if he answered that they should pay taxes, then he would become unpopular with the people.

But Jesus saw through their tricks. "Show me a denarius*," he said, and when someone handed a coin to him, he asked, "Tell me, whose head is on that coin and whose inscription?" The spies replied that it was Caesar's.

Then he said to them, "Then give back to Caesar what is Caesar's, and to God what is God's," and the spies were silent.

*A Roman coin

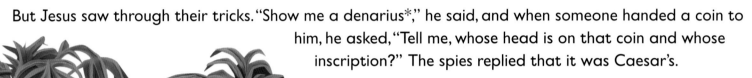

PRAYER

Lord Jesus, I feel so sad that people whom you had made could treat you so badly. I can't understand why they were so mean. I am glad that you are all-knowing and all-wise.
Amen

THE WIDOW'S OFFERING

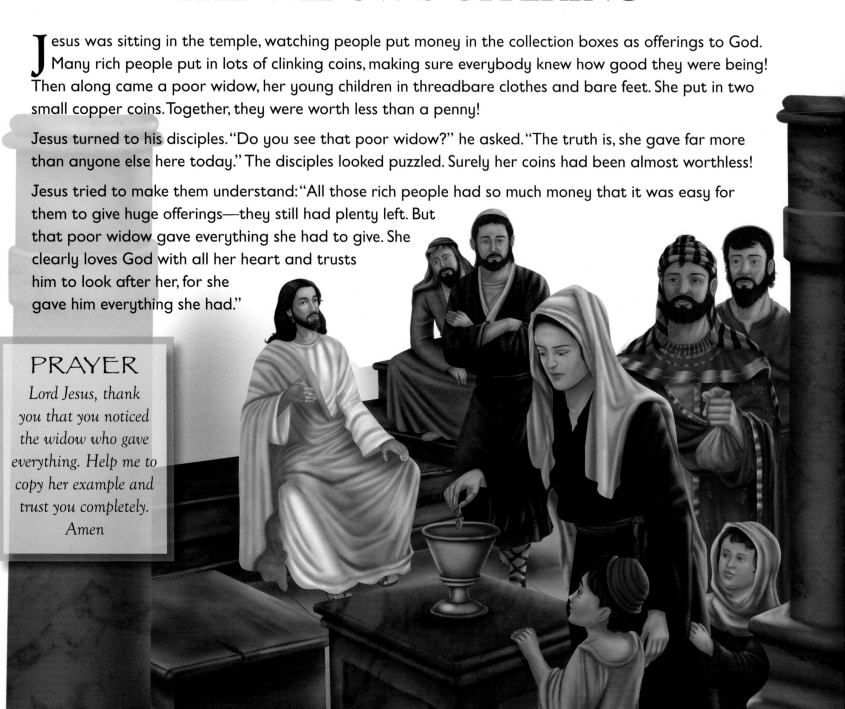

Jesus was sitting in the temple, watching people put money in the collection boxes as offerings to God. Many rich people put in lots of clinking coins, making sure everybody knew how good they were being! Then along came a poor widow, her young children in threadbare clothes and bare feet. She put in two small copper coins. Together, they were worth less than a penny!

Jesus turned to his disciples. "Do you see that poor widow?" he asked. "The truth is, she gave far more than anyone else here today." The disciples looked puzzled. Surely her coins had been almost worthless!

Jesus tried to make them understand: "All those rich people had so much money that it was easy for them to give huge offerings—they still had plenty left. But that poor widow gave everything she had to give. She clearly loves God with all her heart and trusts him to look after her, for she gave him everything she had."

PRAYER

Lord Jesus, thank you that you noticed the widow who gave everything. Help me to copy her example and trust you completely.
Amen

BE READY!

As Jesus was leaving the temple, some of his disciples stopped to admire the building. "These buildings may well look impressive," Jesus told them, "but I tell you that not one stone will be left standing; they will all be thrown down!"

They asked him later when that time would come, and what sign there would be. "You must beware," Jesus answered. "There will be many false prophets trying to deceive you. There will be wars, earthquakes, and famines. You must be on your guard.

"The gospel must be preached throughout the world. You will be persecuted and hated, but stand firm to the end and you will be saved. When I do come, you must be ready. Just like the servants who have been left to look after their master's house when he is away, you must keep watch. For you don't know when the master will come back—it could be early in the morning, late at night, or anytime at all. Don't let him find you sleeping when he does return!"

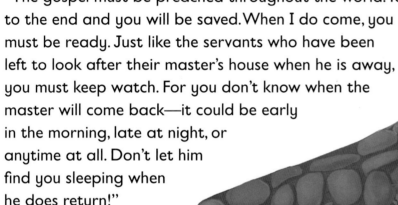

PRAYER

Thank you, Lord Jesus, that I live in a place where I can read your book and pray. I do want to be busy for you when you come back. Please be with Christians today who are persecuted. Keep them strong.
Amen

SHEEP AND GOATS

Jesus told his disciples, "When the Son of Man comes again, he will divide all the people into two groups, like a shepherd separating his sheep from his goats. He will say to the good people, 'Come and enjoy your kingdom, for you gave me food when I was hungry, water when I was thirsty, and shelter when I had no place to stay. When I was sick you cared for me and when I had no clothes you gave me something to wear. For anything that you did for any of my people, you did for me.'

"To the bad people he will say, 'God will punish you, for you gave me no food or water when I was hungry or thirsty, nothing to wear when I was naked. When I had no shelter you didn't take me in, and when I was sick you didn't care for me. For whatever you did not do for any of my people, you did not do for me.'

"Then those people will be sent away to eternal punishment, but the good people will enjoy eternal life."

God wants us to be filled with love and kindness and show that love in the things we do for others.

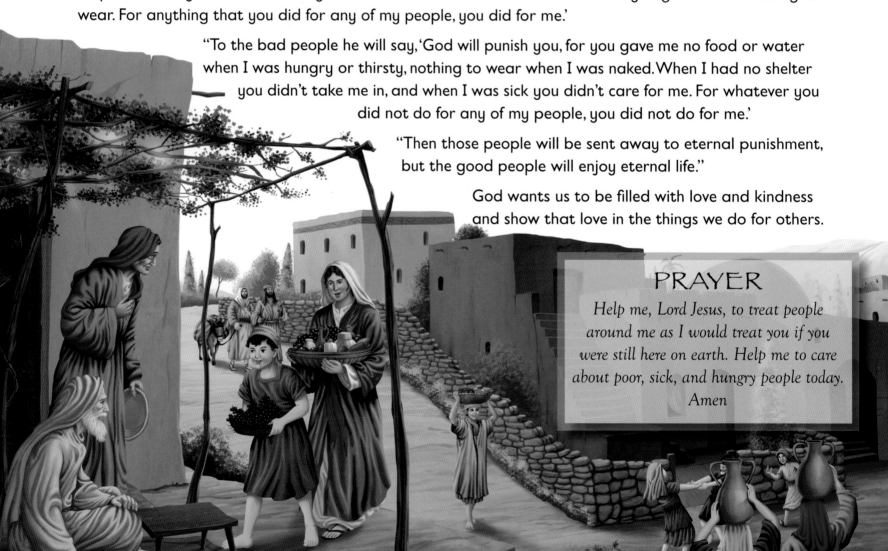

PRAYER

Help me, Lord Jesus, to treat people around me as I would treat you if you were still here on earth. Help me to care about poor, sick, and hungry people today.

Amen

BETRAYAL

Jesus knew that the Pharisees and those who hated and feared him were waiting for any opportunity to arrest him. He spent the days in Jerusalem in the temple, but each night he returned to Bethany to sleep. Yet even among his dearest friends there was one who would be his enemy.

Judas Iscariot, the disciple in charge of the money, was dishonest. He kept some for himself instead of giving it to those who needed it. His greed made him do a very bad thing. Judas went to the chief priests in secret and asked them how much they would give him if he delivered Jesus into their hands.

The priests couldn't believe their ears! They knew that Judas was one of Jesus' closest, most trusted friends. They offered him thirty pieces of silver…and Judas accepted! From then on, Judas was simply waiting for the opportunity to hand Jesus over.

PRAYER
Lord Jesus, I feel hurt that one of your close friends became your enemy. I feel so sad about this story. Please give me your peace in my heart to know that you were in control of everything, even on that dreadful day.
Amen

LIKE A SERVANT

It was nearly time for the Passover feast, and a kind man had set aside a room for the disciples to prepare for it. That night, when they were eating, Jesus left the table, wrapped a towel around his waist, filled a basin with water, and then, kneeling on the floor, began to wash and dry the disciples' feet like a servant.

The disciples were speechless, but when he knelt before Simon Peter, the disciple protested, "Lord, you mustn't wash my feet!"

Jesus replied gently, "You don't understand what I'm doing, but later it will be clear to you. Unless I wash you, you won't really belong to me," to which Peter begged him to wash his hands and head too!

But Jesus answered, "If you have bathed, then you only need to wash your feet; your body is clean."

Jesus had washed their feet like a servant so that they could learn to do the same for one another.

PRAYER

Lord Jesus, you were the most humble servant, even washing the feet of your friends. Help me to copy your example of humility and never to imagine that I am too important for any jobs you give me.
Amen

THE LORD'S SUPPER

Jesus knew he would soon have to leave his friends. He was sad and troubled. "Soon, one of you will betray me," he said sorrowfully. The disciples looked at one another in shock. Who could he mean?

"The one who dips his bread with mine is the one," said Jesus, and when Judas Iscariot dipped his bread into the same bowl, Jesus said softly, "Go and do what you have to do," and Judas left. But the others didn't understand.

Then Jesus handed around some bread, saying "This is my body, which will be broken." Next, he passed around a cup of wine, saying, "Drink this. It is my blood, which will take away sin," and he told them he would soon be leaving them.

Simon Peter cried out, "But Lord, where are you going? Why can't I follow you? I would readily lay down my life for you!"

"Would you, my friend?" asked Jesus gently. "And yet you will disown me three times before the cock crows!" Peter was horrified. He felt this could never happen.

PRAYER

Lord Jesus, I am so sad that your close friends let you down so badly. I don't want to let you down, but I know I am weak too. Please give me courage to always confess you as my Lord.
Amen

THE WAY TO THE FATHER

Jesus tried to comfort the disciples, saying that he was going ahead to prepare a place for them in his Father's house, and that they would know how to find their way there. When they asked how, he replied, "I am the way and the truth and the life. The only way to the Father is through believing in me. If you really know me, you will know my Father as well.

"I am the vine, and my Father is the gardener. He will cut off branches that bear no fruit but look after those that do. You are the branches and will bear fruit, so long as you remain in me.

"As the Father has loved me, so have I loved you. And I give you this command: Love one another, just as I have loved each of you, and everyone will know that you are my disciples. There is no greater love than to lay down one's life for one's friends.

"And remember that if the world seems to hate you, it hated me first. It is because you don't belong to it that it will hate you!"

PRAYER

Thank you, Lord Jesus, that you truly are the way to God the Father. Thank you for the wonderful home you are preparing for all who love you. Thank you that you are taking care of those I love who are already in your home.

Amen

A NIGHT OF PRAYER

Jesus and the disciples left the city to go to a quiet garden called Gethsemane. Jesus prayed to his Father for his disciples and for all those who would come to believe in him because of the message they would spread throughout the world.

Then Jesus went to one side, but he took Peter, James, and John with him, asking them to keep him company. He went a little way away from them to pray in private.

"Father," he cried out in anguish, "if it is possible, may I not have to go through this!" Yet his very next words were, "Yet let it not be as I will, but as you will, Father," for Jesus knew that God wasn't making him do anything: He had chosen freely to do it.

When he returned to his friends, they were sleeping. "Couldn't you men keep watch with me for just one hour?" he sighed. He went again to talk to his Father, but when he returned, the disciples were fast asleep again. This happened once more, and this time when he woke them, he said, "The hour has come. You need to get up, for the one who has betrayed me is here!"

PRAYER

Thank you so much, Lord Jesus, that you willingly came to be our Savior, and you chose to give your life to pay for our forgiveness. Teach me how to pray like you for God's will, rather than my own.
Amen

BETRAYED WITH A KISS

A crowd of people burst into the garden, many armed with weapons. At the head of them was Judas Iscariot. He had told the chief priests that he would kiss Jesus so that they would know whom to arrest. As Judas approached him, Jesus said sadly, "Oh Judas, would you betray the Son of Man with a kiss?"

Peter drew his sword, but Jesus told him to put his sword away, and he allowed the soldiers to arrest him. "I'm the one you have come to find," he said quietly. "Let these others go. You had no need to come here with swords and clubs. You could easily have taken me when I was in the temple courts."

When the disciples realized that Jesus was going to allow himself to be taken prisoner, they fled in fear and despair.

PRAYER

Lord Jesus, I don't like this part of your story. It's all so unfair. I know that today good people are also being betrayed, and I ask that you will be close to them and make them strong.
Amen

A COCK CROWS

When the soldiers took Jesus to be questioned, Simon Peter followed them to the courtyard of the high priest. He waited outside miserably along with the guards warming themselves at the fire. As one of the servant girls was walking by, she caught sight of Peter by the fire. "Weren't you with Jesus of Nazareth?" she asked him. "I'm sure I saw you with him."

"No, you've got the wrong man!" Peter hissed quietly, hoping no one else had heard, for he feared what would happen if they believed he was one of Jesus' disciples.

The girl shrugged and walked away, but on her way back, she said to one of the guards, "Don't you think he looks like one of Jesus' followers?"

"I don't have anything to do with him!" panicked Peter.

Now the other guards were looking at him. "You must be one of them," said one. "I can tell from your accent you're from Galilee."

"I swear I've never even met him!" cried Peter, his heart racing. At that very moment, a cock crowed. Peter remembered what Jesus had said, and he broke down and wept in dismay.

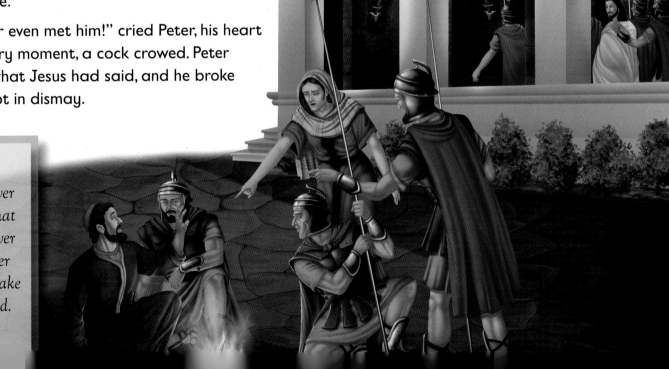

PRAYER

Lord Jesus, help me never to be ashamed to say that I belong to you. Wherever your followers are under pressure today, please make them bold and unafraid.
Amen

PASSED AROUND

The priests and Pharisees spent the night questioning Jesus. They asked him if he was the Messiah, the Son of God, and Jesus replied, "You have said so. But from now on you will see the Son of Man sitting at the right hand of God."

They were furious, but only the Roman governor, Pontius Pilate, could order his death. So they dragged him before Pilate, but although Pilate asked Jesus many questions, he could find no reason to put him to death. "But he's a troublemaker!" the priests complained. "He started in Galilee and made his way here!"

When Pilate realized that Jesus came from Galilee, he saw a way of getting rid of the problem, for Herod was in charge of that area. So Jesus was taken before Herod. But however many questions Herod asked, Jesus remained grave and silent. In the end, Herod grew tired of his silence. Then he and his soldiers made fun of Jesus before sending him back to Pilate.

PRAYER

Lord Jesus, help me never to be found among those who make fun of you. Also, please help me to know when to speak and when to keep quiet.

Amen

PILATE WASHES HIS HANDS

Pilate was under pressure to order the execution of Jesus, but there was one possible way out. During Passover it was the custom to release one prisoner. At that time, there was a man named Barabbas in prison for rebellion and murder. Pilate called the priests and the people before him and asked who they wanted him to release, and the crowd answered, "Barabbas!" for they had been told to say this.

"What shall I do with the one you call King of the Jews?" Pilate asked them.

"Crucify him!" roared the crowd.

"But why?" continued Pilate. "For what crime?" But the crowd only shouted all the louder.

Pilate didn't want to order the execution, but neither did he want a riot! He sent for a bowl of water and washed his hands in it to show that he took no responsibility for Jesus' death. Then he released Barabbas and had Jesus handed over to be crucified.

PRAYER

Lord Jesus, I know that a bowl of water can never take away wrongdoing. Thank you that by your death, you have made a way for true forgiveness.

Amen

MOCKED

Jesus was taken away by the soldiers. "Since you are the King of the Jews, let's dress you for the occasion!" they mocked, and they dressed him in a purple robe, the color worn by kings, and put a crown of thorny branches upon his head. Then they beat him and spat in his face before putting him back in his own clothes and leading him through the streets toward Golgotha, the place where he was to be crucified.

They made him carry the wooden cross on his back, but it was large and heavy, and Jesus had been dreadfully beaten. When he could do it no longer, they snatched someone from out of the crowd to carry it for him. And so the dreadful procession made its way out of the city to the hill of Golgotha.

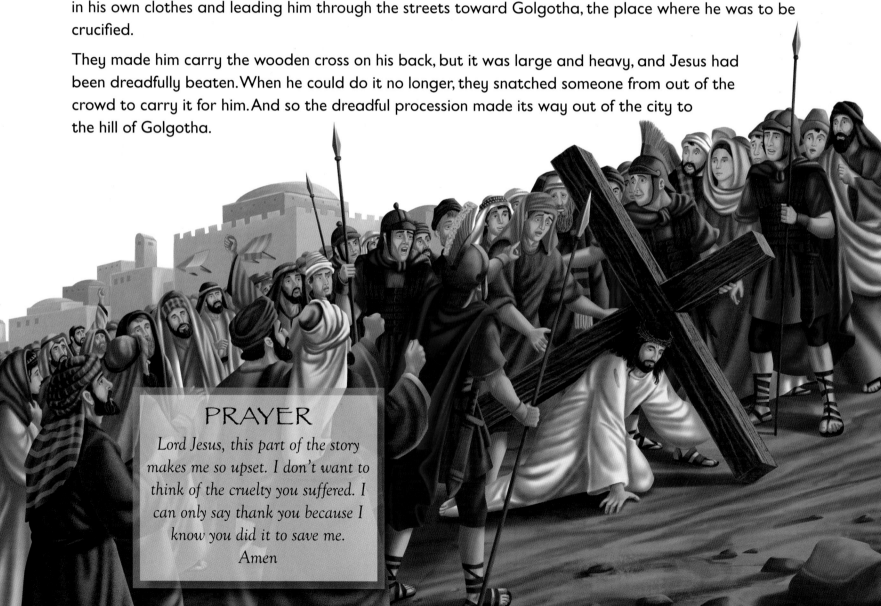

PRAYER

Lord Jesus, this part of the story makes me so upset. I don't want to think of the cruelty you suffered. I can only say thank you because I know you did it to save me.

Amen

THE CRUCIFIXION

Soldiers nailed Jesus' hands and feet to the cross and placed above his head a sign saying, "JESUS OF NAZARETH, KING OF THE JEWS." As they raised the cross, Jesus cried, "Father, forgive them. They don't know what they're doing."

Two thieves were crucified beside him. The first sneered at him, but the other said, "Be quiet! We deserve our punishment, but this man has done nothing wrong." Then he turned to Jesus and said, "Please remember me when you come into your kingdom," and Jesus promised he would be with him that day in Paradise.

The guards drew lots to see who would win Jesus' clothes while the priests and Pharisees taunted him. "If you come down from the cross now, we'll believe in you!" they mocked.

PRAYER

Lord Jesus, I know that the day you died was the most important day in history. I know that people are divided by your cross: Some still want to make fun of you, but I want to always honor your sacrifice.

Amen

THE DEATH OF JESUS

At midday, a shadow passed across the sun and darkness fell over the land for three long hours. At three o'clock in the afternoon, Jesus cried out in a loud voice, "My God, why have you forsaken me?" Then he gave a great cry, "It is finished!" and with these words, he gave up his spirit.

At that moment the earth shook, and the curtain in the holy temple was torn from top to bottom. When the Roman soldiers felt the ground move beneath their feet and saw how Jesus passed away, they were deeply shaken. "Surely he was the Son of God!" whispered one in amazement.

PRAYER

Thank you, Lord Jesus, Son of God, for dying on the cross. Thank you for finishing the work of salvation. Thank you for opening the way to God and heaven.

Amen

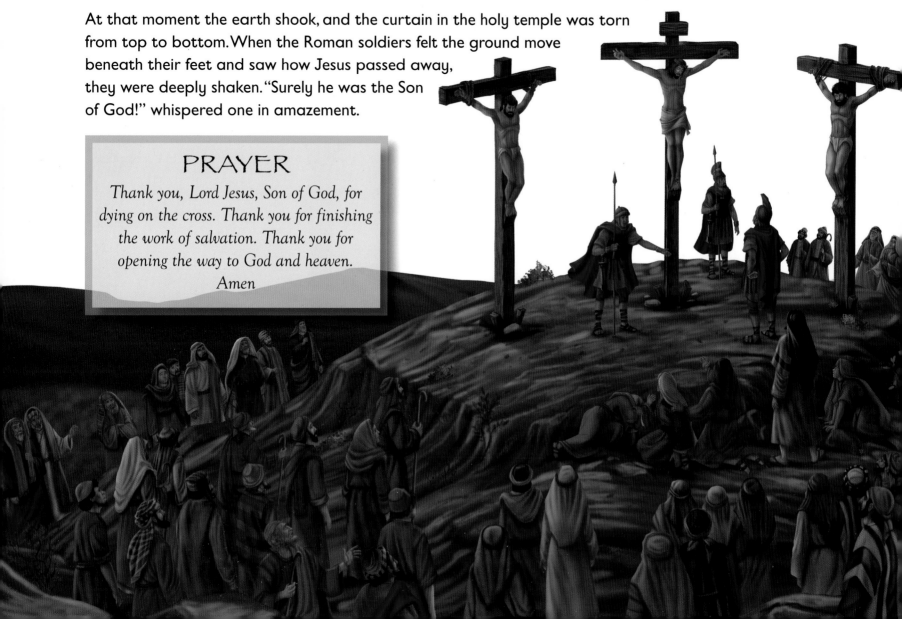

THE BURIAL

B ecause the next day was to be a special Sabbath, the Jewish leaders didn't want the bodies left on the crosses, and so they asked Pilate to have them taken down. A man named Joseph of Arimathea asked permission to take Jesus' body away, and so Jesus' friends carefully wrapped the body in linen and spices, and then placed it in a tomb that Joseph had had built for himself. Then they rolled a large stone in front of the entrance to the tomb and sadly left.

But the very next day, the chief priests and the Pharisees went to Pilate and asked him to place a guard on the tomb and to seal it, for they remembered that when he was alive Jesus had said, "After three days I will rise again." They believed that his disciples might come and steal the body and then try to persuade the people that he had been raised from the dead. Pilate told them to make the tomb secure, and they did.

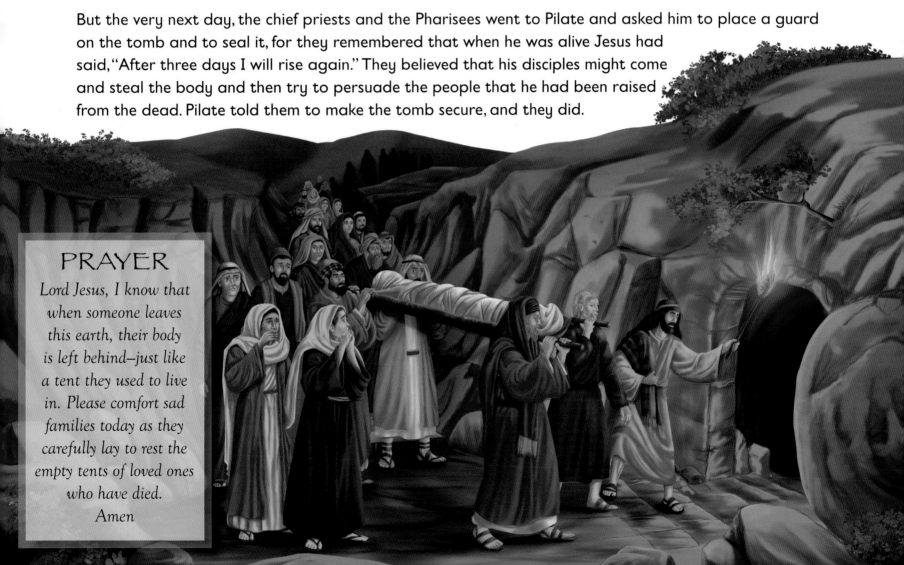

PRAYER

Lord Jesus, I know that when someone leaves this earth, their body is left behind—just like a tent they used to live in. Please comfort sad families today as they carefully lay to rest the empty tents of loved ones who have died.

Amen

THE EMPTY TOMB

Early on the first day of the week, before the sun had fully risen, Mary Magdalene and some other women went to anoint the body. As they came near to the tomb, the earth shook, the guards were thrown to the ground, and the women saw that the stone had been rolled away from the entrance. And inside the tomb, shining brighter than the sun, was an angel!

The terrified women fell to their knees, but the angel said, "Why are you looking for the living among the dead. He is not here—he has risen! Don't you remember that he told you this would happen? Look and see, and then go and tell his disciples that he will meet them in Galilee as he promised."

So the women hurried away to tell the disciples the news, afraid yet filled with joy.

PRAYER

Lord Jesus, I have been waiting for this story. I am so glad that the story of Easter is true. You have defeated death, and you have risen! Help me to celebrate Easter all through the year.

Amen

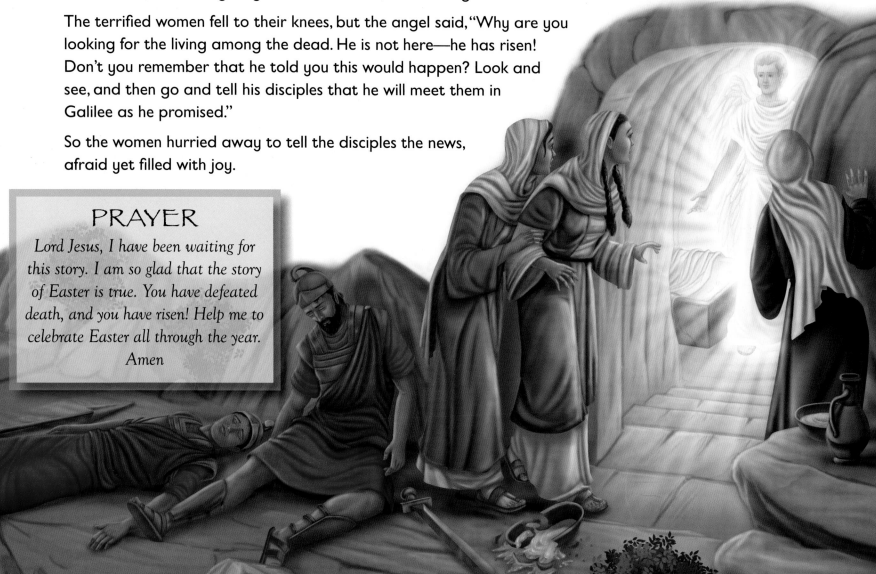

ALIVE!

Mary Magdalene stood outside the tomb. Peter and another disciple had come, had seen the empty tomb and had left, in wonder and confusion. Now she was alone. She missed Jesus! Just then she heard steps behind her, and a man asked, "Woman, why are you crying? Who are you looking for?"

Thinking this must be the gardener, she begged, "Sir, if you have moved him, please tell me where he is, and I'll get him." In reply, the man only spoke her name, "Mary," but instantly she spun around. She recognized that clear, gentle voice!

"Teacher!" she gasped, and reached out toward Jesus.

Jesus said, "Don't hold on to me, for I have not yet ascended to my Father. Go and tell the others!"

So Mary rushed off with the amazing news that she had seen Jesus alive!

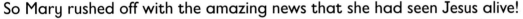

PRAYER

Thank you, Lord Jesus, living Savior, that the sadness of Good Friday was overtaken by your wonderful resurrection. Thank you that my faith rests on the fact that you are alive forever. Help me to share this wonderful news.
Amen

A STRANGER ON THE ROAD

That same day, two of Jesus' followers were traveling along the dusty road from Jerusalem to a village. They couldn't stop talking about the last couple of days. Soon, another man approached them and asked what they were talking about.

"Where have you been?" they asked in amazement, and they went on to tell him excitedly all about Jesus, the amazing things he'd taught, and the miracles he'd performed. Then, more somberly, they told of his death and his disappearance from the tomb.

"How slow you are to believe what the prophets told you!" said the stranger. "Don't you see that the Messiah had to suffer these things and then enter his glory?" And he began to talk to them about everything that had been said in the Scriptures about Jesus. They were enthralled, for he made everything so clear.

At the village, they urged him to dine with them. As they were eating, he took some bread and, giving thanks for it, broke it into pieces and handed it to them. Suddenly, they realized who this stranger really was—Jesus himself! And then he vanished!

The friends hurried back to Jerusalem. They couldn't wait to tell the disciples the good news.

PRAYER

Lord Jesus, I would love to have heard you explain the Bible. Thank you that you have given me parents, pastors, teachers, and friends who teach me today.

Amen

DOUBTING THOMAS

That same evening, Jesus appeared to the disciples. At first, they couldn't believe it. Was he a ghost? But he spoke to them, reassuring them and showing them his hands and feet with their scars. "Touch me and see," he said. "A ghost doesn't have flesh and bones!" Then he went on to explain the Scriptures to them, and they were filled with joy and wonder.

Now, Thomas was not with the others, and when they tried to tell him about it, he couldn't believe them. "Unless I put my finger where the nails were and touch the wound in his side, I will not believe."

A week later, Thomas was with the disciples when suddenly, Jesus was among them again. Turning to Thomas he said, "Put your finger in the wounds in my hands. Reach out and feel my side. Stop doubting and believe!"

Thomas fell to his knees, overcome with joy. Now he believed!

Jesus said, "You only believed because you saw me yourself. How blessed will people be who believe without even seeing!"

PRAYER

Dear Lord Jesus, you know that sometimes my faith is not so strong. Thank you for your gentleness with Thomas —and with me. Thank you that one day I will really see you.
Amen

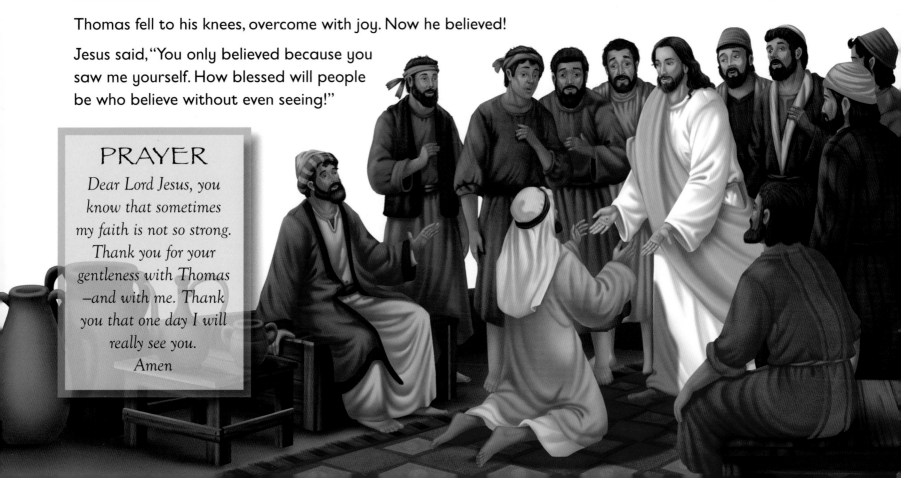

BREAKFAST WITH JESUS

Soon after this, some of the disciples went fishing, but in the morning they came back empty-handed. As they approached the shore, a man called out, "Haven't you caught anything, my friends?" When they shook their heads, he told them to throw their net over the right-hand side of the boat. Shrugging their shoulders, they did so, and were amazed when the net was so full of fish that it was too heavy to haul in!

"It's Jesus!" cried John, and Simon Peter leaped into the water! The others followed in the boat, and by the time they landed, they saw that Jesus was cooking a meal for them. He told them to bring more fish to cook—they had plenty!

After they had eaten, Jesus turned to Simon Peter and asked him if he loved him most. The disciple replied, "Yes, Lord," but was filled with shame, remembering how he had denied Jesus. Jesus asked the same question two more times. Then Simon Peter said in a hurt voice, "Lord, you know everything; you know I love you."

Jesus said, "Then I have work for you. You will take care of my followers," for Simon Peter would be an important leader in the years to come.

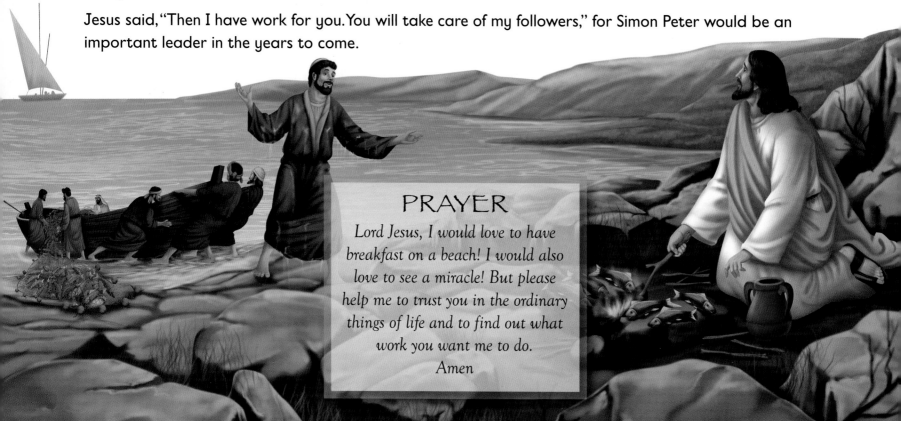

PRAYER

Lord Jesus, I would love to have breakfast on a beach! I would also love to see a miracle! But please help me to trust you in the ordinary things of life and to find out what work you want me to do.

Amen

THE ASCENSION

Jesus and his friends were on a hillside outside Jerusalem. The time had come for Jesus to leave the world. In the time since his resurrection, he had made many things clearer to them and had told them a little about what the future would hold.

Jesus turned to his disciples. "You must stay here in Jerusalem for now and wait for the gift that my Father has promised you, for soon you will be baptized with the Holy Spirit. Then you must spread my message not only in Jerusalem and Judea and Samaria, but in every country."

He held up his hands to bless them and then, before their eyes, he was taken up to heaven, and a cloud hid him from sight.

As they stood looking upward in wonder, suddenly two men dressed in white stood beside them. "Why are you looking at the sky? Jesus has been taken from you into heaven, but he will come back again in the same way that he left!"

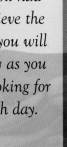

PRAYER

I know, Lord Jesus, that you had to go back to heaven. I believe the message of the angels that you will come back in the same way as you went away. I want to be looking for you and living for you each day.
Amen

THE HOLY SPIRIT

It was ten days since Jesus had been taken up to heaven. The twelve disciples (for they had chosen a man named Matthias to join them to take the place of Judas Iscariot) were gathered together when suddenly the house was filled with the sound of a mighty wind coming from heaven. As they watched in wonder, tongues of fire seemed to rest on each person there. They were all filled with the Holy Spirit and began to speak in different languages—languages they had never spoken before or studied!

Hearing the commotion, a huge crowd gathered outside. Great was their amazement when the disciples came out and began talking in different languages! "How can this be?" they exclaimed. "There are people here from Asia and Egypt, from Libya and Crete, from Rome and Arabia—how can we all be hearing them using our own languages to tell us about God?"

Some people only wanted to make fun of what was happening. "They've all been drinking too much wine!" they mocked.

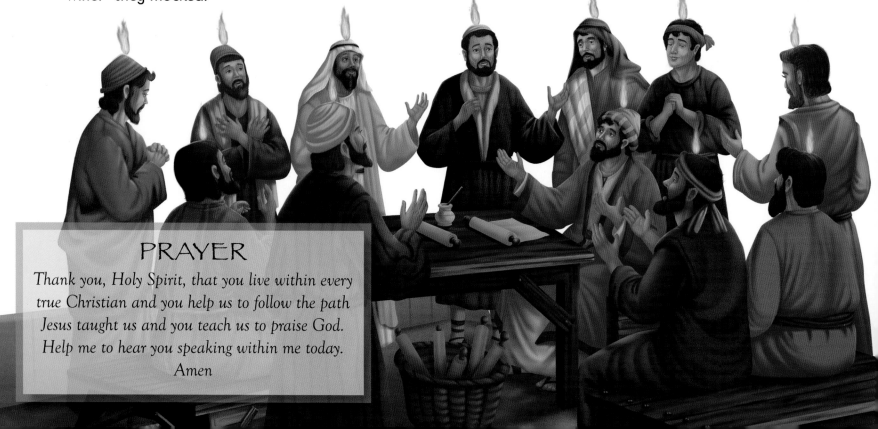

PRAYER

Thank you, Holy Spirit, that you live within every true Christian and you help us to follow the path Jesus taught us and you teach us to praise God. Help me to hear you speaking within me today.

Amen

NEW RECRUITS

Then Peter stepped forward. "Listen!" he said clearly. "Of course we are not drunk—we have been filled with the Holy Spirit! Just a few weeks ago Jesus from Nazareth died on a cross. Yet any one of us can tell you that God has raised Jesus to life! This was all part of God's plan. You know that Jesus was sent to you by God, for he worked many miracles and showed you many signs. But God had planned that Jesus would be handed over to you, so you rejected him and had him killed by evil men. Yet death could not hold him! God made this Jesus, whom you crucified, Lord and Messiah!"

The people looked worried and distraught. What had they done? And how could they make it better?

"If you really are sorry," Peter went on, "then repent. Be baptized in the name of Jesus Christ, and your sins will be forgiven. And you will receive the gift of the Holy Spirit. This promise is not just for you, but for your children, too, and for people who are far away—God's gift is for everyone!"

PRAYER

Thank you, Holy Spirit, that you made Peter bold to explain God's message. Please help me to be bold, and give me words to share with others to help them believe in Jesus.
Amen

THE LAME MAN

A man sat begging outside the temple gates. He had been lame ever since his birth, and he spent every day there, hoping for a spare coin or two. Now, as Peter and John passed by on their way to pray, he looked up hopefully.

The two disciples stopped in front of him, and Peter spoke to the man. "I'm afraid I don't have any money," he said. "But I can give you something far better!" As the lame man looked puzzled, Peter continued, "In the name of Jesus Christ, I order you to get up and walk!" And to everyone's astonishment, he helped him to stand up. The man tried a few cautious steps, and then a few more, and then walked straight into the temple to give thanks to God! People couldn't believe this was the same man who had sat outside the temple every day to beg, and when Peter explained that it was faith in the name of Jesus that had healed him, they stopped to listen.

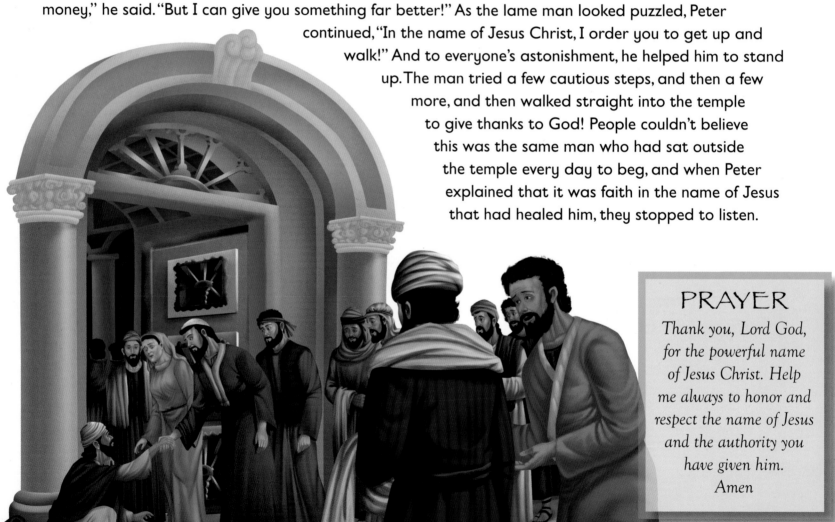

PRAYER

Thank you, Lord God, for the powerful name of Jesus Christ. Help me always to honor and respect the name of Jesus and the authority you have given him.
Amen

TROUBLE!

It wasn't long before the Jewish leaders heard about the miraculous healing and saw the disciples talking to the people. They didn't like what they were saying, and they arrested Peter and John and threw them into prison. The next morning they were brought before the priests, who asked, "Who gave you the right to do this?"

"It is by the name of Jesus Christ that this man has been healed," replied Peter, and when the priests told him not to speak anymore about Jesus, he answered bravely, "What do you think would be right—for us to do as you say, or as God tells us? Anyway, we simply can't stop talking about what we have seen and heard!" The priests and leaders didn't know what to do—everyone had seen the lame man walk, so they couldn't deny it. In the end, the two men were set free.

PRAYER

Lord Jesus, I know there are places in the world where rulers forbid people to speak of you and your name. I pray that you will show your love and kindness to the people who live in those places.

Amen

FREED BY AN ANGEL

After this, the apostles would meet each day to talk to the people about Jesus and heal people in his name. Many people became Christians, and the Jewish leaders became very angry. They wanted people to listen to them—not the apostles!

One day, they threw the apostles in jail. But during the night an angel opened the doors of the jail and brought them out, telling them to go back to the temple courts and spread their message.

The priests sent for them the next morning, only to find the jail locked but the cell empty! When the apostles were found and brought before them, the priests accused them of disobeying their instructions. But Peter and the others bravely replied, "We must obey God rather than human beings!"

Some priests wanted to have them executed, but one said wisely, "If they are just stirring up rebellion, in the end it will all fizzle out. But if they really are from God, then you won't be able to stop them and will find yourselves fighting against God!" So the apostles were released under strict instructions not to talk about Jesus anymore—but of course they did!

PRAYER

Lord Jesus, I love this story—but I also know that you don't always work a miracle to bring Christians out of prison. Wherever believers are in prison for their faith today, please care for them and encourage them.

Amen

LYING TO GOD

Many came to believe in Jesus. They pulled together, sharing what they had. Some even sold houses or land so that the money could be used where it was most needed. But not every new believer was honest. Ananias and his wife Sapphira sold part of their land. They decided that they would keep some of the money for themselves and give the rest to Peter, believing he would never know.

But when Ananias brought the money, Peter looked him in the eye and said, "Why have you lied and kept some back? The land was yours before you sold it, and the money was yours too. Why lie? You haven't just lied to me, but to God himself!" And Ananias fell down dead on the spot!

When his wife came in unaware a bit later, Peter asked if she had given him all the money, and when she answered 'yes', he sighed. "Oh, Sapphira, how could you lie like that? Can't you hear that sound?" (Footsteps were heard outside the room.) "Those men have just buried your husband—and now they will carry your body away too!" And at that, Sapphira fell down dead!

The story of the lying couple spread far and wide and filled everyone with fear and awe.

PRAYER

Dear Lord God, I know that you see everything in my heart. Help me to be honest before you and the church. Help me never to pretend to be what I am not.
Amen

DAY

DAY
318

STONED TO DEATH

Stephen was one of seven wise and good men in charge of distributing food among the new Christians. He was filled with the Holy Spirit and performed such wonders that soon he made enemies among those who hated Jesus. He was taken before the Jewish Council, where false witnesses gave evidence against him.

He faced his accusers bravely, his face shining brightly, like an angel's. "Throughout our history you have persecuted our prophets and refused to listen to them. Now you have betrayed and murdered God's greatest messenger. You have been given the law by angels and have not obeyed it!" Filled with the Holy Spirit, he continued, "Look up! I can see heaven and the Son of Man standing at the right hand of God!"

This was too much for the Council. They dragged Stephen out of the city and began to stone him. But even as they were stoning him, Stephen prayed, "Lord Jesus, receive my spirit." Then he fell on his knees and cried out, "Lord, don't hold this against them," and with these words, he died.

PRAYER

Thank you, Lord Jesus, that nothing was more important to Stephen than speaking of you. Help me to learn from his example. Thank you that he is in heaven with you now. Amen

PHILIP AND THE ETHIOPIAN

One of the onlookers was a man named Saul who hated the followers of Jesus. He wanted to put a stop to their preaching and believed he was doing God's will. Many Christians had to flee to avoid imprisonment, but they spread the word wherever they went.

Among them was Philip. Called by an angel to travel south from Jerusalem, Philip came across a powerful and wealthy man, the treasurer to the queen of Ethiopia, who was reading from the book of Isaiah as he traveled in his fine carriage.

The Ethiopian was frustrated. He was reading Isaiah's words about how God's servant was led like a sheep to the slaughter, and he wanted to know whom the prophet was talking about. Philip explained that it was written about Jesus and went on to tell him all about God's Son.

The official wanted to become a Christian right away, and so Philip baptized him in a river by the roadside! God took Philip away to preach the gospel in many other places, but the Ethiopian continued on his way, filled with joy and happiness.

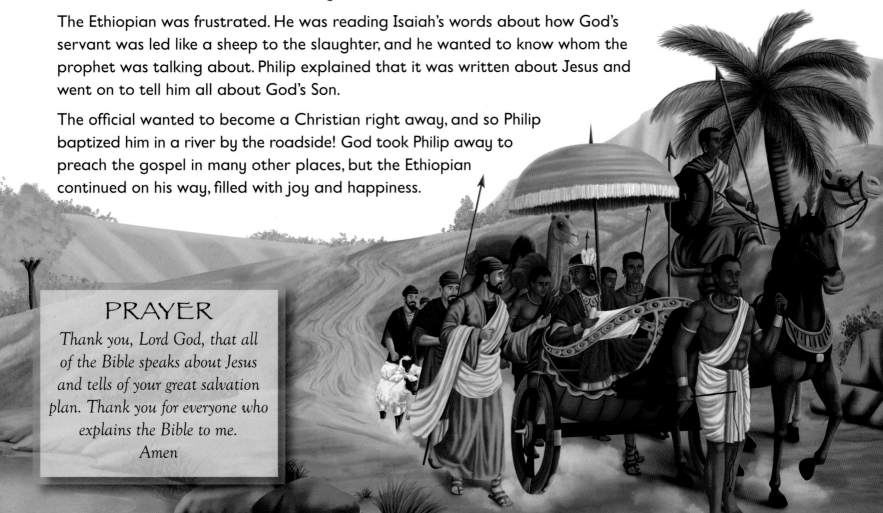

PRAYER

Thank you, Lord God, that all of the Bible speaks about Jesus and tells of your great salvation plan. Thank you for everyone who explains the Bible to me.
Amen

THE ROAD TO DAMASCUS

Meanwhile, Saul was still determined to stop Jesus' followers. Knowing that many had fled to the city of Damascus, he set off to arrest them. Suddenly, a blinding light from heaven flashed down. Saul fell to the ground, covering his eyes. Then he heard a voice say, "Saul, why do you keep on persecuting me?"

Saul began trembling. He thought he knew who was speaking, but he had to ask.

"I am Jesus," replied the voice. "Get up and go into the city, and you will be told what you must do."

Saul struggled to his feet, but when he opened his eyes, he couldn't see a thing! His guards had to take him by the hand and lead him into the city. There he stayed for three days without eating or drinking, spending his time in prayer.

PRAYER

Lord Jesus, thank you that you stopped Saul on the road to Damascus and he became a great missionary. Please speak today to many who are against you, and may they turn around and become your children.

Amen

A CHANGED MAN

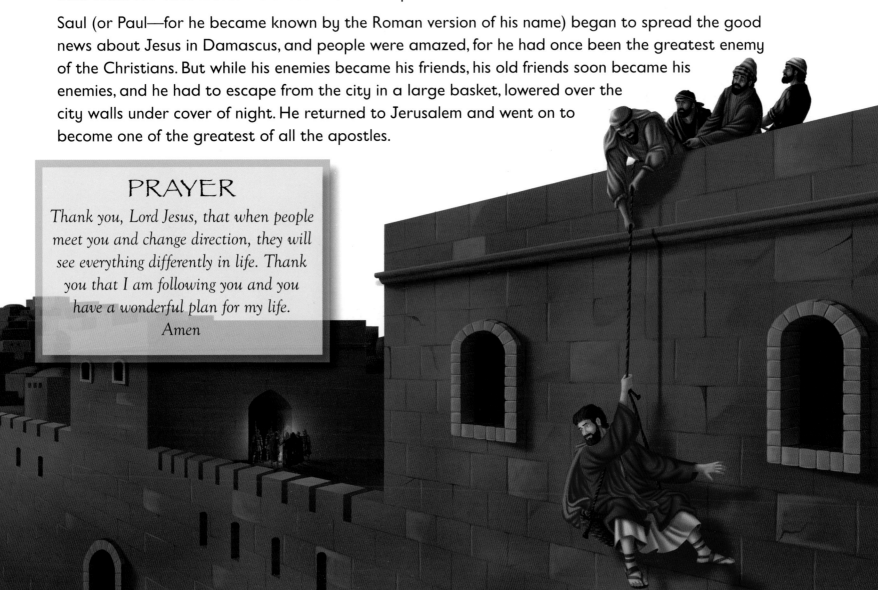

God had great plans for Saul. He sent a Christian named Ananias to the house where he was staying. When he got there, Ananias laid his hands on Saul, saying, "Jesus sent me so that you might see again and be filled with the Holy Spirit!" Suddenly, it was as if scales had fallen from his eyes, and Saul could see once more! He arose and was baptized.

Saul (or Paul—for he became known by the Roman version of his name) began to spread the good news about Jesus in Damascus, and people were amazed, for he had once been the greatest enemy of the Christians. But while his enemies became his friends, his old friends soon became his enemies, and he had to escape from the city in a large basket, lowered over the city walls under cover of night. He returned to Jerusalem and went on to become one of the greatest of all the apostles.

PRAYER

Thank you, Lord Jesus, that when people meet you and change direction, they will see everything differently in life. Thank you that I am following you and you have a wonderful plan for my life.
Amen

PETER AND TABITHA

Kind Tabitha (in Greek her name was Dorcas) lived in Joppa. She spent her days helping others, especially the poor, for whom she made clothes. Sadly, she became ill and passed away. The other Christians mourned her bitterly. They tenderly washed her body and placed it in a room to await burial.

Tabitha's friends sent a message to Peter, begging him to come. When he entered the room in which they had laid her body, Peter was met by a crowd of weeping widows. He soothed them and then sent them from the room. Once he was alone, he fell to his knees and prayed with all his heart. Then he turned toward the dead woman, saying, "Tabitha, get up!"

At this, Tabitha opened her eyes and sat up! Peter led her down to her friends. Amazed and overjoyed, they could hardly believe their eyes! When the news spread, many more people came to believe in Jesus.

PRAYER

Thank you, Lord Jesus, that your love is shown through human care. Thank you for all those today who work tirelessly to relieve the sick and poor worldwide. Please bless their work.

Amen

THE SHEET OF ANIMALS

One day, while praying on the roof under the hot sun, Peter fell asleep and had a strange dream. In his dream, there hung before him a huge white sheet being lowered from heaven by its corners. It was filled with all sorts of animals, reptiles, and birds. Looking closely, he realized they were all creatures that Jews were forbidden to eat, for they were considered "unclean." Then he heard God's voice saying, "Get up, Peter. Kill and eat."

PRAYER

Thank you, Lord God, that you speak in many ways—even in dreams. I pray that you will speak today to many people. As I read the Bible, please speak to me.
Amen

"Surely not, Lord!" Peter replied in horror. "I have never eaten anything unclean!"

The voice spoke again, "Don't call impure what God has made clean."

This happened three times, and then the sheet was pulled back up to heaven.

STRUCK BLIND

God told Paul and Barnabas to go on a journey to spread the good news to people who had not yet heard about Jesus. They went first to Cyprus, where they traveled around the island proclaiming the word of God, until they came to the city of Paphos, the home of the Roman governor. The governor was keen to hear the word of God, and he sent for Paul and Barnabas to come and speak with him.

However, one of the governor's attendants was a man named Elymas. Now, Elymas was a sorcerer and a false prophet, and he tried to stop the governor from listening to the two men.

But Paul was filled with the Holy Spirit, and he looked straight at Elymas, saying, "You are a son of the devil and an enemy of everything that is right! You are full of all kinds of evil tricks, and you always keep trying to turn the Lord's truths into lies! Now the hand of the Lord is against you, and you will be struck blind!" Sure enough, in that instant, the prophet's eyes clouded over, and he couldn't see a thing. He groped about, trying to find someone's hand to take hold of!

The island governor was so amazed that he became a Christian.

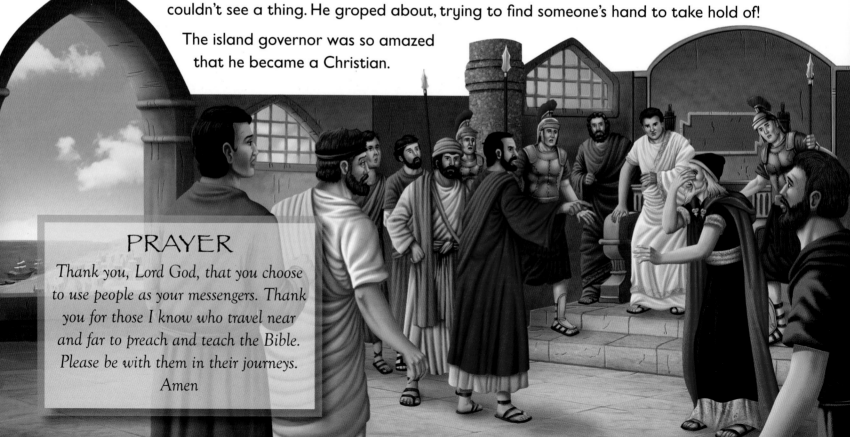

PRAYER

Thank you, Lord God, that you choose to use people as your messengers. Thank you for those I know who travel near and far to preach and teach the Bible. Please be with them in their journeys.
Amen

MISSIONARIES

Next, Paul and Barnabas sailed to the land we know as Turkey, going from town to town, preaching the good news. They went to the synagogue in Pisidian Antioch, where they spoke at length to the people. The next week, practically the whole city turned out to hear what they had to say. But the Jews were jealous and began to say bad things about Paul and contradict his teaching.

Paul and Barnabas told them firmly, "If you won't listen to the word of God, when we came to you first, then we will go and teach the Gentiles, for this is what the Lord commanded us."

The Gentiles were eager to listen to what the apostles had to say, and they took it to heart. Paul and Barnabas made many friends on their travels. But not everyone liked their message or how popular they were becoming, and they made many enemies too! Sometimes they were thrown out of a city, and sometimes stones were thrown after them! But each time, they would pick themselves up and carry on with their mission.

PRAYER

Lord Jesus, it's great to read of these amazing adventures! Please help me to be a young missionary in the places you send me day by day. Help me to speak of you at home or school or wherever I am.

Amen

TAKEN FOR GODS

In Lystra, where few people knew of the one true God, Paul healed a lame man. The excited crowd believed that he and Barnabas were gods! The priest of Zeus brought bulls and wreaths to the city gates because he and the crowd wanted to offer sacrifices to the apostles! Barnabas and Paul had a hard job explaining that they were ordinary men and trying to tell them about God!

Soon after this, some Jews turned the people of Lystra against the apostles. They stoned Paul and left him for dead outside the city, but after the disciples had gathered around him, he got up and went back to preach as if nothing had happened.

After that, Paul and Barnabas visited the city of Derbe, before slowly making their way back to Antioch, stopping in towns along the way to encourage those they had already spoken to and to help them as they set up new churches.

PRAYER

Lord Jesus, I am amazed at how strong your Holy Spirit made Paul and his friends. Thank you that they didn't give up even when it was so hard, and they even went back to the same places later.
Amen

HEALING A SLAVE GIRL

Paul spent some time in Antioch but was then off on his travels once again. This time, he took a man named Silas with him to Asia Minor. After they had passed through the land, strengthening the new churches, Paul had a strange dream of a man from Macedonia standing and begging him, "Come to Macedonia and help us!"

The very next day they got ready to leave for Macedonia, in modern Europe, where they were joined by a doctor named Luke. In the city of Philippi, they were followed around by a slave girl who was possessed by a spirit. She ranted and raved so much that in the end, Paul commanded the spirit to leave her in the name of Jesus Christ.

Instantly the spirit left her, but her owners were angry, for she was no longer able to foretell the future—and they had made a lot of money out of her predictions! They had Paul and Silas dragged before the city magistrates. The crowd joined in the attack, and Paul and Silas were whipped and beaten and thrown into prison with their feet locked in stocks.

PRAYER

Thank you, Lord God, that your Holy Spirit, who filled Jesus, can also perform miracles through Christians. Thank you that your Spirit always overcomes evil.
Amen

SINGING IN PRISON

It was midnight. Paul and Silas were lying in the stocks. The chains were tight and the wood was heavy, but they didn't despair. Instead, they were praying and singing hymns. The other prisoners could hardly believe their ears.

Suddenly a violent earthquake shook the prison, the cell doors flew open, and everyone's chains came loose! Fearing punishment if his prisoners escaped, the jailor was about to kill himself. But Paul called out, "Don't harm yourself! We're still here!" The astonished jailer took Paul and Silas to his own house, where he and his family spent the night learning about Jesus. They became Christians that very night!

Paul and Silas returned to the prison, and when officials came the next morning, Paul told them they were Roman citizens and had not been given a trial. The worried magistrates came to apologize but also to ask them to leave.

Paul traveled on through many lands to tell people his wonderful message. He spent time in Athens, where the people loved debating, and in Corinth, where he earned a living making tents. Then he traveled to Ephesus and Caesarea before settling for a while in Antioch at the end of his second missionary journey.

PRAYER

Dear Father God, help me to praise you not only when things are going well, but also to have a song in my heart in difficult times.
Amen

RIOT AT EPHESUS

Paul was in Ephesus, on the third of his missionary journeys, when trouble erupted. The people there worshipped the goddess Artemis and had built a wonderful temple in her honor. People came from afar to visit it, and the city was full of silversmiths selling silver images of the goddess.

But when Paul started preaching, many people became Christians and stopped buying the images. The silversmiths were furious, and soon the whole city was in an uproar! The angry mob grabbed hold of two of Paul's friends and dragged them to the open-air theater, where they shouted and argued until a city official managed to calm everybody down.

After this, Paul realized that it would be safer for everyone if he left the city, and so he set off to return to Jerusalem, first heading to Macedonia and then Greece.

PRAYER

Thank you, Lord God, that you are the one true God, the Creator of all things. I pray that people will turn away from all kinds of idols that they put in your place, and turn to worship you.
Amen

THE GREAT FALL

Paul wanted to return to Jerusalem to help the Jewish Christians there. On his way, he spent the night in a town called Troas. The Christians there were thrilled that Paul was among them. They crowded into an upstairs room to listen to him, and he talked long into the night.

One of his listeners was a young man named Eutychus. He wanted to hear everything that Paul was saying, but he was dreadfully sleepy and could hardly stay awake. He was sitting by the window, hoping that the fresh air would keep him awake, but at last he could keep his eyes open no longer and dozed off—plummeting three floors down to the hard ground! When people realized what had happened, they rushed downstairs, only to find him dead. But Paul, coming behind them, knelt by the young man and gathered him in his arms. Turning to the crowd, he smiled, "Don't worry. He's alive!"

People could hardly believe what had happened and were filled with joy at the miracle. They went back upstairs, and Paul carried on talking to them until daybreak!

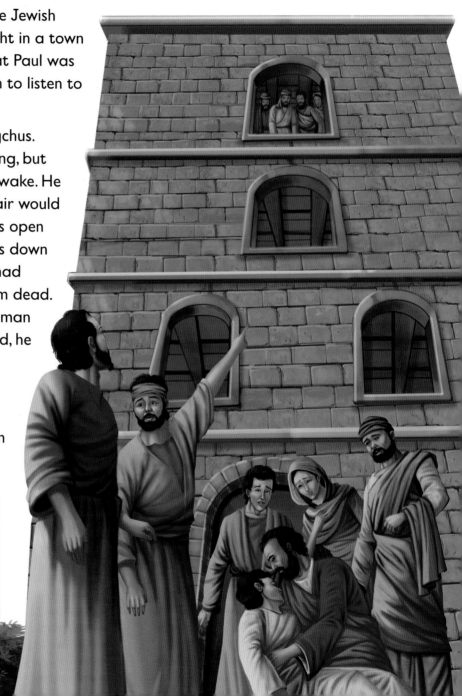

PRAYER

Dear Lord God, I don't usually fall asleep in church—but sometimes my thoughts do wander. Please help me to concentrate, to listen, and to learn when someone is teaching about you.

Amen

"PLEASE DON'T GO!"

Paul's friends didn't want him to go to Jerusalem. They all warned him that it would be very dangerous for him—they feared that he would be imprisoned there and probably killed. "Please don't go!" they begged.

But Paul shook his head sadly. "Please don't try to change my mind with your tears. This is what I have to do. I'm ready not only to be put in chains for Jesus, but to die for him."

Even though he knew in his heart that hardship and suffering were ahead of him, Paul would go where God wanted him to go. Before he boarded the ship that would carry him onward, Paul knelt with his friends and prayed. They all wept as he sailed away. They knew that they would never see him again.

PRAYER

Thank you, Lord Jesus, that you understand all human emotions. You know how hard it is for friends and families to be separated. Please encourage all who have to say goodbye to those they love.

Amen

TROUBLE IN JERUSALEM

Paul received a warm welcome from his friends in Jerusalem, but all too soon trouble flared up. Many Jews didn't like the message that Paul was preaching. When they came upon Paul in the temple, they stirred the crowd up and told lies about him. The crowd dragged him from the temple, and he would probably have been killed then and there if it hadn't been for the Roman governor of the city, who learned about the uproar and sent in troops.

The commander of the soldiers tried to find out what Paul had done, but one person shouted one thing and another screamed something else, and there was so much uproar that the commander thought he had better get Paul out of there quickly and into the barracks. The soldiers had to lift him up to stop the crowd from getting to him!

Before he was taken away, Paul asked the commander if he could speak to the people. He just wanted to explain his story and how God had spoken to him, but the people were furious with him, and in the end the Roman soldiers took him away.

PRAYER

Dear Lord God, help me to know that you are in control even if everything in life seems to be going wrong. Thank you that I can always trust you to sort things out.
Amen

CONSPIRACY

The Roman commander had ordered his soldiers to flog Paul and question him to find out why the people hated him. When Paul told them that he was a Roman citizen, they were alarmed, because they knew they couldn't flog a Roman citizen who hadn't even been found guilty of anything! The commander himself was worried when he realized that he had put a Roman citizen in chains. He wanted to find out exactly what Paul was being accused of, so he sent him before the chief priests and the Jewish council—maybe they could find out what was going on.

But the council only argued among themselves, and Paul was sent back again.

However, he was still in danger. Some of the Jews hated Paul so much that they swore an oath not to eat or drink until they had killed him! They planned to have him brought out for further questioning and murder him then. By good fortune, Paul's nephew heard about the plot. He went to the fort and told the commander about it. That very night the commander smuggled Paul out of the city with an armed guard under cover of darkness. Now Paul was on his way to the Roman headquarters at Caesarea.

PRAYER

Thank you, Lord God, that you know everything about my life. I am so glad to be your child and to know that you can protect and provide for me, just like you did for the apostle Paul.

Amen

CONFUSION

Some days later, Paul found himself facing his accusers before the Roman governor, Felix. They told Felix that Paul was a troublemaker who had stirred up riots among the Jews all over the world. They claimed he was the ringleader of the Nazarene sect and even that he had tried to desecrate the temple at Jerusalem.

When Paul was allowed to speak for himself, he did so with honesty and courage. He explained that he had come to Jerusalem only to worship, and that the accusations were false and couldn't be proved. He did willingly admit that he was a follower of Jesus, but he told Felix that he was still worshipping the same God and believing what the prophets had said, and he had the same hope in the resurrection of good and bad people. He had done nothing wrong!

Felix knew that Paul's accusers could prove nothing, but he still kept Paul under guard, as did the governor who came after him, a man named Festus. In the end, Paul demanded that his case be heard by the emperor in Rome. Festus was unhappy about sending a prisoner to Rome without being able to say what he was charged with, and he encouraged King Agrippa to question Paul. But after talking to him, Agrippa could only say that if Paul hadn't already demanded to go to Rome, then surely he should have been set free.
As it was, to Rome he must go.

PRAYER

Dear Lord God, I am amazed at the way you arranged for Paul to meet so many rulers! Please still send Christians to speak your message to people in high authority and government. Amen

STORM AT SEA

Paul was traveling to Rome aboard a ship. Julius, the Roman centurion in charge, took a liking to Paul and treated him kindly, and some of Paul's friends had chosen to travel with him. However, bad weather and stops delayed their voyage, and the stormy season was upon them. When they lay at anchor at a harbor in Crete, Paul warned Julius and the captain that it would be dangerous to sail onward and that they would be heading for trouble. But the captain ignored his advice, and the ship set sail.

Soon they found themselves in the middle of a dreadful storm. For days the ship was at the mercy of the angry sea, dragged along by the towering waves and the fierce winds. In despair, the crew began throwing cargo over the side to try to save the ship, and after several days passed without sight of the sun or stars, all hope seemed lost.

It was then that Paul spoke to the crew and the other passengers to give them comfort. "You should have listened to me when I warned you of this, but nevertheless, now you need to keep up your courage because an angel has spoken to me and has promised we will all reach land alive. Only the ship will be lost. Have faith in God as I do. We will be saved."

PRAYER

Thank you, Lord God, that you gave words of comfort to the apostle Paul, which he shared with the travelers. Please give comfort today to those who are in deep trouble.
Amen

SHIPWRECKED!

After two whole weeks at the mercy of the storm, the sailors sensed that they were approaching land. Some of the sailors tried to leave in one of the lifeboats, as they feared that they would be dashed upon the rocks, but Paul told the captain and the centurion that they would all have to stay with the ship to be saved, so the soldiers cut the ropes that held the lifeboat and let it drift away.

Just before dawn Paul urged them all to eat. He took some bread himself and, thanking God, began to eat, and so the other passengers were encouraged to eat too.

Everyone was excited when the coastline finally came into sight, but just as things seemed to be looking up, suddenly the ship struck a sandbar. The bow stuck fast, and the ship began to be broken to pieces by the surf!

The soldiers planned to kill the prisoners to prevent any of them from swimming away and escaping, but Julius ordered everyone who could swim to make for land, and told those who could not swim to cling to pieces of the wreckage and float ashore. In this way, everyone reached land safely. Every last one of the two hundred and seventy-six people on board was saved, just as God had promised!

> ## PRAYER
> *Dear Lord God, I would love to be the kind of person who helps others when they are struggling. Please teach me how to see the needs of others and be a good encourager.*
> *Amen*

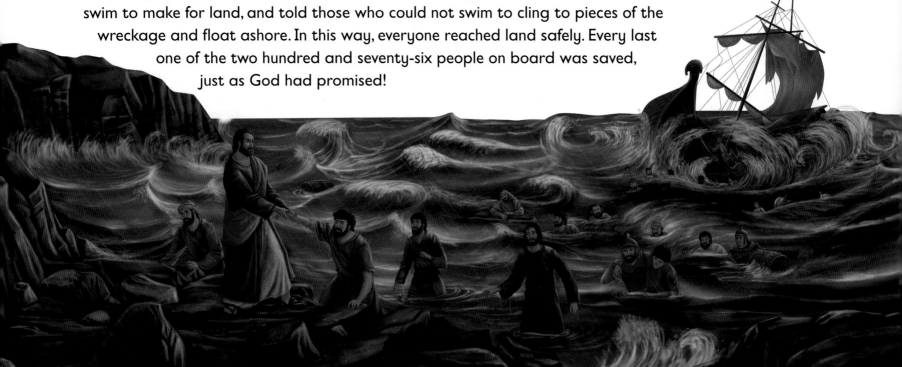

ROME AT LAST

Paul and his companions found themselves on the island of Malta. They were cold and wet, but they were alive! Some islanders came to help. They lit a huge fire to warm them. While Paul was putting some extra wood on the fire, a poisonous snake slithered out and fastened itself on his hand. Paul calmly shook the snake off and carried on as if nothing had happened. The astonished islanders thought he must be a god!

After three months, they set sail once again for Rome. While he waited for his case to be heard, Paul was allowed to live by himself with a soldier to guard him. Although he was not allowed out, he could have visitors, and so he was able to carry on spreading the message to new people. He also wrote letters to the Christians he had met during his travels, to encourage and help them as they set up their churches. It is not known for sure how Paul died, but many believe that he was executed while in Rome.

PRAYER

Thank you, dear Lord God, for older Christians and the encouragement they can offer. When they can no longer travel around and have to spend many hours at home, please bless them. Please help me to make time to listen to old people.

Amen

THE LOVE OF GOD

Paul's letters and those of others make up a large portion of the New Testament. Some were written to one individual, or to one group of people, or to talk about a particular problem, while others were more general. But these letters speak to all Christians even today, for many of the problems we face and the fears we have are the same, and the advice given is as relevant today as it was then, while the comfort offered is as true as ever.

Paul wrote to the believers in Rome before he went to the city. His words helped to explain how our faith in Jesus Christ will save us. We can't save ourselves from our sins, but God, in his loving-kindness, sent us his Son so that we could be saved by accepting Jesus as our Savior, Gentiles as well as Jews: "When we were God's enemies, we became his friends through the death of his Son. So how much more, now that we are God's friends, shall we be saved through his Son's life!"

Paul knew that life could be hard, but he told them that they would be rewarded in the end: "I believe our present suffering is not worth comparing with the glory that will be revealed in us— and suffering produces perseverance, and so character and hope!"

He went on to reassure them: "If God is for us, who can be against us? He didn't even spare his own Son but gave him up for us all. If he did this, won't he freely give us all things? There is nothing that will ever be able to separate us from the love of God which is ours through Jesus—not hardship, or persecution, or hunger, or poverty, or danger, or death."

PRAYER

Thank you, Lord God, for your great love for me. Thank you that whatever happens in my life, there is absolutely nothing that can ever separate me from you love.
Amen

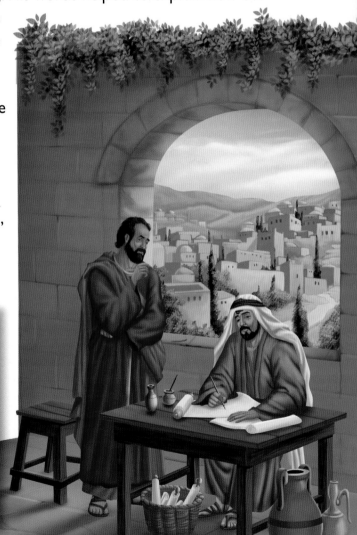

LOVE IN ACTION

PRAYER

Dear Lord God, I do want to follow your pattern for living. Please help me to think good thoughts and give my whole life to you. I want to find ways to put love into action every day.

Amen

In his letter to the believers in Rome, Paul encouraged them to live good lives, filled with love and kindness. "Don't try to be like everyone else—don't live the way they live," he told them. "Change the way you think, and make your life a living sacrifice to God—all you are, all you have, and all you do. He has given you so much!"

"Love must be sincere," he continued. "Hate what is evil; cling to what is good. Think about other people before yourselves. Love and respect one another, be joyful in hope, patient in suffering, and faithful in prayer. Share what you have with those in need. Live in peace, and if someone does something bad, don't think about retribution or revenge—leave that up to God. Don't be overcome by evil, but overcome evil with good."

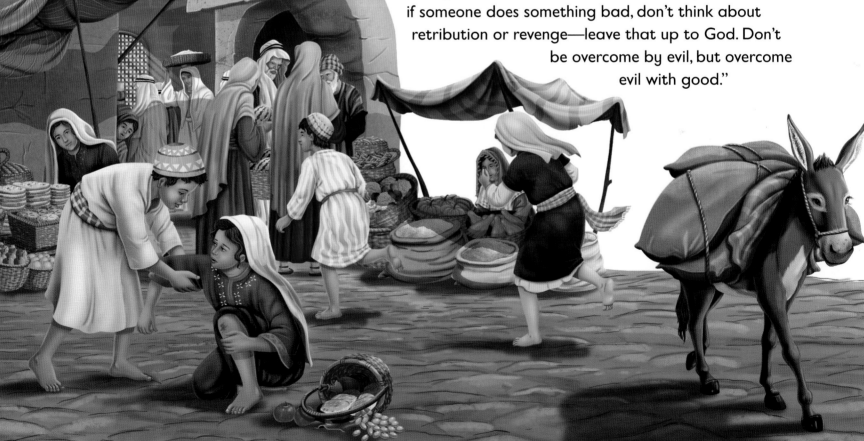

TEETHING PROBLEMS

Paul wrote a stern letter to the believers in Corinth. He had helped to set up the church there some time before, but the Christians were having problems. Corinth was a busy seaport, and many bad things went on in the town. Paul told the Corinthians that they mustn't mix with bad people.

They were also divided over leadership. Some believed what Paul had told them, while others had listened to what others had to say. Paul told them firmly that they needed to focus on Christ and not his messengers. He said that while he may have been the one to plant the seed, and that another apostle may have watered it, they were only servants and had nothing to boast about at all, for it was God alone who made it grow. The people needed to see the big picture and not squabble about details!

PRAYER

Dear Lord God, thank you for the church family. Please help those who lead churches and encourage Christians to keep their eyes on Jesus and to carefully follow your ways.

Amen

ONE BODY

Paul explained to the people in Corinth that they shouldn't argue or boast about who was better at one thing, or who was better at another. He told them that all their different talents and abilities came from God, and that they were all equally important: "Many of you have been given wonderful gifts by the Holy Spirit. Maybe you can speak in foreign languages, or prophesy, or teach, or heal. None of these is better than the others, so don't get bigheaded!"

To make it easier for them to understand, he described the followers of Christ as many parts of one body. It would make no sense for the eye to say to the hand, "I don't need you!" or for the head to say to the feet, "I don't need you!" If the whole body were an eye, where would the sense of hearing be? If the whole body were an ear, where would the sense of smell be? Even those parts of the body that don't seem to have such a big role, or seem weaker, are just as important.

Paul was saying that we should all respect and take care of one another and work together without quarreling.

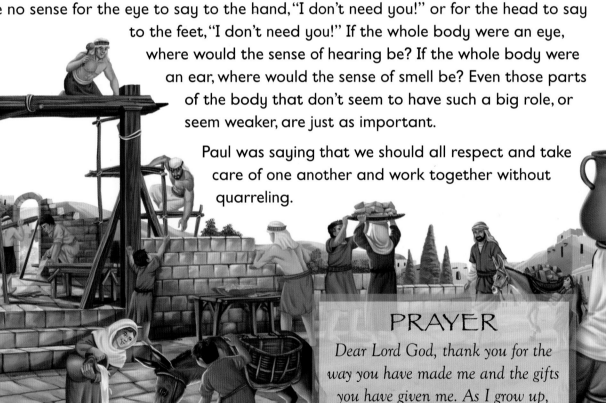

PRAYER
Dear Lord God, thank you for the way you have made me and the gifts you have given me. As I grow up, help me to see the place you have for me in the church family and the jobs I can to do bless others.
Amen

THE GREATEST OF THESE

In his letter to the Corinthians, Paul went on to write one of the most beautiful passages of the whole Bible: "If I could speak every single language in the world and even talk with angels, but didn't love others, I would be no more than a noisy gong. If I had the gift of prophecy, or knowledge, or such great faith that I could move mountains, it would mean nothing if I didn't have love. I could give all I owned to the poor and suffer great hardship, but it would be meaningless if I didn't feel love for the people I was doing it for.

"Love is patient and kind. It isn't jealous, boastful, proud, or rude. It doesn't insist on having its own way, or become irritable, or seek revenge, or feel happy when someone else fails. Love protects, and trusts, and hopes. It is steady and true, and it never, ever gives up. Three things will last forever—faith, hope, and love—and the greatest of these is love."

PRAYER

Lord God, I know there is a relationship of perfect love within the trinity of Father, Son, and Holy Spirit. Through your Holy Spirit in me, please teach me to build my life on your true love that lasts forever.
Amen

A HOUSE IN HEAVEN

We believe that Paul wrote several letters to the church in Corinth. Things weren't running smoothly there, and it was his love for them that drove Paul to send them words of correction and encouragement.

Paul told the Corinthians, "God comforts us in our troubles so we can comfort others. The more we suffer for Christ, the more God will comfort us through Christ. We are surrounded by troubles but are not crushed. We will never give up! The troubles we face now are small and will not last, for when we leave these earthly bodies, we will have a house in heaven and an eternal body made for us by God himself!"

Paul told them to focus on heaven and not on the present moment, for "what can be seen is temporary, but what cannot be seen is eternal."

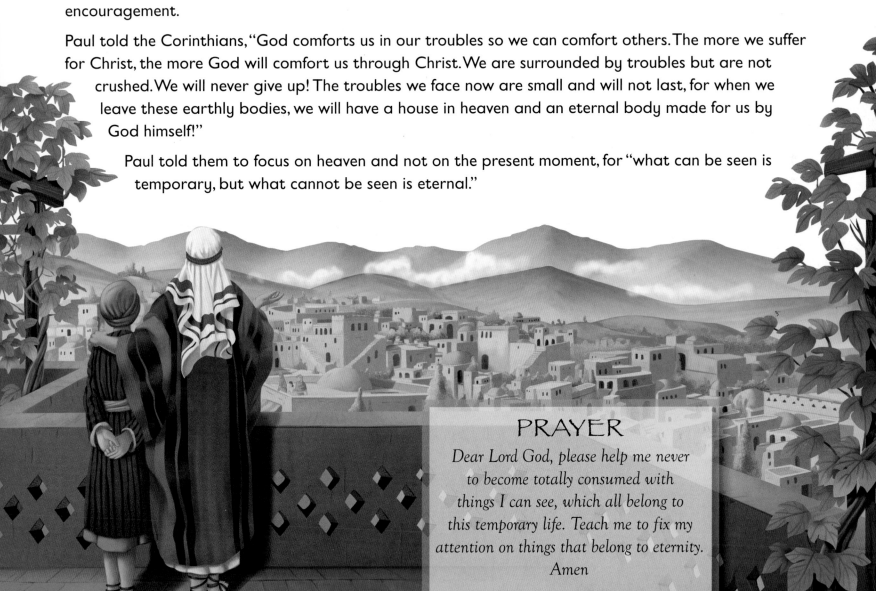

PRAYER

Dear Lord God, please help me never to become totally consumed with things I can see, which all belong to this temporary life. Teach me to fix my attention on things that belong to eternity.

Amen

A THORN IN MY FLESH

Paul's letter to the Corinthians was very personal. He truly spoke from his heart. He told them that suffering is part of being a Christian. He, too, had suffered. He had experienced oppression and persecution, and he referred to his very own "thorn in the flesh," which was something unpleasant that he lived with every day. We don't know if it was something wrong with his body, or an emotional problem, or something else altogether, but that doesn't matter. The point was that God had a purpose for this thorn. It kept Paul humble. Paul explained that he had begged God to take it away from him, but that God had told him that his grace was enough for him and that his power was make perfect in weakness.

Paul wrote, "That is why, for Christ's sake, I delight in weaknesses, in insults, in hardships, in persecutions, in difficulties. For when I am weak, then I am strong."

Paul understood his own weaknesses and was happy to admit them. He knew that he should look to God alone for the grace that would give him strength to do what God wanted him to do. God doesn't need us to be strong, and he doesn't want us to think that we are powerful or clever or faultless. All the good things we do, we do by the grace of God.

PRAYER
*Dear Lord God,
please help me to be
humble and accept my
weaknesses. Thank you
that your grace and
kindness will always be
enough for my needs.
Amen*

SLAVES NO MORE

Paul was worried that many believers were going back to their old ways and thinking too much about rules and rituals, when the true path to God is through belief in Jesus. He wrote to the church in Galatia: "A person is made right with God by faith in Jesus Christ, not by obeying the law. If keeping the law was enough, there wouldn't have been any need for Christ to die! You didn't receive the Holy Spirit by obeying the law of Moses, but because you believed the message about Christ! So why are you now trying to be perfect? Don't you understand? Christ took upon himself the curse for our wrongdoing. You were slaves before, but now you are no longer slaves, but God's own children. And since you are his children, God has made you his heirs!

"Jesus set us free! Make sure you stay free, and don't become slaves to the law again!"

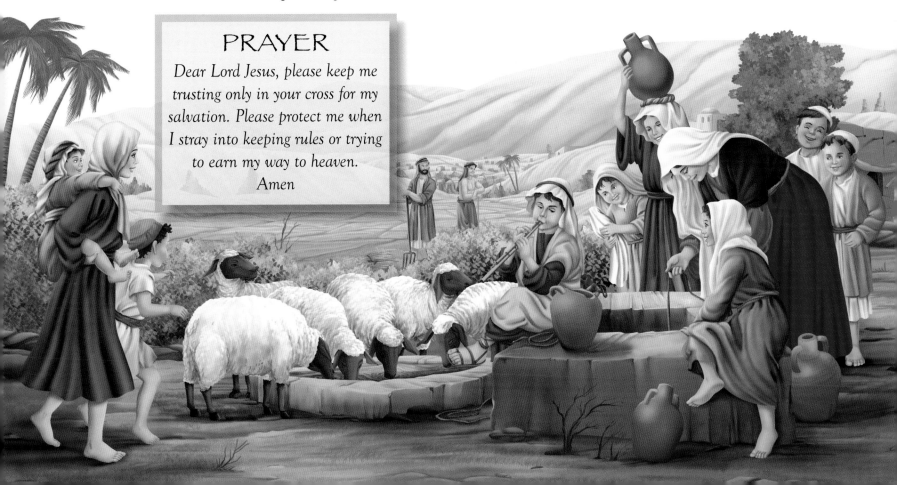

PRAYER

Dear Lord Jesus, please keep me trusting only in your cross for my salvation. Please protect me when I stray into keeping rules or trying to earn my way to heaven.
Amen

DAY
348

THE GIFT OF GOD

Ephesus was a bustling port city in the Roman province of Asia Minor, which today is Turkey. It was an important trade city, and Paul had set up the church there. Paul wanted the Ephesians to understand that our salvation is something that God planned from eternity and that he planned it in such a way that it would show the glory of his grace.

The people of Ephesus knew that before Paul had come to tell them all about Jesus, their city had been a wicked one, full of people doing bad things. They knew that their salvation had come about purely through the grace, power, and kindness of God. Paul explained that God had saved them by his grace through their faith in Jesus. They couldn't possibly have done it by themselves, but God did it for them. So none of them could boast that he had saved himself, for the good things that we do can't save us—only the gift of God himself can do this!

And if we do good things, they are only what God had in mind for us all along—he made us so that we could do them.

PRAYER

Dear Lord God, thank you for your great gift of salvation, which can never be earned. Please help me to respond to your grace by living to please you.
Amen

PUT ON GOD'S ARMOR

Paul sent the people of the church in Ephesus some wonderful words of encouragement: "Be strong in the Lord. Our enemies aren't made of flesh and blood, so put on every piece of God's armor. Then you can stand firm, with the belt of truth buckled around your waist and the breastplate of righteousness on your chest. Let your feet be shod with the readiness that comes from the gospel of peace, and take up the shield of faith. Put on the helmet of salvation, and take hold of the sword of the Spirit, which is the word of God."

What a wonderful image! God's word and God's love are our protection against all that life can throw at us.

PRAYER

Dear Lord God, when I feel under attack or tempted, please remind me to rely on your word, your truth, your righteousness, and your salvation. Thank you that I am secure when I am trusting in you.

Amen

REJOICE!

The people of the church in Philippi were some of Paul's strongest supporters. They had sent gifts to Paul when he was in prison, and Paul sent them a letter to thank them and to encourage them about practical matters. He also told them that he had found true contentment despite all his troubles and despite his current imprisonment. He realized that compared to the wonderful joy of knowing Jesus Christ, nothing else mattered at all. He wasn't saying that he had reached his goal, but that he was pressing on daily toward the prize that he knew God had planned for him in Jesus. He said that Christians could find true joy in believing in Jesus and in serving God.

He also told his friends not to be anxious. If they felt anxious, then they should talk to God, and by praying to him and thanking him, they should let him know what they were feeling. He also advised them to spend their time thinking about good things—whatever is true or noble, pure or lovely, excellent or praiseworthy—and at all times they should rejoice in the Lord!

PRAYER

Dear Lord God, I am so glad to be in your family. I have so much to rejoice in. Help me never to worry, but to fill my mind with the beautiful things that belong to your kingdom.

Amen

THE THINGS OF HEAVEN

Paul wanted to warn the people of the church in Colossae not to believe those teachers who told them to focus on the law. Some teachers were saying that believing in Jesus was not enough to get into heaven and that you had to follow many extra rules. Paul wanted to set things right: "Don't spend too much time thinking about all the old rules. Think about the things of heaven, not the things of earth!"

Rules such as "Don't eat this" or "don't touch that" had only to do with earthly things that didn't last. They were rules made by humans, and while they might make people look as though they are being humble and punishing themselves, they don't actually stop anyone from doing bad things. Paul wanted to explain to them that they would never be able to keep enough rules or do enough good things to earn a place in heaven. Only Jesus can save us and give us a new life.

PRAYER

Thank you, Lord God, that you have provided everything I need in Jesus. Thank you that I am saved simply by trusting in Jesus—and nothing else.

Amen

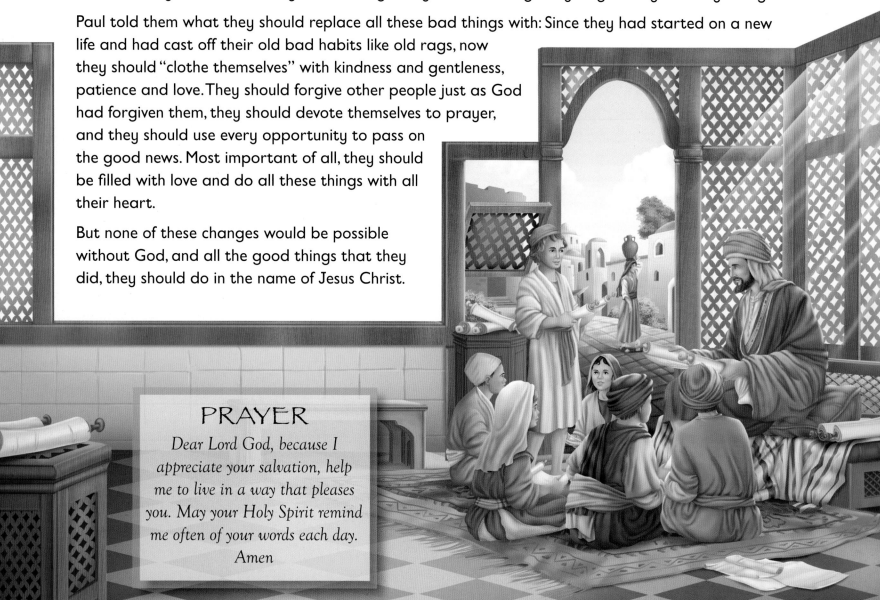

A FRESH START

Now that Jesus had saved the people of Colossae from their sins, Paul wanted to remind them how to live a good life. He told them that they must stop losing their temper and being angry about things, and that they mustn't lie or say hurtful things. They shouldn't be greedy or give way to nasty thoughts.

Paul told them what they should replace all these bad things with: Since they had started on a new life and had cast off their old bad habits like old rags, now they should "clothe themselves" with kindness and gentleness, patience and love. They should forgive other people just as God had forgiven them, they should devote themselves to prayer, and they should use every opportunity to pass on the good news. Most important of all, they should be filled with love and do all these things with all their heart.

But none of these changes would be possible without God, and all the good things that they did, they should do in the name of Jesus Christ.

PRAYER

Dear Lord God, because I appreciate your salvation, help me to live in a way that pleases you. May your Holy Spirit remind me often of your words each day.
Amen

FIRM IN FAITH

Paul had been forced to leave his new converts in Thessalonica, the capital city of Macedonia, sooner than he wanted to as he had faced severe opposition. So he had sent a friend, Timothy, back to check on them. Timothy returned with good news—the Christians there were bravely standing firm in their faith even though they had many enemies. Paul wrote them a letter offering comfort and encouragement. He told them that they were an example to all believers in Greece.

He advised them on practical ways to be ready for the time when Christ would come again, by living good lives so that they would not be caught unprepared, for the day of the Lord will come like a thief in the night.

He also answered some questions they had about the resurrection. He told them not to grieve over those who had died, and he reassured them that everyone who believes in Jesus Christ will be united with him in death and live with him forever.

PRAYER

Thank you, Lord God, that you have prepared a wonderful eternal home for those who die now as believers and also for those who are living when Jesus comes again. Help me to enjoy this life while looking forward to eternity.
Amen

THE WORK OF THE LORD

Paul wrote another letter to the Thessalonians about a year later. People had been saying that the day of the Lord had already come and that there was no point working. Paul wanted to set the record straight. He told them that certain things must happen before the day of the Lord could come to pass and that in the meantime they must stay busy doing the work of God. They mustn't become lazy and expect others to provide for them.

He told the church in Thessalonica that the people there had been chosen by God to share in the glory of Jesus Christ, and that they must stand firm and never, ever tire of doing good. For God loves us and through his grace has given us a wonderful hope and comfort that has no end.

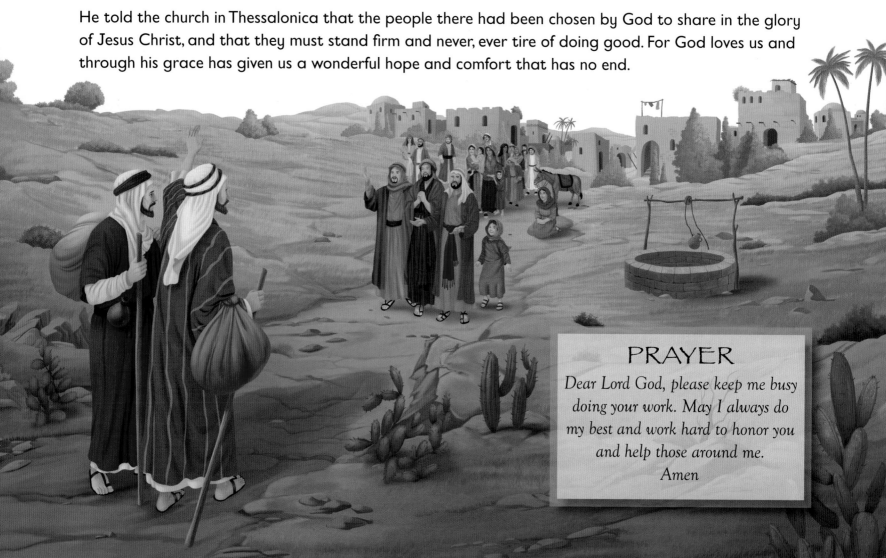

PRAYER

Dear Lord God, please keep me busy doing your work. May I always do my best and work hard to honor you and help those around me.

Amen

MONEY, MONEY, MONEY

Timothy was very special to Paul. He thought of him like a son. When Paul was in prison in Rome, he wrote to Timothy to encourage him. He told him not to listen to people when they said he was too young for the work he was doing, but to continue to set a good example in everything he said and did.

He also talked about silly people who thought that they could become rich by being a Christian. In fact, he said, giving your life over to God could indeed make you rich, but not in the way they thought! We all come into this world with nothing, and when we die we take nothing with us. So we shouldn't be longing for money and expensive clothes and possessions. The love of money, said Paul, is the root of all evil. So many people stop thinking about what is really important because they want more and more money, more and more things. But this only leads to unhappiness. We should be content with what we have and feel rich in God. And if we do have lots of money, we should do good things with it and help those who are not so well off!

PRAYER

Dear Lord God, as I grow up, please help to have a right view of money and possessions. Help me to be faithful to you in whatever circumstances you place me, whether rich or poor.

Amen

A GOOD FIGHT

Toward the end of his life, Paul wrote to Timothy: "I am suffering and have been chained like a criminal, but the word of God cannot be chained. I am willing to endure for the sake of God's chosen people so that they, too, may obtain the salvation that comes through Jesus Christ and brings eternal glory. Remind everyone of this saying:

"'If we die with him, we will also live with him.

If we endure hardship, we will reign with him.

If we deny him, he will deny us.

If we are unfaithful, he remains faithful,

for he cannot deny who he is.'

"As for me, my life has been an offering to God. The time of my death is near. I have fought a good fight, I have finished the race, and I have kept the faith. Now I look forward to my reward, which the Lord will give me on the day of his return—a reward not just for me but for all who eagerly await his coming!"

PRAYER

Thank you, Lord God, for the great example of the apostle Paul, who kept his faith to the very end of life. Please teach me to persevere in faith and to continue all the good things I start.
Amen

A GOOD EXAMPLE

Paul wrote a letter to his friend Titus, whom he had left in Crete to keep an eye on the church there. One of Titus' jobs was to select church leaders, and Paul knew how important it was to have the right people at the head of the church, setting a good example. He gave Titus lots of advice about what sort of man he should be looking for: an honest, honorable man who was patient and self-controlled, who didn't get angry, and who wasn't too bossy. It was especially important that he pass on God's message honestly and truthfully and that he believe in it himself, and he must live the message he preached and do nothing to attract criticism.

Good leaders would make the church strong and would earn respect for it, while bad leaders would help to destroy it. We must all lead by example.

In addition to this, Paul told Titus that the people themselves must use their lives, not to fight or gossip or drink too much, but to do good things and to help others, so that their lives would not be empty, and God would be pleased.

PRAYER

Thank you, Lord God, for the leaders of my church. Please give them wisdom, kindness, and patience as they encourage Christians in godly living.
Amen

THE RUNAWAY SLAVE

This short, personal letter is a wonderful story of forgiveness and the power of Christian brotherly love. In it, Paul asks his old friend and fellow believer Philemon to forgive his runaway slave, Onesimus, whom Paul had met in Rome.

Paul could demand Philemon's forgiveness, but he chooses not to. Instead, he asks for it, "for love's sake," knowing that Philemon's Christian love for the slave will lead him to do the right thing. Even though Philemon would have been within his rights to have the slave executed for running away, Christians believe that we should forgive those who sin against us, just as God forgives us our sins. When Peter asked Jesus how many times he should forgive a brother who had sinned against him, suggesting seven times, Jesus answered, "seventy times seven." Paul believes that he can trust Philemon to not only forgive Onesimus, but to welcome him back as a brother in Christ.

Paul goes so far as to say that if Onesimus has stolen anything from Philemon, he, Paul, will gladly repay him. He is willing to put himself on the line for the runaway slave and pay his debt, just as Jesus paid the debt of our sin.

PRAYER

Thank you, Lord God, for your wonderful forgiveness and the freedom this gives me. Help me to copy you in blessing anyone who asks me for forgiveness. Help me to be a peacemaker where I can.

Amen

RUN THE RACE

We cannot be certain who wrote the book of Hebrews, although some believe it might have been Paul. In Hebrews we're told, "Faith is the confidence that what we hope for will actually happen. Our ancestors had faith: Noah built a boat when everyone was laughing at him; Sarah believed she would have a child even though she was old; Moses took his people out of Egypt just because God told him to.

"Let yourself be filled with faith. Cast off the things that weigh you down so you have the strength and endurance to run the race set before us!"

PRAYER

Thank you, Lord God, for the heroes of faith who have gone before us. Thank you that you are always pleased when I have faith. Remind me, dear Father, that I can never please you without faith.

Amen

The writer knew that our Christian journey would not be an easy one, but if we depend on Jesus for help we will grow stronger.

REAL FAITH

Other writers also had inspiring words to say about faith. The apostle James wrote, "What good is it to say you have faith but don't show it by your actions? Words are not enough, faith is not enough, unless it produces good deeds." James told his readers that they should ask God for the things they needed but that when they asked, they really had to believe and not doubt, because if you doubt, then you are like "a wave of the sea, blown and tossed by the wind."

Peter went on to say, "You face hardship and suffering—but don't despair! Instead, be glad, for these trials make you partners with Christ in his suffering. They will test your faith as fire tests and purifies gold, and remember that there is wonderful joy ahead! Don't be disheartened if it seems a long time in coming—God is being patient, for he wants everyone to repent. But the day of the Lord will come unexpectedly, so be prepared!"

PRAYER

Dear Lord God, please help me to have strong faith and to show it by how I live. Please help me always to do good whenever I can—but to rely only on Jesus and never to think that good works will get me to heaven.

Amen

GOD IS LOVE

The apostle John wrote, "God is love. He loves us so much that we are called children of God! He showed how much he loved us by sending his one and only Son into the world so that we might have eternal life through him. Since he loved us that much, let us make sure that we love one another so that God can live in us and we can live in God. And as we live in God, our love will grow more perfect, and when the day of judgment comes we will not have to fear anything.

"Perfect love drives out all fear! We love one another because he loved us first. All love comes from God!"

PRAYER

Dear Lord God, thank you for showing your great love by giving Jesus for us. Please help me to show my love for others in the way I give time, money, and care to them.

Amen

JOHN'S AMAZING VISION

The very last book of the Bible is Revelation. Many believe it was written by the disciple John. The author had an amazing vision to pass on: "On the Lord's day the Spirit took control of me, and I heard a loud voice, coming from behind me, saying, 'Write down what you see and send it to the seven churches.'

"When I turned, I saw seven golden lampstands, and among them I saw a being like the Son of Man, dressed in a long robe, with a golden sash round his chest. His head and hair were white as snow, and his eyes were like blazing fire. In his right hand he held seven stars, and out of his mouth came a sharp double-edged sword. His face shone like the brightest sun.

"I fell at his feet, but he told me not to be afraid. 'I am the First and the Last,' he said. 'I was dead, and behold I am alive for ever and ever! And I hold the keys of death and Hades.'"

In John's vision, the seven lampstands were the seven churches of Asia Minor, and the Lord wanted John to send a message to those churches, to correct and encourage them. But this was not all. He also sent John a vision of the future . . .

PRAYER

Thank you, Lord Jesus, that you are now exalted in heaven and are alive forever. Thank you that death is defeated. I bow and worship you now, risen, glorified Son of God.
Amen

THE THRONE OF GOD

John found himself before the throne of God. A rainbow resembling an emerald encircled the throne, and it was surrounded by twenty-four other thrones, on which sat twenty-four elders, dressed in white, with crowns of gold.

From the throne came flashes of lightning and peals of thunder, and seven lamps blazed before it. Around it were four living creatures—one like a lion, one like an ox, one with a face like a man, and one like an eagle in flight—all covered with eyes. They each had six wings and chanted incessantly, "Holy, holy, holy is the Lord God Almighty, who was, and is, and is to come!"

The one on the throne held a scroll covered with writing and sealed with seven seals. At first it seemed that no one could be found who was worthy to open it, but one of the elders declared that the Lion of the tribe of Judah, the great descendant of David, could break the seals and open the scroll. Then John saw a Lamb standing in the center of the throne, and the four beings and all the elders bowed down in praise and were joined by many angels and all the creatures in heaven and earth.

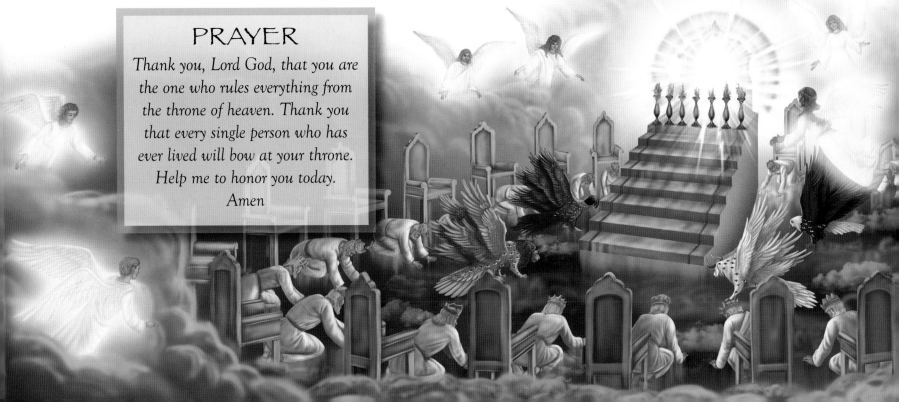

PRAYER

Thank you, Lord God, that you are the one who rules everything from the throne of heaven. Thank you that every single person who has ever lived will bow at your throne. Help me to honor you today.

Amen

THE END OF DAYS

In John's vision, the seven seals were broken off one by one, and many dreadful things happened to the earth, but those who were faithful to Jesus were protected by the seal of God.

Then seven trumpets were sounded. Hail and fire rained down, the waters were poisoned, and the world plunged into darkness. Locusts with thunderous wings covered the earth, tormenting all but those with God's seal. An army of horsemen released dreadful plagues of fire, smoke, and brimstone upon the land. Then, when the seventh trumpet was blown, the temple of God opened in heaven, and the ark of his covenant could be seen. There was lightning, thunder, an earthquake, and terrible hail.

John saw that a terrible time was to follow, but finally all that is evil will be destroyed, and God's kingdom will reign. After the final judgment, a new heaven and earth will replace the old.

PRAYER

Thank you, Lord God, that I don't need to worry about the future. Thank you that you have a plan where good will overcome all evil. Help me to trust in you for time and eternity.
Amen

"I'M COMING SOON!"

John wrote, "Then I saw a new heaven and earth, and I saw the Holy City coming down out of heaven like a beautiful bride. I heard a loud voice speaking from the throne: 'Now God's home is with his people! He will live with them. They shall be his people, and he will be their God. There will be no more death, no more grief, or crying, or pain. He will make all things new! For he is the first and the last, the beginning and the end.'

"And I was shown the Holy City, shining with the glory of God. It had a great high wall with twelve gates and twelve angels in charge of them. Its temple is the Lord God Almighty and the Lamb. The city has no need of the sun or the moon, because the glory of God shines on it, and the Lamb is its lamp. The people of the world will walk by its light, and the gates will never be closed, because there will be no night there. But only those whose names are written in the Lamb's book of life will enter.

"'Listen!' says Jesus. 'I'm coming soon!'"

Let it be so! Come, Lord Jesus, come soon!

PRAYER

Thank you, Lord God, for the wonderful place called heaven. Thank you for those I know who are already there. Thank you that it is a place of joy and singing and light. I want heaven to be my goal all through my life.

Amen

Here are some more words of wisdom from the book of Proverbs

Trust in God with all your heart: never rely on what you think you know.

God sees all that we do, good or bad. He can see what is inside our hearts.

Being wise is better than being strong.

Make fun of wisdom, and you'll never find it.

The easier you get money, the sooner you will lose it.

If you have to choose between reputation and wealth, choose reputation.

Being lazy will make you poor; hard work will make you rich.

Thoughtless words can wound as deeply as a sword, but wisely spoken words can heal.

Even fools can seem smart if they keep their mouths shut.

No one who gossips can be trusted with a secret.

If you're wronged, don't try to get even: Trust God to make it right.

If you want people to like you, be forgiving.

When parents correct their children, it shows that they love them.

Listen when God corrects you: He corrects those he loves.

Anger is cruel and destructive, but jealousy is far worse.

Peace of mind makes the body healthy; jealousy is like a cancer.

A simple meal with people you love is better than a feast where there is hatred.

Love is always ready to overlook the wrongs that people do.

If you don't listen to the cry of the poor, your own cry for help will not be heard.

Whenever you possibly can, do good to those who need it, even if they are your enemies

You do yourself a favor when you are kind: If you are cruel, you hurt yourself.

Don't mix with people who'll pass on bad habits.

Sometimes only a painful experience makes us change our ways.

Pride leads to destruction, and arrogance to downfall.

The poor have a hard life, but happiness lies in being content.

PRAYER

Dear Lord God, please help me to put
these ideas into my life day by day and
to know that this is the best way to live.
Help me to travel the road of good people.
May I learn the secret of contentment as
I trust you to meet all my needs.

Amen

Your word is a lamp for my feet, a light on my path.

Psalm 119:105